Red Book, Middle Way

Red Book, Middle Way

How Jung Parallels the Buddha's Method for Human Integration

Robert M. Ellis

SHEFFIELD UK   BRISTOL CT

Published by Equinox Publishing Ltd

UK: Office 415, The Workstation, 15 Paternoster Row, Sheffield, South Yorkshire S1 2BX
USA: ISD, 70 Enterprise Drive, Bristol, CT 06010

www.equinoxpub.com

First published 2020

© Robert M. Ellis 2020

All rights reserved. No part of this publication may be reproduced or transmitted in any form or by any means, electronic or mechanical, including photocopying, recording or any information storage or retrieval system, without prior permission in writing from the publishers.

British Library Cataloguing-in-Publication Data
A catalogue record for this book is available from the British Library.

ISBN-13 978 1 80050 008 2 (hardback)
       978 1 80050 009 9 (paperback)
       978 1 80050 010 5 (ePDF)

Library of Congress Cataloging-in-Publication Data
Names: Ellis, Robert M, author.
Title: Red book, middle way : how Jung parallels the Buddha's method for human integration / Robert M. Ellis.
Description: Bristol, CT : Equinox Publishing Ltd, 2020. | Includes bibliographical references and index. | Summary: "Red Book, Middle Way offers a new interpretation of Jung's Red Book, in terms of the Middle Way, as a universal principle and embodied ethic, paralleled both in the Buddha's teachings and elsewhere" -- Provided by publisher.
Identifiers: LCCN 2020019346 (print) | LCCN 2020019347 (ebook) | ISBN 9781800500082 (hardback) | ISBN 9781800500099 (paperback) | ISBN 9781800500105 (ebook)
Subjects: LCSH: Jungian psychology--Religious aspects--Buddhism. | Jung, C. G. (Carl Gustav), 1875-1961. Liber novus. | Jungian psychology. | Eightfold Path. | Gautama Buddha.
Classification: LCC BF173.J85 E45 2020 (print) | LCC BF173.J85 (ebook) | DDC 159.19/54--dc23
LC record available at https://lccn.loc.gov/2020019346
LC ebook record available at https://lccn.loc.gov/2020019347

Typeset by S.J.I. Services, New Delhi, India

The God calls me toward the right and the left, his voice calling out to me from both sides. Yet the God wants neither the one nor the other. He wants the middle way. But the middle is the beginning of the long road.

C.G. Jung, *The Red Book*, Liber Secundus 138

Contents

List of Illustrations	xi
Acknowledgements	xii
Introduction	1
a. Jung's *Red Book*	1
b. The Middle Way	3
c. Interpreting the *Red Book*	5
d. Outline of this book	6
e. Note on references to the *Red Book*	10
1. The Middle Way in the *Red Book* and in the Buddha's Quest	11
a. Jung and Izdubar	11
b. The universal Middle Way	15
c. The Buddha's quest	17
d. No final goal	20
e. Understanding the extremes	22
f. The individual way	24
g. Scepticism	27
h. Meaningful symbols and the brain	30
i. Facing the unholy alliance	33
2. God as Integrative Archetype	37
a. God's death and rebirth	37
b. The New God and Middle Way values	39
c. Archetypes	42
d. Integrating the God archetype	46
e. Varying names for the Self	48
f. Is the New God impotent?	49
g. Is the New God solipsistic?	53

3. The Wise: Elijah and Philemon 56
  a. The Wise Old Man 56
  b. Jung and Elijah 58
  c. Jung and Philemon 61
  d. Does Philemon become dogmatic? 64
  e. The Middle Way of authority 66

4. Christ as the Middle Way 69
  a. The Christ archetype 69
  b. Suffering for creativity 71
  c. Eating flesh and drinking blood 74
  d. The imitation of Christ 76

5. The Tree of Life and the Mandala 81
  a. The Tree of Life 81
  b. The bidirectional tree 85
  c. Destruction and regeneration 87
  d. The meaning of mandalas 88
  e. Combining mandala and tree symbols 89
  f. Mandala as city 94
  g. Mandala with archetypes 96

6. Integrating the Shadow 100
  a. The nature of evil 100
  b. Mara and the absorption of evil 102
  c. Good's dependence on evil 104
  d. The Cabiri and the sword 106
  e. The shadow of destitution 107
  f. How to talk to the devil 108

7. The Soul and the Anima 112
  a. Jung's view of the soul 112
  b. Salome 115
  c. The serpent and the bird 117
  d. The hidden daughter in the castle 118
  e. The proposal of marriage 121

f. Hanging on the tree of life	122
g. The abodes of Brahma	124

8. Death of the Hero — 127
   a. The murder — 127
   b. The motif of sacrifice — 129
   c. The hero as an object of imitation — 131
   d. Magic and the heroic — 133
   e. The rebirth of the hero — 136
   f. Integrating the hero — 137

9. Embodied Meaning and the Scholars — 139
   a. The scholars — 139
   b. Embodied meaning and the image — 140
   c. Embodiment and the Buddha's breakthrough — 143
   d. The hidden daughter and the right hemisphere — 144
   e. The spirit of the depths — 148
   f. Symbols from the depths — 150
   g. Conversations with Ammonius — 152
   h. The tower of confidence — 155
   i. The dancing devil — 156

10. Complaints of the Dead — 159
   a. The effects of the dead — 159
   b. Acceptance of death — 160
   c. The irruption of the dead — 162
   d. The instrumentality of the dead — 164
   e. The hanged man — 166
   f. Integration of the dead — 167

11. Gnostic versus Agnostic — 170
   a. The two Jungs and the trouble with metaphysics — 170
   b. Gnostic metaphysics — 172
   c. Philemon's inadequate answers — 175
   d. Psychological interpretations of the Seven Sermons — 180
   e. Jungian agnosticism — 183

12. Towards a Jungian Integrative Ethic 184
   a. Jung as a moral thinker 184
   b. Middle Way ethics 186
   c. Integration and responsibility 188
   d. Self and other 191
   e. The Middle Way on moral rules 193
   f. Forethinking and the paradox of hedonism 196
   g. Cultivation of the integrated self 202
   h. Towards a Jungian integrative ethic 206

Conclusion 209

Bibliography 211

Index 214

List of Illustrations

1. Jung's illustration from *Red Book* facsimile LS 32   35
2. Author's diagram of archetypes as functions   46
3. Jung's illustration from *Red Book* facsimile LS 64   51
4. Jung's picture of Philemon from *Red Book* facsimile LS 154   63
5. Jung's mandala from *Red Book* facsimile LS 127   73
6. Jung's bidirectional tree from *Red Book* facsimile LS 22   85
7. Jung's illustration from *Red Book* facsimile LS 135   87
8. Jung's mandala from *Red Book* facsimile LS 80   90
9. Jung's mandala from *Red Book* facsimile LS 84   91
10. Jung's mandala from *Red Book* facsimile LS 96   93
11. Jung's mandala from *Red Book* facsimile LS 163   95
12. Jung's mandala from *Red Book* facsimile LS 105   97
13. Aloka: Mandala of the Five Buddhas   98

Acknowledgements

The author would like to thank Susan Averbach, Pablo Nagel, Graham Mummery and Ian Rees for their reading and comments on this book prior to publication.

A large number of quotations throughout this book, as well as illustrations 1 and 3–12, are taken from *The Red Book* by C.G. Jung, edited by Sonu Shamdasani, translated by Mark Kyburz, John Peck, and Sonu Shamdasani. Copyright © 2009 by the Foundation of the Works of C.G. Jung. Translation copyright © 2009 by Mark Kyburz, John Peck, and Sonu Shamdasani. Used by permission of W.W. Norton & Company, Inc.

Illustration 2 is a diagram created by the author, incorporating 'Devil Goat' by Rex Diablo, Creative Commons CC BY-SA 3.0. All other images used in this diagram are public domain. The author allows this diagram (only) to be re-used under the same share-alike creative commons license.

Illustration 13 is the 'Five Buddha Mandala' by Dharmachari Aloka, used by permission of Ian Linn.

Introduction

a. Jung's *Red Book*

Imagine one of the great creative figures of the past whose experiences have ignited a whole new world-view: Buddha, Jesus, or Muhammad, say. Imagine that, rather than themselves writing nothing, and being dependent on others to record their experiences, one of these figures was able to write down their own experiences extensively, and even add pictures. Imagine, too, that rather than being absolutised by religious traditions with a vested interest in winning quick converts, one of these figures was able to be quite explicit that his aim was not to set up a new set of claims about ultimate 'truth', but rather to help people develop in relation to the cultural and religious frameworks they already found themselves in. Imagine, too, that rather than being at best narrowly educated in one tradition, one of these figures had a wide understanding of the arts and the sciences, and had a rich familiarity with both Christian tradition and the critical debates of nineteenth-century German thought, together with an openness to other traditions from around the world.

Such is the position with Jung's *Red Book*, which I would personally judge to be one of the most remarkable, and above all helpful, documents yet produced by Western civilisation: not because it is perfect but because of its self-recognised imperfection, profound ambiguity, and intense appeal to our most vivid and insightful selves. The *Red Book* offers Jung's own practical conclusions, based on direct experience, as to how individuals can develop in their adequacy of response to the world by engaging in a personal integration process. It consists of a series of visions, reflections, and paintings, primarily based on Jung's intense visionary period between September 1913 and April 1914, but then worked over and interpreted during a further fourteen-year period until 1928.

The *Red Book* contains accounts of visions that Jung cultivated using his own technique of active imagination, often recalled in striking detail. It also contains his own reflections on those visions, filled with insights that are expressed in solemn and universal language. These are all the more valuable and striking because they were never compromised to meet the expectations of any particular audience, not being published until 2009, nearly fifty years after Jung's death.

The *Red Book* is a book of vision and wisdom. It is not a book of theory, unlike the remainder of Jung's substantial corpus of writings; but all the more useful for that, because instead it generally maintains the right degree of ambiguity to be both intensely personal and intensely universal. It is helpful to make use of Jung's subsequent theory in interpreting the *Red Book*, but that might also have the effect of obscuring how much the *Red Book* consists of a set of developing intuitions taking a more open form than Jung's subsequent theory. Where the *Red Book* does start to develop a set of claims about the universe (in the 'Seven Sermons to the Dead' towards the end), as I shall argue, Jung's judgement starts to become much more questionable.

It is also not in the least a book about analytical psychology, which is never mentioned. It seems to be mainly a historical accident, due to the field in which Jung primarily worked, that the *Red Book* has been most discussed so far by psychologists, rather than, say, philosophers, or scholars and practitioners of religion, literature, or art. If Einstein had produced a prophetic book in his youth, that would not make it physics. The study and interpretation of the *Red Book*, insofar as it is an academic matter at all, needs to be very much an inter-disciplinary affair. More than this, however, it is a document of personal practice that should be of interest to anyone who feels themselves to be engaged on a spiritual or integrative path.

The fact that it was never published during his lifetime makes the Jung we meet in the *Red Book* apparently much more adventurous, provisional, experimental and sceptical than the Jung of the psychological writings, who wished to be taken seriously as a scientist and scholar. Always impatient with binary extremes, Jung consistently seeks out a subtle position between them, but very often the *Red Book* records a process of questioning established beliefs in order to seek such 'mediating' positions. For example, he does not rest content either with Christian orthodoxy or with Nietzschean rejection of God, nor with thinking as opposed to feeling, nor with masculine identity as opposed to feminine.

In the process of questioning and seeking, he sometimes appears to be contradicting himself and occasionally strikes false notes. It is easy to misread his failure to accept a given position as the embrace of its opposite, which he generally tried to avoid. It is also too easy to read contradictions into the *Red Book*, because one can easily forget the particularity of its assertions, which work for Jung *at the particular point he had reached* in his development, and are obviously not intended to be final. Once one learns to accept this, the text will seem all the richer for the fact that it records a *process* rather than offering unrealistic finality.

However, the *Red Book* is just as much a book of (often startling) visionary experiences as it is of reflection. Jung meets all sorts of characters inside his own head. He puts a wounded god into his pocket to smuggle it home. He eats the liver of a murdered child in order to acknowledge the commonality of human guilt. He argues about Nietzsche with a musty librarian, and about the meaning of words with a desert hermit. He is accosted by a crowd of obsessive dead Anabaptists tearing about the world between prayer venues. He regularly falls in love with his own soul in female form. He seeks out a magician to learn magic, only to find that the magician has retired. The incidents in the *Red Book* could potentially be turned into a stack of intriguing novels and films, rich in twists, but the stories also nearly always point one towards a direct and dramatic appreciation of startling and subtle insights, often even before the ensuing reflections begin to unpack them.

b. The Middle Way

On first reading the *Red Book* myself, it seemed to me that I had hit upon, not just an extraordinary book, but something approximating to a religious scripture that was about the Middle Way. The Middle Way is a principle that I have cultivated and developed in the form of practical and critical philosophy for around twenty years now, initially within the context of Buddhist tradition where the term 'Middle Way' originates, but more recently in a more universal way beyond any one particular tradition. Though I was already aware that Jung offered many resources for understanding the Middle Way, I didn't yet think of his work as being directly *about* the Middle Way until I read the *Red Book*.

The central principle of the Middle Way is the reliance on imperfect experience, integrated over time and critically reflected upon, to support provisional beliefs about both facts and values. To remain in this uncertain but productive space, though, we also need to avoid our tendency to absolutise, which means to set up certain claims as finally 'true' or 'false' rather than incrementally justified. Absolutisation can be either positive or negative, affirming or denying some claimed 'truth' which is generally promoted by a group and used as a tool of power. Thus the Middle Way requires us to stay in that ambiguous zone between ultimate affirmation and ultimate negation, affirming and denying only for provisional and practical reasons.

This account of the Middle Way is a reasonable practical interpretation of the Buddha's Middle Way as offered in the Buddhist scriptures of the Pali Canon, as I have argued fully in my recent book, *The Buddha's Middle Way*. It is illustrated particularly by the progress of the Buddha in the story of his early life, from the absolute assumptions represented by the Palace and the Forest, to the point where he explicitly recognised the Middle Way as independent of either. Rather than being based on conventional obedience to social expectations on the one hand, or the repressive exercise of will on the other, the Middle Way is built on recognition of the body and the conditions it creates as the starting point of a path of autonomous and experiential judgement. The Buddha's 'silence' in the face of metaphysical questions, and his famous raft simile, showing that no teaching is an end in itself, are also crucial to the understanding of the Middle Way in Buddhism.

The Middle Way Philosophy I have been developing in other books, however, is independent of any appeal to Buddhist tradition or authority. It takes seriously a point that many Buddhists seem to recognise only theoretically – that the Middle Way is universal. It offers tools for the critical assessment of the helpful and unhelpful elements in any religion, as well as other traditions (such as political, scientific, or artistic). It offers the potential to unite people from a variety of backgrounds in a critical type of universalism – one that does not blandly assert that all traditions are of equal value, but rather subjects those traditions to practical tests that they are likely to pass only to varying degrees.

Apart from the obvious influence of the Buddha and Buddhist practice, Jung has been a major influence on Middle Way Philosophy from the beginning of my work on it. His concept of integration or individuation is a central element of Middle Way Philosophy, providing a positive account of how human judgement can improve, not just through the avoidance of absolutising dogmas, but also through the overcoming of both internal and external conflict. This Jungian concept can be further refined today using developments in cognitive psychology, embodied meaning, and neuroscience, and is beginning to gain purchase well beyond explicitly Jungian circles. I have also made much use of Jung's concept of archetypes, which I find astonishingly fruitful. A wide variety of different scientific resources can now be brought together in support of some of Jung's key insights, especially including that of Daniel Kahneman and his associates on biases, of Iain McGilchrist on brain lateralisation and its implications, and of George Lakoff and Mark Johnson on embodied meaning.

I will be making some connections with these new forms of scientific insight in this book, but for more details you will have to look at my *Middle Way Philosophy* series.[1] Rather than following through the interpretation of all Jung's psychological theory in detail, my main aim here is instead to interpret the *Red Book* as a resource of the most direct and inspiring kind – let us say, a scripture – of the Middle Way. The *Red Book* is not easy to read and interpret, and I suspect that many of those who have an intuition of its great significance are somewhat at a loss as to how to interpret it in a way that is relevant to their lives. I am aiming to offer an interpretation of the *Red Book* that makes it of universal practical value by drawing out the Middle Way Philosophy that I find there.

c. Interpreting the *Red Book*

I am happy to acknowledge that the *Red Book* can potentially be interpreted in a variety of ways, and that each individual who engages with it will need to go through their own process of interpretation. My own experience, however, is that when I read the *Red Book* I find Middle Way Philosophy apparently already there shaping it. As we will see, there are a number of explicit references to the Middle Way

---

1 Embodied meaning and Jungian archetypes are discussed in volume 3 (2013), cognitive biases in volume 4 (2015, section 3) and McGilchrist's (2009) work on brain lateralisation at frequent intervals throughout.

itself in it, as well as a whole integrative approach and recognition of the role of archetypes that fits the Middle Way's implications in other respects. Jung's approach is profoundly anchored in a recognition of the need to gradually integrate opposing forces wherever they are found, in a way that acknowledges and harnesses both forces dialectically rather than attempting to impose one upon the other.

Like any other human, I am subject to confirmation bias, and to an extent will find what I seek when I interpret the text. I do not have a final interpretation of it, but then the text itself largely eschews the type of approach that claims to have a final position. Nor can a final position be based on historical facts about Jung himself. I do not claim to know Jung's 'real' intentions, nor would these necessarily change my response if I somehow knew them, as a book can surpass its author.[2] However, what I am confident of is the *practical* value of a Middle Way approach in interpreting this text. If you can follow me to the extent of at least including the Middle Way within your repertoire of interpretations, you should be able to modify your understanding of the *Red Book* in ways that help to make human judgement more, not less, adequate. Of course, I also hope that my interpretation may provide a way in, both for Jungians to recognise and explore Middle Way Philosophy, and for those interested in the Middle Way to explore Jung.

d. Outline of this book

The structure of this book is thematic rather than following the order of the *Red Book* itself. This is a more effective way of bringing out the relationship of the text to aspects of the Middle Way approach, and in any case the role of a commentary following the order of the text has already been filled by Sanford L. Drob's *Reading the Red Book*.[3] Whilst I disagree with Drob's occasional tendency to interpret Jung metaphysically, and there are surprising limits to his grasp of the more difficult parts of the text, there is also a good deal of useful information in his book, and it raises a variety of issues relating to

---

2 Jung himself shows appreciation of this point in his discussion of his 'son' (symbolising his work) from the final drafted section of the *Liber Secundus* that was never added to the final version: LFT 327-9, RE 449-55.

3 Drob (2012).

the text of the *Red Book*. If your interest is primarily in the relationship between the *Red Book* and Jung's psychology, Jung's life, his sources and the cultural background behind his symbols, you will generally be better turning to books like Drob's, or writings by other Jungian scholars (including Sonu Shamdasani's introduction to the text). I have a larger task here that is more reflective of the text's original purpose: that is, to expound a practical philosophical approach for which the *Red Book* can offer a major source of inspiration.

To do this, I shall begin with the Middle Way itself, drawing out the ways that Jung himself presents it both explicitly and implicitly, and also including some comparison with the Middle Way as it is presented in the Buddha's quest. Even the explicit treatments of the Middle Way in *the Red Book* appear to have entirely escaped the notice of scholars so far, but they are clearly there for those who look. There is no mention of the *Buddhist* Middle Way in the *Red Book*,[4] and Jung's explorations of Buddhism generally developed later in his life, so it seems most likely that the Middle Way as it is presented in the *Red Book* is not at all a product of Buddhist influence, but rather an instance of another thinker independently developing approaches that parallel those of the Buddha – in the process providing further evidence (if it should be needed) that the Middle Way is not a Buddhist monopoly but a more general description of a practically valuable approach to human judgement. Like the archetypes, the Middle Way is universal because it is a product of the very structure of human responses, appearing in a variety of cultural guises that are nevertheless functionally similar.

The next seven chapters are all concerned with what might be called the archetypes that feature prominently in the *Red Book*, even though Jung does not use the term 'archetype' at this stage. These are the God archetype (or what Jung would later call the 'Self'), the shadow represented by Satan, the anima or soul, and the hero. All of these archetypes are represented by characters that Jung finds within himself. At one and the same time he regards them as 'real' because they represent genuine forces in his experience, but also as

---

4   There is a brief mention of the Buddha in the text at LP vi(r), LFT 248, RE 184, which is expanded a little in Jung's commentary at LFT 367, RE 570. However, this focuses entirely on the Buddha's enlightened status as transcending pleasure and suffering, making no mention of the Middle Way by which the Buddha is said to have achieved that state.

symbolic because they represent characters within himself rather than beyond. Any of these archetypes can be absolutised and projected, mistaken for external realities, but they can also be engaged with positively as aspects of oneself.

The God archetype, that Jung refers to as 'the God', 'my God', or 'the New God' (and later 'the Self') represents Jung's own capacity for integration, and must thus encompass all the other archetypes. It does not represent an external, supernatural or metaphysical entity, for the important reason that to take it to be thus would be an act of projection in conflict with the integration process itself. Nevertheless, this God does not lose an inch of his power in experience. In the *Red Book,* the God archetype is also encountered in the forms of wise old men (like Elijah and Philemon), Christ (who also has elements of the hero archetype), the Tree of Life, and the mandala, all of which are explored here in successive chapters. The next three chapters after these are on the three other archetypes.

Jung encounters Satan and talks of descent to Hell in the *Red Book*, laying much stress on the importance of acknowledging Satan as an aspect of God. This is basically because we can only integrate the evil within us by recognising it as part of ourselves, and indeed as essential to what is good in ourselves. In this lies a whole implicit challenge to the inadequate ethics that has become traditional in Western culture, where 'good' is recognised as ideal but set apart from what is practically feasible. If we are ever to make ethics practically effective, it is necessary to integrate the shadow.

Jung also constantly encounters his soul, a female figure he would later call the anima and that is represented by the attractive other. The soul leads him on to the God archetype, but at the same time challenges him with the recognition that his idea of the attractive other is interdependent with the rejected and repulsive other. Jung's dialogues with the figure of Salome in the *Red Book* reflect this difficulty in the path of integration.

The other archetype in the *Red Book* is the hero, who represents the egoistic quest, the desire to win through and fulfil one's goals. *The Red Book* is preoccupied with the motif of the death of the hero, representing the ways in which we may need to let go of our current goals in order to fulfil more integrated and more adequate goals. Nevertheless, the acknowledgement and channelling of desire has a positive and appropriate place in Jung's emerging philosophy.

With all of these archetypal figures, I shall stress that the usefulness of Jung's approach to them depends on the role of the Middle Way. It is only if we avoid absolutising these characters, whether as 'real' or 'unreal', that we are able to work with them helpfully as aspects of our experience.

The chapter on embodied meaning draws on the many references to meaning in the *Red Book*, and argues that they implicitly fit the account of embodied meaning that has more recently been developed by Lakoff and Johnson. The 'meaning' Jung refers to throughout is not 'merely' emotive, nor is it readily compatible with the representationalist accounts of meaning that still dominate in science and philosophy, in our time as in Jung's, falsely dividing the cognitive from the emotive, thinking from feeling, as they do. Jung's visionary encounters with dusty scholars and the linguistically obsessed ascetic Ammonius emphasise this point.

The dead also have a role in the *Red Book*, particularly those returning unfulfilled from Jerusalem who are then addressed in the 'Seven Sermons to the Dead' near the end. The dead are unfulfilled because they have been given unintegrated, absolutised religion, and Philemon becomes Jung's mouthpiece in addressing them with a vision for a revitalised religion that draws heavily on Gnosticism. Since I find this section of the *Red Book* incompatible with the insights of the rest of it, I am reluctantly obliged in the penultimate chapter to make my case against it, concluding that Jung here made some unfortunate mistakes in spite of his huge achievements in the rest of the *Red Book*.

Overall, though, Jung's *ethical* intentions in the *Red Book* are clear. He presents us with a revaluation of good and evil, in which good is integrative and evil is disintegrative. This type of ethical approach appears to have been almost totally ignored by moral philosophers, despite its clear practicability and potential for resolving a whole range of moral problems. It thus seems important to conclude with an exploration of the moral and practical implications of the *Red Book,* and at least a glimpse of the far-reaching implications of a Middle Way ethics. Though focused on intense individual experience, the *Red Book* has plenty of implications for social and political as well as individual ethics, and these as yet remain insufficiently explored.

e. Note on references to the *Red Book*

The English edition of the *Red Book* has been published by Norton in two forms: first, the expensive large-format edition of 2009, which includes the full facsimile of the original book in German, plus an English translation; then the Reader's Edition of 2012, which provides a far more affordable and convenient source for the text, but unfortunately does not include even reduced versions of the pictures (a mistake on Norton's part, I think). The variation between these two editions, plus the absence of the pictures from the translated text and the fact that Jung started off by numbering his first book like a medieval manuscript, makes referencing the *Red Book* complex and potentially confusing. If one references the original text, there is a different numbering system for the *Liber Primus* (the first part of the *Red Book*), which goes i(r), i(v), ii(r), ii(v) etc., as opposed to the *Liber Secundus*, which follows more conventional numbering from its beginning. Such referencing of the original text is also a clumsy instrument for pinpointing something in the English translation, because each page covers a large amount of text. The alternative adopted by commentators such as Drob is to give page numbers from the translation. However, the page numbers for the translations in the original large format edition and in the Reader's Edition do not match up, so quoting only one of them will be irritating for anyone who possesses only the other.

My somewhat cumbersome solution to this bibliographic headache is to reference all three of them in footnotes. I shall thus first quote a facsimile page number preceded by LP (Liber Primus) or LS (Liber Secundus); then a page number in the English translation of the large-format 2009 edition, preceded by LFT (large format translation); then a page number in the (identical) English translation of the Reader's Edition, preceded by RE. Thus, for example, the opening words of the *Red Book* ('The way of what is to come') will be referenced LP i(r), LFT 229, RE 117. Where pictures have been referenced, these of course can only be given references from the facsimile. *Scrutinies*, the third part of the *Red Book*, does not occur in the facsimile, so only LFT and RE references are given for that section.

References to Jung's other work, published in his *Collected Works*, are given in the form CW (Collected Works) followed by the volume number and paragraph number (§) or chapter.

1. The Middle Way in the *Red Book* and in the Buddha's Quest

1.a. Jung and Izdubar

One of the most striking visions in the *Red Book* is that of Jung's encounter with the bull-god Izdubar, recounted in the chapters headed 'First Day' and 'Second Day'.[1]

Jung came out of 'my Western land, where the men are rich in knowing and doing, and I began to suffer from the sun's empty darkness. And I threw everything from me and wandered toward the East, where the light rises daily.'[2] He wanders through the desert and finds his way blocked by a mountain range, through which the only way is a path through a narrow gorge with a path that is ice on one side and red-hot iron on the other. Having passed this, he follows a narrow path up a mountain ridge.

> *As I approach the top, a mighty booming resounds from the other side of the mountain like ore being pounded. The sound gradually swells, and echoes thunderously in the mountain. As I reach the pass, I see an enormous man approach from the other side.*
>
> *Two bull horns rise from his great head, and a rattling suit of armour covers his chest. His black beard is ruffled and decked with exquisite stones. The giant is carrying a sparkling double axe in his hand, like those used to strike bulls. Before I can recover from my amazed fright, the giant is standing before me. I look at his face: it is faint and pale and deeply wrinkled. His almond-shaped eyes look at me astonished. Horror takes hold of me: this is Izdubar, the mighty bull-man. He stands and looks at me: his face speaks of consuming inner fear, and his hands and knees tremble. Izdubar, the powerful bull trembling? Is he frightened?*[3]

Izdubar is indeed even more frightened of Jung than Jung is of him, and with good reason. Jung tells him about the sun lying in

---

1 LS 37–49, LFT 277–84, RE 277–98.
2 LS 40, LFT 279, RE 283.
3 LS 37, LFT 278, RE 277–8.

empty space, and Izdubar, whose power is closely associated with the sun and with light, is devastated. It seems that his whole mythical understanding of the world has been instantaneously destroyed by being informed of science and its evidential conclusions. He smashes his weapon (symbolic of his loss of power), and is 'lamed' and 'paralysed' by Jung's 'poison'. Jung is shocked.

> *I: Oh Izdubar, great and pitiable one, had I known that my knowledge could cut you down, I would have held my tongue. But I wanted to speak the truth.*
>
> *Iz: You call poison truth? Is poison truth? Or is truth poison? Do not our astrologers and priests also speak the truth? And yet theirs does not act like poison.*[4]

Jung manages to console Izdubar temporarily by suggesting that 'Our truth is that which comes from the knowledge of outer things. The truth of your priests is that which comes to you from inner things.'[5] He also says that Westerners have no choice but to 'swallow the poison of science' and get used to it over time.

> *This poison is so insurmountably strong that everyone, even the strongest, and even the eternal gods, perish because of it. If our life is dear to us, we prefer to sacrifice a piece of our life force rather than abandon ourselves to certain death.*[6]

Jung and Izdubar find temporary unity from the lighting of a fire, which warms them both and that becomes symbolic of the way beyond their opposition.

> *An old secret fire burns between us, giving sparse light and ample warmth.*
>
> *The primordial fire that conquers every necessity shall burn again, since the night of the world is wide and cold, and the need is great.*
>
> *The well-protected fire brings together those from far away and those who are cold, those who do not see one another and cannot reach one another, and it conquers suffering and shatters need.*
>
> *The words uttered at the fire are ambiguous and deep and show life the right way.*[7]

A little later Jung also adds this sentence:

---

4 LS 38, LFT 278, RE 280.
5 Ibid.
6 LS 39, LFT 279, RE 282.
7 LS 42, LFT 280, RE 286.

The high-blazing flame is the middle way, whose luminous course runs between the human and the divine.[8]

What is this middle way, and why is it being compared to a fire? It is not an absolute or magical solution to the opposition between 'East' and 'West' as Jung represents them: that is, between the assumptions of traditional and modern societies, or between the respective 'truths' of the scientists and the priests. Rather, fire is an energy, a process that reproduces that of the sun on a small scale, with the same warming effects. It creates emotional engagement and social or psychological unity in a limited context. East and West have not resolved their cosmic contradictions, but rather put both axe and poison aside to focus on the practical conditions of the moment, when they are caught in temporary isolation between the sustaining social contexts of each.

By the fire, the 'two truths' have declared a truce, and Izdubar is at least temporarily consoled by the idea that one of them refers to inner things and the other to outer. But the Middle Way does not consist in the mere recognition of 'two truths'. This would merely mean that 'truth' changes its meaning to abandon all pretension of representing a universally consistent state of affairs, and we have not been told what else 'truth' means if it is not this. Jung's formulation is a makeshift, and as often in the *Red Book*, we should not interpret it as representing any kind of final philosophical position. Rather we need to take our interpretation from the whole direction of the story.

It is in the *judgements* of the following day that the Middle Way is most directly represented. Jung and Izdubar sleep by the fire, but in the morning the temporarily optimistic mood has lifted and Jung is instead placed in a dilemma. Izdubar's temporary recovery by the fire proves to be misleading, as he is 'silent and stiff'.

I paced the mountain ridge, pondering, and looked back to my Western lands, where there is so much knowledge and so much possibility of help. I love Izdubar, and I do not want him to wither away miserably. But where should help come from? No one will travel the hot-cold path. And I? I am afraid to return to that path. And in the East? Was there possibly help there? But what about the unknown dangers that loomed there? I do not want to go blind. What use would that be to Izdubar?[9]

---

8 LS 43, LFT 281, RE 289.
9 LS 46, LFT 281–2, RE 291–2.

The hot-cold path seems to represent the extremes that one must engage with to find the Middle Way. Very often we have to be pitched from side to side, thinking first in terms of one contradictory world-view, then the other, before we find any kind of balancing position, and it is difficult to see where the balance lies until we have experienced the extremes. In the West, it seems, we prefer to stay in our secure certainties (whether these are the beliefs of scientific naturalism, or any other beliefs) rather than hazard this process. If he goes further East, however, Jung will be blinded by the sun. This is symbolic of the inability of those enmeshed in the certainties of traditional societies to look beyond their borders. He could abandon Western science entirely and throw himself into an exclusive religious cult, for example, thus finding meaning and security, but at the price of curiosity and adaptability.

After further pondering, however, Jung hits on a solution. At first he expresses this clumsily to Izdubar, provoking an angry reaction: 'I think that you are not at all real, but only a fantasy.' However, he then hits on a better way of putting it that Izdubar is eventually persuaded to find more acceptable: 'I do not mean to say that you are not real at all, of course, but only as real as a fantasy. If you could accept this, much would be gained.'[10]

Like truth, 'reality' does not admit of degrees. A thing is either real or it isn't. Again, Jung's words should not be taken as a metaphysical description, but rather interpreted within the terms implied by the practical situation in which they are used. The situation is one of lucid fantasy, in which Jung is aware that he is engaging in a situation apart from the normal assumptions of the rest of his life. Izdubar has an important *meaning* for Jung, representing aspects of his own experience and motivation, but that meaning is not accompanied by the kinds of beliefs about consistent and predictable objects and processes that tend to accompany 'reality' in our everyday lives. He knows that he could leave this fantasy at any time, even though its outcome is important to him. Jung was rightly adamant that fantasies are not 'unreal' in any final sense, because to say this usually functions as a way of dismissing their meaning and importance. However, to say that Izdubar is 'only as real as a fantasy' can be seen as a form of *practical* advice, namely that he should be treated as a meaningful and important symbol but not assumed

10 LS 47, LFT 282, RE 293.

to have the same consistent features as objects or processes in the 'physical' world we more normally experience.

By treating Izdubar as 'only as real as a fantasy', Jung resolves the practical situation. He says to Izdubar 'You have become light, lighter than a feather. Now I can carry you.'[11] Jung then carries him without difficulty back to the West, and back to his house. Given Izdubar's size, Jung then worries about getting him through the door, but is able to squeeze him into the size of an egg and put him into his pocket.

This is a demonstration of the Middle Way, not as any kind of intermediate 'reality', but as a form of *judgement*. Confronted with the rigidity of a dualism between two extremes, both of which are tied into ideas of 'reality' and sources of social power, Jung reframes his understanding of the situation so as to avoid the rigidity of the two extremes, in the process allowing the resolution of a conflict between two opposed desires. In some measure, both his desires are fulfilled: he wants to preserve Izdubar and yet also return to the safety of his home. Yet in the process he has to reconsider both what Izdubar means and what bringing him into modern society means. This is just one such move in the process of integration charted by the *Red Book*, through which Jung identifies conflicts within himself and finds ways of resolving them by reframing his understanding of the situation. Reducing the God to the size of an egg does not prove to be the final solution, but it is a step along the way, adequate to the practical conditions.

1.b. The universal Middle Way

I have already quoted Jung as explicitly using the term 'middle way' – not capitalised, but then capitalisation is a minor issue.[12] He uses it (or the similar 'middle path') in a number of other places in the *Red Book*,[13] though in his other work it only appears in *Psychological*

---

11 LS 47, LFT 282, RE 294.

12 It is my own practice to capitalise the term 'Middle Way' because we tend to capitalise concepts that refer to unique entities, whether or not these are considered proper names, e.g. God, Psychology (when referring to a university department), or the Moon. The Middle Way is a unique process for each individual consisting in unique optimal judgements at each moment, as discussed below.

13 These include (1) LS 53, LFT 284, RE 300; (2) LS 99, LFT 293, RE 331; (3) LS 112, LFT 301, RE 357; (4) LS 138, LFT 311, RE 393.

Types,[14] which he was working on at a similar time to the *Red Book*. Only in *Psychological Types* is there anything approaching a formal account of what he means. There he discusses a 'flow of libido' towards 'a vital optimum' between 'pleasure and the necessary limitations of pleasure'.[15] This account is sketchy and does not seem to have been fleshed out in any of his other theory. It remains overwhelmingly an intuition found in *The Red Book* rather than a formalised Jungian teaching.

It is difficult to tell whether in using the term 'middle path' Jung was to any extent influenced by Buddhism, or whether he developed it independently and then discovered an affinity with Buddhism: but, whichever of these is the case, it is very clear that his understanding of it is very much his own and expressed in his own authentic terms. The *Red Book* thus provides a striking piece of evidence in support of my wider thesis that the Middle Way is a universal phenomenon rather than merely the teaching of Buddhism. In my view it can be found *implicitly* in all kinds of different places,[16] but of course claims about the implicit can be very easily disputed. For Jung to have developed the Middle Way *explicitly* and independently, however, suggests that the resources may exist for human beings to develop the conception in a wide variety of contexts, even if the cultural expressions of the Middle Way differ.

In understanding that wider conception, however, it is important to remain steadfastly with the understanding of the Middle Way as a method of judgement, and to resist all temptation or pressure to turn it into a claimed metaphysical truth about the universe. As we have already seen in the example of Izdubar, the practical operation of the Middle Way as a method of judgement requires us to be able to question the absoluteness of a pair of opposing descriptions of a situation that are being otherwise interpreted as necessarily the only way of understanding it. However much someone may assert that the way they are understanding a situation *is* the only possible way of understanding it, we must maintain a critical perspective. It is thus impossible to maintain any belief in an absolute

---

14 Jung CW 6 §326, 356, 357.
15 Jung CW 6 §356.
16 See Ellis (2019) section 7 for an example list of such places, including Pyrrhonism, Scientific Falsificationism, Systems Theory, Embodied Meaning Theory, and the 'mindfulness' of Ellen Langer.

or metaphysical truth whilst practising the Middle Way, and to treat the Middle Way itself as a metaphysical absolute contradicts and undermines it as a method. Statements about the Middle Way are helpful and provisional generalisations whose worth must be assessed in practice, not 'truths'. Nor, on the other hand, are they falsehoods.

Nevertheless, the tendency to absolutise, and to turn the reasonable generalisation of one moment into the metaphysical dogma of the next, is one that humans apparently find very difficult to resist. It may well be the case that Jung himself sometimes failed to resist the temptation to turn the Middle Way into metaphysics (though this is a highly debatable point, and one that I will return to), despite his clear disavowal that any of his work involved metaphysical claims.[17]

1.c. The Buddha's quest

It is also helpful in this regard to make some comparison with the treatment of the Middle Way in Buddhism, where the same tendency is constantly evident. Rather than starting only with Buddhist doctrine about the Middle Way, we are more likely to find the Middle Way as a method of judgement in the process of a narrative where a character has to encounter dilemmas and make judgements. The prime narrative that exemplifies the Middle Way in Buddhist tradition is that of the Buddha's quest leading up to his enlightenment. The story has been much embellished by Buddhist tradition, but since it is not its historicity but its value as a symbol of the Middle Way that is at stake, there is no harm in considering the story as the tradition tells it[18] rather than as scholars or revisionists may prefer to tell it.

The Buddha (Siddhartha Gautama) was said to have been born a prince in the land of the Shakyas, and to have had an extremely protected upbringing, closeted in a beautiful palace and its grounds.

---

17 E.g. Jung CW 5 §95, CW 14 §7.

18 The earliest sources for this story are in the Pali Canon: *Digha Nikaya* 14, Walshe (1995) p. 199 ff; *Anguttara Nikaya* 3:38, Nyanaponika and Bodhi (1999); *Majjhima Nikaya* 26 and 36, Ñanamoli and Bodhi (1995). A more popular and highly embellished later source is Ashvaghosha's *Buddhacarita* ('Acts of the Buddha'), Johnston (1972).

He grew up, received a princely education, married and had a child, all without leaving the palace or encountering the suffering beyond it. His life is said to have been filled with distracting pleasure.

However, one day he told his charioteer to drive him outside the palace, and there he encountered the 'four sights' (an old man, a sick man, a corpse, and a religious mendicant) that made him aware of the torments of suffering and of alternative ways of life. He thus renounced his life as a prince, left the palace and went forth into the forest as a spiritual mendicant, seeking enlightenment as a solution to suffering.

In the forest he received spiritual instruction from two successive teachers, Alara Kalama and Udaka Ramaputta, and learnt much from them, but was not satisfied with their answers as the final ones. He then fell in with five ascetics, who were engaged in austerities in the belief that inflicting pain and hardship on themselves in this life would lead to a better rebirth in future. Though he was said to have excelled in these austerities, Siddhartha then realised that they would not help him, but merely weaken his body. His body was necessary for any spiritual development. It is then that he is said to have recognised the Middle Way between that of the palace and that of the ascetics. He gave up fasting, allowed his body to become stronger, and then gradually moved towards enlightenment by using techniques of meditation and reflection that increased his awareness.

The parallels between this story and Jung's encounter with Izdubar may not be immediately apparent, but they are nevertheless striking. Jung leaves 'the West' because he is dissatisfied with the meaninglessness of life there, 'the sun's empty darkness', just as the Buddha leaves the Palace. Both the West and the Palace are enclosed places of certainty, where people are absorbed in conventions that they take to be all there is to life, even though they are ignoring important conditions beyond that enclosed sphere. Jung seeks 'The East' for a solution, just as the Buddha seeks the Forest. Both encounter fear, difficulty, and obstacles. Both come to recognise the flaws and weaknesses of an absolutised religious perspective, which proves to be another enclosed place of certainty ignoring important conditions. Both reach a 'halfway' point before fully embracing the absolutised religious perspective, realising that it would destroy their quest. Both start to practise the Middle Way by reframing the situation to deal with a dilemma, recognising that there are third alternatives to the opposed absolutes they have been presented with, and that these third alternatives will address the conditions better and allow them to develop.

In Buddhist tradition, however, this story is normally told only as a prelude to the central event of the Buddha's attainment of enlightenment (nirvana, or awakening), which he is said to have achieved by means of the Middle Way. Enlightenment is often described as the awakening to a reality that is not otherwise appreciated by the unenlightened. This attainment then provides the Buddha with revelatory authority as the founder of Buddhism. The promise is held out that we all, too, could attain enlightenment through the practise of the Middle Way, but this creates an important conflict: that the absolute status of the Buddha's achievement itself has to remain questionable for the Middle Way to be practised. If our personal path encounters the Buddha's own authority as one of the extremes to be questioned and reframed, we will need to be able to set aside that authority in order to practise the Middle Way.

In my experience, some Buddhists accept this point, whilst others do not. Some recognise that following the Buddha's insight may actually be incompatible with 'Buddhism' in the sense of unconditional allegiance to the authority of the Buddha or of the tradition he is said to have founded. The Buddhist tradition itself (particularly in the Mahayana schools of Tibet, China, and Japan) tries to neutralise this authority by using a great deal of paradoxical language. They say that the enlightened state is ultimately identical to the unenlightened, both being ultimately 'empty',[19] or even that if we meet the Buddha on the road, we should be prepared to kill him.[20] However, it is practical judgement that tests the worth of such paradoxical language. If you are a member of a group, maintaining membership of which in practice requires you to accept the authority of the Buddha, you are not likely to be able to practise the Middle Way unless you can make your membership of that group conditional – unless you are prepared to participate in that group insofar as it helps you on the middle path, rather than treading a way that is presented as the middle path because that is what the group does.

---

19 See any of the *Prajñaparamita* (Perfection of Wisdom) literature, e.g. the *Diamond Sutra*, Price and Mou-Lam (1969).
20 Zen ko'an attributed to ninth century master Lin Chi.

1.d. No final goal

These contradictions in Buddhism are created not only by the appeal to the Buddha's authority, but by the belief in a final goal for the Middle Way on which it depends. When we follow a literal path, we are generally doing so in order to reach a particular destination that we have in mind, so of course it becomes habitual to also ask that question even in relation to the metaphorical path such the Middle Way. As goal-oriented creatures, we are very likely to have goals in mind when following the Middle Way, such as overcoming difficulties with relationships, achieving greater happiness, or becoming more like a model character who has inspired us. These goals are compatible with the Middle Way as long as they are not absolutised: as long as we are prepared to combine them with, or even abandon them for other goals that come to seem more important in later experience. However, a final goal for the Middle Way as a whole, when it becomes an object of belief rather than just a meaningful symbol, immediately becomes an absolute goal, and one that is incompatible with the Middle Way itself. The Buddhist insistence that we follow the Middle Way *in order to achieve enlightenment* fatally undermines it, because we can still sincerely believe that we are following the Middle Way when we are merely making judgements on grounds that the word 'enlightenment' or 'Buddha' has become abstractly attached to. There have been Sinhalese fundamentalists engaged in terrorist acts against Tamils,[21] and Zen leaders who supported Japanese fascism during the Second World War,[22] who could all have claimed to be following the Middle Way merely because they were following Buddhism.

In the *Red Book*, however, Jung evidently surpasses mainstream Buddhism by showing an appreciation of this problem. He appears to grasp the nettle by recognising that the Middle Way cannot have a final goal. At one point Jung imagines what it would be like to have reached the end of the path, and asks questions about the implications:

> *How will it be, now that God and the devil have become one? Are they in agreement to bring life to a standstill? Does the conflict of opposites belong to*

[21] Bartholomeusz and Da Silva (1998).
[22] Victoria (1997).

the inescapable conditions of life? And does he who recognises and lives the conflict of opposites stand still?[23]

In a bizarre and comic episode, he then sends his soul on a mission to dig up answers to these questions. His soul digs out the Holy Trinity and Satan; but it is only Satan, though irascible, who is prepared to offer any answers. Satan tells him that he agrees with the feelings Jung has already experienced about the end of the path, finding 'this standstill unbearable'. He urges him to 'revoke your completely harmful innovation' (of ending opposition) because 'the absolute is boring and vegetative'.[24] In other words, complete integration of opposing desires is incompatible with life, which requires conflict to continue. Jung accepts Satan's characterisation of absolute unity as incompatible with life, which seems to apply equally well at the individual and the cosmic level. The end of conflict in the universe would be entropy, and in the individual it would be a 'standstill' – a loss of stimulating energy.

Satan's recommendation to stop ending opposition (which Jung does not follow) represents a common response to this type of argument, which is to take it as a reason for rejecting the Middle Way as a whole, and thus as a justification for dismissing the Middle Way approach, regardless of its obvious value in more immediate experience. However, rather than undermining the Middle Way as a process, what the argument shows is the incompatibility of the Middle Way with any final achievement, and the importance of understanding it only as a method of judgement forming part of a process. The justification for the Middle Way lies in our experience of it working in each specific context, not in any final achievement. It is incompatible with any absolute justification because it involves the setting-aside of absolute justifications.

Nevertheless, it is possible to develop confidence in the Middle Way on the basis of experience – confidence of a kind that is more practically grounded and justified because it is embodied and imperfect, and stronger in practice than the brittle certainties one may build through appeal to the remote achievements of a distant historical figure, or appeal to scriptural revelations, or abstract deductions from assumptions about the metaphysics of the universe as a whole.

---

23 LS 160, LFT 318, RE 420-1.
24 LS 161-4, LFT 319-20, RE 420-3.

Jung shows unshakeable confidence of this kind throughout the *Red Book*, whose constant theme throughout many varied experiences is the importance of integration of opposing desires in the psyche. Jung recognises that integration can only occur through constant stretching of his own assumptions, which could never occur if he abandoned the Middle Way by taking any position as absolute.

Given that the Middle Way is a practice that needs to be adaptable to every new situation, the balancing of openness of judgement with closure is a further factor that helps to avoid the problem of 'standstill'. The Middle Way does not require us to suspend judgement indefinitely, but only as long as possible, so as to avoid 'fast' thinking (to use Daniel Kahneman's term[25]) when 'slow' thinking (which is more aware and reflective) can be used. However, some situations obviously require us to think fast and to fall back on trained procedures that we first developed slowly. Not all fast thinking is absolute thinking, but it is quite often a sign that we are falling back on absolutising shortcuts. The need to limit the amount of information and the range of values we consider for practical reasons is recognised by Jung in a striking passage where his soul dredges up all kinds of terrible but also wonderful things from the depths, representing human history from old armour to epidemics to temples. Jung continually says that he will accept it all, whatever the soul dredges up, but then finally snaps and changes his mind, saying 'That is an entire world – whose extent I cannot grasp. How can I accept it?' He then concludes that he must limit himself, and his soul instructs him to 'Be content and cultivate your garden with modesty.'[26]

1.e. Understanding the extremes

Another problematic aspect of the Middle Way as it is interpreted in the Buddhist tradition is the limitation of formulations as to which opposing extremes the Middle Way seeks to unite. The opposing positions are in Buddhism called 'eternalism' and 'nihilism' (or 'annihilationism') and are normally explained as opposing positions concerning the continuation of the essential self after death, with 'eternalism' (the belief of the five ascetics) affirming such

---

25 Kahneman (2010).
26 LS 124, LFT 305–6, RE 374–5.

continuation, and 'nihilism' (the belief in the palace) denying it. Each of these extremes, focused on this one essential belief that defines it, is then also associated with other absolute beliefs and moral qualities. Eternalists are associated with rigid codes of ethics, self-denial and asceticism, because they believe that they will be rewarded for these in another life, whereas nihilists are associated with hedonistic self-indulgence, because there are no future consequences for this after death. Mahayana Buddhism then also went on to identify eternalism with belief in an ultimately real world, and nihilism with its denial. However, in order to sustain this model of the Middle Way, Buddhists are obliged to believe in opposing bundles of beliefs, with each element of each bundle taken to necessarily imply all the others.[27]

I discovered the inadequacy of this view of the Middle Way myself the hard way, by writing a PhD thesis which largely consisted of an attempt to classify different types of philosophy as 'eternalist' or 'nihilist'.[28] Even after revising the definitions of 'eternalism' and 'nihilism' from the traditional Buddhist ones to try to make them more adequate, I ended up having to over-stretch each philosophy to make it fit this pre-conceived scheme. Belatedly I realised that though 'eternalism' and 'nihilism' may have been the extremes that the Buddha encountered in his time and place, the Buddhist tradition had made a mistake in assuming that these are the definitions of the extremes that fit *every* time and place. People who have beliefs that involve denying future lives are not necessarily self-indulgent: for example, they could be hard-working but materialist scientists living stringent lives. Likewise, people who believe in future lives after death are not necessarily self-denying and ascetic: they could, for example, be jolly, bibulous monastics after the fashion of Friar Tuck in the tales of Robin Hood. These inadequate assumptions about necessary bundles of absolute beliefs may be one reason for the Middle Way often being effectively ignored, or at least given a very limited role in presentations of Buddhist teachings, by critical modern Buddhists.[29]

Eventually I realised that the extremes avoided by the Middle Way are much simpler, more flexible and more universal than this.

---

[27] The sources for these, as well as the incoherence of the assumptions made about the bundles, are discussed in more detail in Ellis (2019) 4.c.
[28] Ellis (2001).
[29] See Ellis (2019) 4.d for a fuller version of this argument.

It is not necessary to form and defend theories about bundles of absolute beliefs, only to avoid absolute beliefs of all kinds. These do often form interdependent bundles of assumptions, but those bundles do not always form predictable patterns. It would also be bizarre and ironic if the defending of beliefs about the extremes prevented us from actually practising the Middle Way because we started to absolutise those beliefs. I thus concluded that the Middle Way is the practice of avoiding *all* absolute beliefs in our judgements, whether those beliefs are positive or negative, conscious or unconscious.

As in many other respects, though, when I came to read the *Red Book* I found that Jung had long anticipated the conclusions I had reached so laboriously, as well as being well in advance of the thinking I had encountered in the Buddhist tradition. Throughout the *Red Book* he applies the Middle Way to a very wide variety of oppositions, with no indication that it might have ever occurred to him that they were limited. The following particularly beautiful passage explicitly states his openness to overcoming all oppositions:

> *The door should be lifted off its hinges to provide a free passage between here and there, between yes and no, between above and below, between left and right. Airy passages should be built between all opposed things, light smooth streets should lead from one pole to the other. Scales should be set up, whose pointer sways gently.*[30]

The image of the scales is one that implies *incrementality*: that is, the substitution of judgements that are a matter of degree for ones that require absolute opposition. This again requires reframing, and in my own work I have suggested a variety of ways in which this reframing can be achieved with various common but intractable oppositions.[31] For example, absolute oppositions between freewill and determinism can be turned into an incremental scale of degrees of responsibility or of conditioning.

1.f. The individual way

Many other crucial aspects of the Middle Way can be traced in the *Red Book*, with some of these also easily misunderstood. The Middle

---

30 LS 114, LFT 302, RE 361.
31 Ellis (2015) section 4.

Way involves a subtle but consistent practical perspective dependent on a fine balance. In interpreting the *Red Book* it is easy to slip into an absolute on one side or another, and only one such slip can easily begin to confuse one's sense of what Jung is saying.

At the very beginning of *Liber Primus*, Jung uses the heading *'Der Weg des komenden'*.[32] This has been translated as 'The way of what is to come', but it would be easy to read that translation as referring to forecasting of the future. Instead, the term 'the way' (der Weg) is used throughout the *Red Book* to mean the Middle Way. The Middle Way is also 'the way of coming things' because it continually unfurls forwards from the present, consisting of a series of unique judgements. Your path depends on where you start, not only in terms of time, but also in terms of space and in terms of the state of each psyche, and it changes from moment to moment. No absolute description of such a path is possible, which is presumably why Jung says that nothing can justify it. He cannot prove it to others, but nevertheless, having understood it, he feels its overwhelming importance and that he must try to communicate it.[33]

The Middle Way is simultaneously individual and universal. Jung writes 'There is only one way and that is your way' and warns others away from the assumption that their path must be like his.[34] At the same time, however, one individual *functionally* resembles another. Jung's Middle Way resembles my Middle Way and your Middle Way, as long as we are all subject to the same basic human conditions: a similar physical structure, a limited lifespan followed by death, desires accompanied by positive and negative valuation, a capacity for language, assumed beliefs about the world that enable us to operate within it, and the capacity to absolutise those beliefs or to avoid doing so. It does not matter in the least how these conditions came about, as long as we share them. I think this is the underlying reason why Jung's experiences are probably meaningful to all, or at least the vast majority, of his readers. Jung experiences that universality in a more immediate and intuitive fashion:

> *The spirit of this time whispered to me: 'This supreme meaning, this image of God, this melting together of the hot and the cold, that is you and only you.' But the spirit of the depths spoke to me: 'You are an image of the unending*

---

32 LP i(r), LFT 229, RE 117.
33 LP i(v), LFT 229, RE 119.
34 LP ii(r), LFT 231, RE 125.

world, all the last mysteries of becoming and passing away live in you. If you did not possess all of this, how could you know?'[35]

The spirit of this time (which often speaks in a scientific tone) might dismiss Jung's fantasies and reflections as anecdotes with no further necessary implications. If Jung was offering theory, or generalised beliefs based only on one case, that might be correct. But instead, Jung is overwhelmingly offering *meaning*, not belief, talking here of the *supreme meaning* that he also identifies with God. He is offering us a huge range of resources from which to construct our own understanding of the best way to live. These resources take the form of gestalt *images* that are creatively varied with each iteration, rather than descriptions that must be precisely copied.[36]

In contrast to beliefs, which need to be specific to our circumstances to be useful to us, meaning is largely passed on to us from our total heritage – biological, cultural, and linguistic. As will be detailed in chapter 9, Jung's approach can be best understood in relation to embodied meaning, and is liable to be simply dismissed by those who are attached to representationalist theories of meaning that take meaning to be dependent on the potential for belief in some way. Embodied meaning theory makes clear, however, that meaning is not dependent on belief: rather beliefs are built up from the meaning available to us as synaptic links associated with symbols and stimuli. If we do not understand the very possibility of the Middle Way through words and symbols that convey it in its subtlety, it will not be available to us, and the main task involved in communicating the Middle Way (as I have discovered myself) lies in making it meaningful rather than convincing people of it. Once people really understand it, its value seems obvious, and they can forge a Middle Way for themselves.

The spirit of the depths, then, is not conveying belief in some kind of mysterious Platonic imprint of universal truth to be found in each individual. Instead, the meaningful symbols to be found within Jung's inherited experience provide universal resources that equip other individuals with the potential to develop a version of the Middle Way that is unique to their circumstances. The variations between individuals create variations in the way that

---

35 LP i(v), LFT 230, RE 121.
36 Hogenson (2014) explores the role of the idea of *image* in Jung's work.

the Middle Way is expressed, but there is nevertheless universality in the meaning and relevance of the *motif* that is thus varied. The Middle Way can only be understood as theory in *negative* respects that we need to understand in order to avoid its destruction, i.e. in its avoidance of absolutisation, which in turn requires a theory of what absolutisation consists in.

1.g. Scepticism

In order to avoid absolutisation, the Middle Way is also sceptical. The scepticism must be balanced and Pyrrhonian, meaning that it offers doubts about all claims *both* of truth *and* of falsity. Only by doubting one set of 'truths' can we integrate them with their opposite – but we don't achieve that by merely swapping sides and declaring the 'truths' false. Rather we need to adopt a provisional perspective accompanied by a cultivation of awareness, sitting in the middle and attempting to reframe our understanding in a way that avoids the extremes. There is thus nothing negative about scepticism, but it is rather a starting point for creative integration.[37]

In the context of Buddhism, such scepticism can be found in the Buddha's balanced rejection of absolute or final beliefs. For example, in one well-known discourse, he is approached by a disciple called Malunkyaputta who is obsessed by questions such as whether the universe is infinite or eternal, whether or not there is a self or soul, and whether an enlightened person continues to exist after death. He is so obsessed with finding answers to these questions that he threatens to leave the Buddha's following if he is not given answers to them. However, the Buddha refuses to answer such questions. He does not affirm nor deny any of the positions, and in the spirit of the fourfold logic used in that context, also refuses to state whether both or neither of the two alternatives in each case are true. To explain his refusal to answer these questions, he uses the simile of a man struck by an arrow, who asks interminable questions about where the arrow comes from and how it is made rather than pulling the arrow out.[38]

---

[37] For more details on sceptical argument, its implications and the ways these have been traditionally misunderstood, see Ellis (2012a) section 1. Its misunderstanding in a Buddhist context is also discussed in Ellis (2019) 4.a.

[38] *Majjhima Nikaya* 63, Ñanamoli and Bodhi (1995).

It is clear from this story how much the Buddha appreciated that scepticism needs to be adopted for entirely practical reasons: in this case to address the immediate conditions of suffering by pulling out the arrow. Some questions about the arrow may have practical value, but the Buddha's criticism is of the valuation of 'answers' that are purely abstract and bear no relationship to our experience of helpful development.[39] Sceptical argument offers us a tool to avoid being caught up in these abstract and irrelevant questions, as we recognise that there is no justification either for affirming or denying positions about them.

Jung's whole approach in the *Red Book* requires such scepticism, but he never mentions the term, nor shows much interest in the epistemological arguments that underpin it by showing all our beliefs to be uncertain. However, the early importance of scepticism to Jung is made clear by Papadopoulos in his very helpful discussion of Jung's epistemology and methodology. To some extent Jung set this basic scepticism aside during the period between 1906 and 1913, when he was influenced by Freud's materialist positivism, but the *Red Book*, following the break with Freud, marks his return to earlier approaches. Papadopoulos points out that Jung consistently tried to develop a third approach between (positive) metaphysics, and the materialist scientism of Freud (which I would describe as involving negative metaphysics).[40] He also quotes an early epistemological statement reflecting Jung's balanced scepticism from his Zofingia Lectures in the 1890s:

> *The only true basis of philosophy is what we experience ourselves, of our world around us. Every a priori structure that converts our experience into an abstraction must inevitably lead us to erroneous conclusions. Our philosophy should consist in drawing inferences about the unknown on the basis of real experience, and not in drawing inferences about the inner world on the basis of the outer, or denying reality by affirming only the inner world.*[41]

The disentangling of such balanced scepticism from the 'scepticism' of those who adopt sceptical arguments but use them to support negative dogmas has been an ongoing problem of both Jung's time and ours. Jung was clearly familiar with Nietzsche, who

---

39 For further discussion see Ellis (2019) 3.d.
40 Papadopoulos (2006) p. 15.
41 CW Supplementary volume A §175.

uses a good deal of sceptical argument, but whose approach Jung describes in the *Red Book* as 'too agitated and provocative' and 'too oppositional'.[42] So it may be that, like many other Western thinkers, Jung mistakenly associated philosophical scepticism solely with a destructive attitude to traditional resources of human meaning. Nevertheless, Jung constantly takes a sceptical approach in the *Red Book*. Only occasionally does this become more explicit:

> Man strives towards reason only so that he can make rules for himself. Life itself has no rules. That is its mystery and its unknown law. What you call knowledge is an attempt to impose something comprehensible on life.[43]

> He who cannot bear doubt cannot bear himself. Such a one is doubtful; he does not grow and hence he cannot live. Doubt is the sign of the strongest and the weakest. The strong have doubt, but doubt has the weak.[44]

In the second quotation here, Jung recognises the distinction between two types of doubt (a distinction also made in Buddhist tradition). What he describes as the strong having doubt is doubt put into a wider context of awareness and thus enabling reframing and integration. However, 'the weak' are those who do not have a wider context of awareness for their doubt, but are instead obsessed by it. Doubt then becomes an absolutised negative idea about the falsity of a particular claim or the unreliability of oneself or another. However, we have nothing to fear from doubt if it leads us to consider alternatives that might be better.

If we put scepticism together with the distinction between meaning and belief, it becomes evident that the idea of truth can be extremely meaningful to us without us actually having access to true beliefs or claiming to know the truth. It is thus that I interpret the constant references to 'truth' and 'knowledge' in the *Red Book*. 'Truth' can break in on us, in the sense that we acquire new resources of meaning with which to construct more adequate beliefs, but we do not thus acquire certainty that the new, striking and apparently highly applicable words we have gathered together can represent ultimate reality. Although Jung does not discuss truth as an archetype, it seems to me an entirely appropriate subject for archetypal interpretation. 'Our truth' is an archetype that is meaningful for us,

---

42 LS 99, LFT 293, RE 330.
43 LS 108, LFT 298, RE 348.
44 LS 114, LFT 301, RE 361.

but it should not be projected onto the world, nor assumed to be necessarily shared with others in the same form.

Just as we can find 'truth' meaningful in an archetypal fashion without claiming to have it, likewise the metaphysical objects of 'truth' or its denial. One of the foremost of these is God, who gets a great deal of discussion in the *Red Book* and will be the subject of the next chapter. Jung is consistently clear that he does not advocate belief in God as a metaphysical object, but the meaningfulness and power of God in his experience is equally clear throughout: 'it has seized me beyond measure and steadily goes on working in me'.[45] Jung's sympathetic separation of religious experience from religious 'belief' is a massive contribution to human thought, even though, a century later, few seem to have absorbed or even understood the value of that separation, let alone applied it so as to avoid the religious conflict that tends to follow without it. Yet the implications of that separation are even bigger than only the field of religious conflict. Wherever there is absolutisation, whether of factual or value claims, the power of our experience is not enough by itself to justify the dismissal of alternative interpretations of it. Scientists who assert that the 'facts' are obvious, politicians who turn the people's valuation of a term like freedom or greatness into unreflective votes, and addicts who are prepared to burgle a house for the sake of a few moments' oblivion from an underlying anxiety – all take an experience and absolutise it in a way that leads to the destructive dismissal of alternatives. All need a Middle Way that values their experience whilst putting it into a wider perspective.

1.h. Meaningful symbols and the brain

The value of intense experience, beyond the value it may have in itself, is often the inspiration it can offer in recollection. We associate the aroused experience with a symbol (the cross, a lover's nape, the word 'freedom') in a gestalt fashion – that is, taking them as an intuitive whole rather than going through a process of analysis. As long as that symbol remains alive for us, it can motivate new awareness and thus new responses, but as soon as it becomes a mere concept incorporated into a belief, it becomes only a token of conformity to a

---

45 LFT 338, RE 480.

group. It is that transition to mere conceptual tokenhood that marks the death of an ideal, turning a live symbol into an absolute belief. As Jung puts this:

> *Ideals are, according to their essence, desired and pondered; they exist to this extent, but only to this extent. Yet their effective being cannot be denied. He who believes he is really living his ideals, or believes he can live them, suffers from delusions of grandeur and behaves like a lunatic in that he stages himself as an ideal; but the hero has fallen. Ideals are mortal, so one should prepare oneself for their end.... The ideal is also a tool that one can put aside anytime, a torch on dark paths. But whoever runs around with a torch by day is a fool.*[46]

The Middle Way thus does not require anyone to abandon their ideals, as long as those ideals remain alive. When they threaten to die, we will need to revive them through exposure to wider experience. It is only through an ecological relationship with other ideals, allowing the uncomfortable new stimulus of 'truth' that is not merely the reiteration of familiar conceptual claims, that ideals become sustainable. 'Like everything healthy and long-lasting, truth unfortunately adheres more to the middle way, which we unjustly abhor.'[47]

Much light has been shed on this experience we have of live symbols as opposed to dead concepts, as well as on our tendency to absolutise, by Iain McGilchrist's work on the role of the brain hemispheres.[48] This use of information about the brain need not be at all reductive, but on the contrary simply provides us with a further layer of understanding of what we in any case experience. I shall only summarise this neuroscientific perspective briefly here, because it is such a large further subject in itself. The left hemisphere of the brain contains the adjacent tool-using and conceptual language centres of the brain, which tend to be generally dominant over the right hemisphere. However, wider meaning, in the sense of connections to bodily sensation and the senses, associated with symbols in increasingly complex ways through metaphor, is processed in the right hemisphere.[49] Our ability to avoid the death of symbolic meaning and accompanying absolutisation seems to depend

---

46 LS 34, LFT 276, RE 273.
47 LS 99, LFT 293, RE 331.
48 McGilchrist (2009).
49 Ibid. ch. 3.

on the extent of left-hemisphere dominance and the effectiveness of communication between the hemispheres. When symbols are 'live', we have effective connections between the hemispheres that allow us to maintain our awareness of the right hemisphere process, but when they 'die', they are reduced to a flat instrumentality that is indicative of a purely left-hemisphere processing.

Absolutisation seems to depend on the constant reinforcement of this left-hemisphere dominated, 'dead' conceptual belief through a feedback loop that also involves the organs that produce basic drives and anxieties (the striatum and the amygdala) in the 'primitive' or 'reptilian' part of the brain. This part of the brain produces chemical signals such as cortisol and dopamine, which motivate the activity of the more complex and aware front parts of the brain to objects of desire to be sought or of fear to be avoided. When this loop is dominated only by a relationship between the 'reptilian' brain and the linguistic and tool-using centres in the left pre-frontal cortex, the result is a narrow focus of attention and the instrumental limitation of symbols to mere signs, helping us to construct a linguistic model of the world around us that can help us to get what we seek or avoid danger. Because of the urgency of this instrumental state, wider awareness is suspended and the linguistic models we employ become rigid and absolute.[50] Socially, this often also implies absolute reliance on an in-group and the rejection of ambiguous relationships beyond it.

Sometimes we need to be in this kind of mode for practical reasons: for example in a survival situation. However, in a complex and increasingly secure modern society it is more likely to hamper us by shutting off our ability to recognise new information that we need for a more adequate response to our environment. However, our brains fortunately also offer us the capacity to avoid this closed feedback loop. If we can sufficiently relax the activity of the striatum and amygdala so that they do not undermine our responses to the world by over-reacting, and if we can develop sufficiently strong inter-hemispheric communication, we can remain open to new meaning through our bodies, senses and faculty of metaphor, all in the right hemisphere. Though the left hemisphere may remain

---

[50] This account, combining 'front-back' and 'left-right' brain dynamics, is consistent with McGilchrist, as well as the account of different types of integration developed by Daniel Siegel (Siegel 2015, 2006).

dominant, it will then not be over-dominant in a way that undermines our awareness. The feedback loop will be opened to allow new inputs, and we will become more flexible and adaptable. Every time we open the feedback loop as we make a judgement, we are practising the Middle Way.

This type of explanation of the Middle Way can be extremely useful in making us aware of an additional dimension of the conditions that produce it, but it is also dispensable. Jung is a key illustration of this, as he was able to recognise and present the Middle Way with hardly any of the neuroscientific knowledge on which the account in the last three paragraphs is based, all of which has developed in the century since he composed the *Red Book*. Just as it is not the authority of the Buddha that makes the Middle Way helpful and justified, nor is it scientific information, helpful as the presentation of the Middle Way in either of these contexts may be.

A brain-based model of the Middle Way also carries the danger that it will be entirely viewed in the terms of a scientific theory, to be investigated and verified (or disputed) in the light of further observation. Such investigation will be valuable, and may inform our interpretation of the Middle Way and make it more adequate. However, it cannot change the basic relationship of the Middle Way to meaningful experience, or the fact that people need to have meaningful experience of it first, before they can understand it, and make use of scientific observations that relate to it. Once the Middle Way is understood as a practical option, it is then unlikely to be the scientific data that decisively influences their acceptance of it.

1.i. Facing the unholy alliance

Jung's *Red Book* shows an awareness not only of the nature of the Middle Way, but of these difficulties in communicating it. Merely recognising and compensating for past extremes is not enough, and human bias and prejudice will often swing back into operation to distract people even after they have had some intimation of the Middle Way. These problems are directly encountered in confrontations with Jung's interior characters, particularly in the ironic chapter called 'The Remains of Earlier Temples'.[51]

---

51 LS 32, LFT 275, RE 268 ff.

Here Jung re-encounters two figures that he has previously met separately: the Red One (who is identified with the Devil) and Ammonius, the anchorite. In these previous encounters, the Red One has mistaken Jung for a dogmatic Christian, and Ammonius has mistaken Jung for Satan, in each case illustrating the tendency of those entrenched in each extreme to reject all those who challenge them as necessarily being on the opposite side (try introducing a Middle Way perspective into a debate about, say, abortion, or a particularly fraught and contested area of politics, and you are likely to experience this phenomenon).

However, when Jung meets these figures again he is astonished to find them together. It also turns out that his meetings with each of them have impelled the changes. Ammonius, who used to be a hermit, was moved by Jung's suggestion that he might get closer to the higher mysteries in contact with others. The Red One, on the other hand, was affected by Jung's remark about dancing to go and join the church so as to bring dancing into its liturgy. Both of these, it seems, have practised the Middle Way at these points, because they have reframed their assumptions and as a result engaged with desires and beliefs that they had previously rejected, resulting in a more integrated outlook. However, in both cases their new lives sent them down slippery slopes: the monk into hedonistic indulgence and the devil into ascetic excess of dancing. With the benefit of hindsight, they both blame Jung for setting them onto this ruinous course: 'We are not pleased, mocker and adversary, clear off, you robber, pagan!'[52]

This illustrates a phenomenon that any practitioner of the Middle Way will shortly encounter: that of the *unholy alliance*. Those who theoretically oppose each other often prove to have more in common than they suspect, and feel more threatened by someone who questions the paradigm on which their opposition is based than they do by each other. The two 'extremes' thus unite against the middle. The Red One and Ammonius also illustrate the exceptionalism of prejudice, by scapegoating 'the other side', but making an exception for those they know personally who belong to it (just as racists may make an exception for those of their reviled race that they know personally, whom they claim lack the normal negative characteristics of that race).

---

52 LS 33, LFT 276, RE 271.

Illustration 1. Jung's illustration from 'The Remains of Earlier Temples' (*Red Book* facsimile LS 32). Used by permission of W.W. Norton & Company, Inc.

> A: *I must confess I did not fare so badly with the Red One; he's a toned-down type of devil.*
>
> R: *I must add that the monk is hardly the fanatical type, although I've developed a deep aversion against the whole Christian religion since my experience in the monastery.*[53]

Both also cite practical necessity that requires them to associate with a member of the opposite group, but refuse to allow their pragmatic peacefulness to extend to Jung.

All of this goes to show some of the great difficulties attending the practice of the Middle Way. One can set off along it, but once again be halted or even go backwards. One can fail to overcome

53 Ibid.

conflict because others are not ready to do so and persist in their oppositional models. Most ironically, one can be reviled for following the Middle Way itself, either by being lumped in with 'the other side' or even by being singled out for special persecution because one dares to question the basis of the unholy alliance. There is also a reverse danger, not so much illustrated in this story, of the Middle Way being appropriated and assumed to be part of 'our side' so that its challenges are neutralised. Either way, all the phenomena of cognitive bias and cognitive dissonance will be much in evidence.

Jung's painting at the beginning of 'The Remains of Earlier Temples' also strikingly illustrates the theme (**illustration 1**). Within a large mosaic circle, there are two smaller circles at some distance from each other, rather reminiscent of an embryo, and possibly inspired by medical diagrams of embryos, as Joseph Cambray notes.[54] The two smaller circles each have a tiny figure inside with a hat, presumably representing the Red One and Ammonius. Although they both lie within the larger embryonic circle and are equally dependent on it, they are also fortified against each other.

However, we need to bear in mind, as in every vision of the *Red Book*, that all the characters are Jung himself. In response to this episode, Jung turns into a new being:

> This was a laughing being of the forest, a leaf green daimon, a forest goblin and prankster, who lived alone in the forest and was itself a greening tree being, who loved nothing but greening and growing, who was neither disposed not indisposed towards men.... I had absorbed the life of both my friends; a green tree grew from the ruins of the temple.[55]

Both the symbols of vegetation and those of the trickster are part of Jung's rich symbology of the Middle Way. The idea of us growing in the Middle Way like vegetation captures the idea of integrative development as a basis of good, burgeoning in one direction rather than being caught in oppositions. This will reach fuller expression in the image of the Tree of Life, which I will discuss in chapter 5. The trickster, which Jung later developed as an archetypal figure, challenges and breaks up established assumptions unpredictably within the conventions of play and humour. There are a number of places in *Red Book* where Jung moves from his serious, prophetic tone to a lighter one, all in the service of opening our minds.

---

54 Cambray (2014) p. 40.
55 LS 34, LFT 276, RE 272-3.

2. God as Integrative Archetype

2.a. God's death and rebirth

In Nietzsche's *Thus Spake Zarathustra*, a book that seems to have profoundly influenced Jung, the sage Zarathustra famously asserts that God is dead.[1] Nietzsche's fuller statement of this assertion appears in *The Gay Science*:

> God is dead. God remains dead. And we have killed him. How shall we comfort ourselves, the murderers of all murderers? What was holiest and mightiest of all that the world has yet owned has bled to death under our knives: who will wipe this blood off us? What water is there for us to clean ourselves? What festivals of atonement, what sacred games shall we have to invent? Is not the greatness of this deed too great for us? Must we ourselves not become gods simply to appear worthy of it?[2]

For Nietzsche, God is dead because he is no longer relevant. His importance always came from human belief in his necessity, but simply by losing that necessity he is dead. His loss makes way for the idealisation of humanity instead, in the form of the Übermensch that Zarathustra extols.

Jung, who was the son of a pastor, must have taken from this great motif of late nineteenth century German culture the dispensability of the absolute God, but he did not thereby lose his sense of the experiential and cultural importance of God. Indeed, as we have already seen, he felt that God seized him beyond measure. Jung could not accept Nietzsche's conclusion that God is dead, because that would involve the denial of the experience of God, rather than integration of that experience. In the 'Seven Sermons to the Dead', later on in the *Red Book*, he thus has the wise old man figure Philemon directly contradict Nietzsche: 'God is not dead. He is as alive as ever.'[3] Nevertheless, Jung's prophetic yet revisionary tone

---

1 Nietzsche (1933) Prologue §2.
2 Nietzsche (1991) §125.
3 LFT 348, RE 516.

in the *Red Book* rather reflects that of Nietzsche, as he proclaims not the death, but the *rebirth* of God.

> *The spirit of the depths opened my vision and let me become aware of the birth of the new God.*
>
> *The divine child approached me out of the terrible ambiguity, the hateful-beautiful, the evil-good, the laughable-serious, the sick-healthy, the inhuman-human and the ungodly-godly.*
>
> *I understood that the God whom we seek in the absolute was not to be found in absolute beauty, goodness, seriousness, elevation, humanity or even in godliness. Once the God was there.*
>
> *I understood that the new God would be in the relative. If the God is absolute beauty and goodness, how should he encompass the fullness of life, which is beautiful and hateful, good and evil, laughable and serious, human and inhuman? How can man live in the womb of the God if the Godhead himself attends only to one-half of him?*
>
> *If we have risen near the heights of good and evil, then our badness and hatefulness lie in the most extreme torment. Man's torment is so great and the air of the heights so weak that he can hardly live anymore. The good and the beautiful freeze to the ice of the absolute idea, and the bad and hateful become mud puddles full of crazy life.*[4]

This new God is a not a supernatural entity loaded with perfection, omnipotence, omnipresence, absolute goodness and ultimate creativity. Rather he is a symbol of the Middle Way and the potentials it opens up. He is 'in the relative' in the sense of being found in ordinary imperfect experience, but not 'relative' in the sense of making all ways of equal worth. The Middle Way may need to be found by each individual in their own context, but is nevertheless the best way for them, which is different from other ways they might have taken. The best way will be the integrative way, the one that engages with what we have rejected as well as with the ideals we hold. The best way will take into account our contradictory feelings and take a sustainable path, rather than one that merely accords to a fixed concept of 'good' or 'truth' that dictates to our understanding at that moment.

---

4   LP v(r), LFT 243, RE 166.

2.b. The New God and Middle Way values

Jung's proclamation here also reflects Nietzsche in the attempt to go 'beyond good and evil' – at least in the sense that we have traditionally understood good and evil. However, where Nietzsche could only offer an alternative ethics based on the power, superiority and self-assertion of the individual, Jung offers instead quite a different and far more adequate new ethic, based on integration. Both Nietzsche and Jung appeal to 'life', but for Jung in the *Red Book* life itself is a symbol of the Middle Way, through the vegetative metaphor of growth and development, whilst for Nietzsche it only involves the sense of power experienced by the dominant and self-disciplined individual.

For Jung, God is still the arbiter of ethics, but divine ethics thus cease to be the institutionalised failure that was created by ignoring people's actual motivations and simply commanding them to behave in one way or another way. God is the spirit within each individual that can actually inspire them to act better, with more adequacy to each context. The new good is a more adequate good, because it takes into account the diverse and contradictory nature of each human psyche, as it veers from one extreme to the other, commits to ideals and fails to fulfil them, faces up to one condition and neglects another but then reverses.

Jung also later articulates more fully how the experience of God can inspire the reframing process by which the Middle Way is found in each moment:

> *On emerging, the God calls me toward the right and left, his voice calling out to me from both sides. Yet the God wants neither one nor the other. He wants the middle way. But the middle is the beginning of the long road.*
>
> *Man, however, can never see this beginning; he always sees only one and not the other, or the other and not the one, but never that which the one as well as the other encloses in itself. The point of origin is where the mind and the will stand still; it is a state of suspension that evokes my outrage, my defiance and eventually my greatest fear. For I can see nothing anymore and can no longer want anything. Or at least that is how it seems to me. The way is a highly peculiar standstill of everything that was previously movement, it is a blind waiting, a doubtful listening and groping. One is convinced that one will burst. But the resolution is born from precisely this tension, and it almost always appears where one did not expect it.*[5]

5   LS 138, LFT 311, RE 393.

If God integrates every quality, how can he guide me one way or another? But the need for God seems to lie in reminding human beings of a wider perspective that lies beyond our tendency to fixate (or absolutise) on one condition at the expense of the others. We can be prompted by our symbolic relationship with God to stop, expand our awareness and reflect, suspending our impulses in a way that may temporarily create all the discomfort that Jung describes. If we allow our intuitions to work by allowing *a symbol* to emerge, rather than only insistent reasons for acting one way or another, we can also become aware of alternatives that would otherwise be closed off to us. Such symbols emerge from our wider and more integrated experience rather than just our egoistic obsessions of the moment, and are thus unexpected. So God, in the terms of our experience, appears to be 'other', but is nevertheless part of our own psyche. Jung appears to be describing what many may practise in the course of silent prayer, meditation, or 'waiting on God'.

The relationship of this state of openness to the Middle Way becomes clear in the use of meditation in the Buddhist tradition. The most basic practice of mindfulness in Buddhism begins with awareness of the body, and we can then build on that body-awareness to become aware of our sensations, emotions, and thoughts.[6] This is a process of moving increasingly into the receptive openness of the right hemisphere's connection with the body, senses, and imagination, rather than the dominant closed loops that characterise left-hemisphere dominated states. Increasing awareness of God, then, should not be seen as dwelling on an abstraction in which we 'believe', but rather the opposite process of broadening out our beliefs through wider awareness to give them the widest possible context. It is only through such an opening to wider awareness that we are able to engage with the experience of God as a symbol, rather than his reification as a concept.

God is thus no longer concerned with obliging one choice rather than another, but rather with developing the judgement itself through the awareness of the person who makes the judgement. Some judgements will be harder and more challenging than others, especially when they involve taking into account new conditions. For example, supposing you are considering a more difficult and

---

6 *Digha Nikaya* 22, Walshe (1995); *Majjhima Nikaya* 10, Ñanamoli and Bodhi (1995).

God as Integrative Archetype

riskier choice, say of studying for a long period of years in preparation for a demanding and competitive profession such as medicine, over the easier option of taking an immediately available job that will keep you in comfort but not stretch you in the longer term. Should you follow a principle of making every effort to fulfil your potential, or should you follow one of limitation and precaution? It is the more difficult choice here that is the harder one to make, and it may be daunting both to decide on and to carry through. You will only be able to carry it through in the long-term if you recruit some of the energies that would otherwise have gone into wishing that you had taken the easier job. To try to get them on board you need to hold those contrary energies in mind, in a wider stillness, listening, and dialogue before you make the decision, and also as much as possible while you are putting it into effect. The decision still takes courage, but the more of you makes the decision, the less likely you are to make absolute assumptions that leave some major factor out of account.

This may be at least a part of what Jung means in the following passage in the *Red Book* (one that was apparently much corrected and worked over in draft):

> *The God holds the separate principles in his power, he unites them. The God develops through the union of the principles in me. He is their union.*
>
> *If you will one of those principles, so you are in one, but far from your being other. If you will both principles, one and the other, then you excite the conflict between the principles, since you cannot want both at the same time. From this arises the need, the God appears in it, he takes your conflicting will in his hand, in the hand of a child whose will is simple and beyond conflict. You cannot learn this, it can only develop in you.*[7]

This passage could be misread as offering a magical solution along the lines of Jung's Old God, one that makes the will simple just by being reassuring and effectively distracting attention from the conflict. However, that would be completely inconsistent with the rest of the *Red Book*. It seems more likely that what Jung meant here is that the will can only become simple when it *has* taken more into account and thus conflict is avoided. Jung's New God is a way of talking about the energy, awareness, and confidence we can experience when we adopt a more integrated response to things. However,

7 LP vii(r), LFT 254, RE 204.

because the process of integration is still a potential, part of the 'way of coming things', we cannot experience it as a whole. Rather we only get glimpses of it in moments of inspiration.

It is thinking practically like this, about the reframing process in judgement, that I suggest will help us most in getting to grips with what is meant by Jung's 'New God'. In one sense, God *is* the Middle Way, in the sense of being that process, though more specifically one could also say that in Jung's personal mythology Christ also represents the aspect of God that actually performs the practical mediation between the divine and the human (see chapter 4). God, though, is also a symbol of the goal or outcome of the Middle Way as far as we can grasp it. I have already argued (in chapter 1) that the Middle Way needs no beliefs about an absolute outcome such as enlightenment, and these are indeed incompatible with it. However, we can nevertheless maintain enlightenment (or those represented as achieving it – Buddhas) as a meaningful symbol of the goal of the Middle Way, and such a symbolisation of enlightenment is also functionally equivalent to God. As a *symbol*, the goal of the Middle Way proves inseparable from its process, though it is only as we engage with the process that we begin to get a fuller understanding of the meaning of the symbol.

2.c. Archetypes

The New God that Jung describes is an *archetype*, so before further exploration of this and other archetypes of the *Red Book* in particular it will probably be helpful to discuss them in general. Though Jung does not use the term 'archetype' within the *Red Book*, it is omnipresent in his other writings, and almost essential for understanding the significance of the *Red Book*. However, I have long held the opinion that the way Jung (and many Jungians) commonly try to explain the concept of archetypes is unnecessarily complex and offers too many hostages to fortune. Confronted with talk of the 'collective unconscious', 'personal unconscious', and even talk of Platonic forms, it is not surprising if many otherwise moderately open-minded folk start to become suspicious about the justification for 'belief' in archetypes. But archetypes are much simpler and easier to justify than this terminology suggests, and do not need to be contentious objects of belief. So I am going to ignore a good deal of the way Jung explains archetypes here[8] and offer my own unorthodox account, in the service of the practical goals of this book. The account I shall give, however, should be just as functionally effective in explaining the archetypes of the *Red Book* as any other.

If one chooses to focus on what they *do* in human experience, rather than on speculations about what they *are,* archetypes can be seen simply as labels for the expression of specific psychological functions that we encounter readily in experience. A psychological function turns desire (biological energy) into certain identifiable forms of expression that can be found in personal experience or behaviour, or in our cultural heritage, which fulfil a wide range of human needs (not only survival or reproductive needs). It is of no practical significance how these functions originated, and whether they are 'collective' or 'personal', for there is no clear way of knowing where the boundary lies in any case. Nor does it matter, for practical purposes, whether they are the result of genes, or environment, or some other mysterious process. It is reasonable to assume that these archetypal functions are shared by all human beings, simply because all human beings share the basic conditions that give rise to them just by virtue of being human beings.

To call the archetypes 'unconscious' today is also possibly to overwork a term that both Freud and Jung found necessary to counteract the assumption of a hugely exaggerated role for consciousness in the thinking of their time. However, 'unconscious', like 'secular', is a term that is probably only of temporary use to counteract previous rigidity in the way its opposite has been adhered to. Consciousness is merely an instantaneous edge to our awareness in which nearly everything remains implicit, even the experiences of a few seconds ago that we are no longer having now but which still influence our current experience. Nearly everything, then, is 'unconscious' in one sense, whilst also being potentially 'conscious', and Jung's achievement lies in telling us about the limitations of consciousness rather than telling us about something distinct called the 'unconscious'. I find 'embodied' a much more useful term than 'unconscious', because it reminds us of the way our experience arises, with varying *degrees* of explicitness, from the body. The archetypes are *embodied*. In chapter 9 I will say more about embodied meaning, and suggest

---

8   In Ellis (2021) 1.e and f I will offer a more detailed argument on the unnecessary assumptions in Jung's account.

that archetypes are a form of schema that is directly experienced as meaningful in the body, but then expressed through a variety of linked metaphors.[9]

The psychological functions from which embodied archetypes spring begin with our basic need to survive as humans, but then also develop in increasingly complex ways, up to and including the need for self-fulfilment. We need to turn our energies towards fulfilling our needs, and we find certain objects, actions, people, and goals ('things') attractive. Other things, however, potentially offer a threat, so we reject them and turn our energy against them. Amongst the things that we find attractive, some are already us or ours, so we will serve and protect these things and their goals. Other things that we find attractive, however, are 'other', being treated as beyond ourselves. We are intrigued by these attractive things that are other, and would like to possess them too, but their attraction also depends on their otherness and thus may be undermined by possession. If there are things that are us or ours that we come to reject, we rapidly come to regard them as 'other' too.

These three psychological functions provide the basis of the three most basic archetypes: the ego or hero archetype (mine and attractive), the anima/animus archetype (other and attractive), and the shadow archetype (rejected). At the most basic level, these are just ways of describing a particular type of meaning we ascribe to things, but this meaning becomes intensified by the degree of difficulty we encounter. For example, if you desire food that you already have in your cupboard, food is both attractive and yours, and you are unlikely to think about it much or tell stories about it. However, if you have to go out and hunt for it and overcome difficulties, your feelings about it and your urge to express them is likely to become stronger, turning you into the hero who is part of a story, fulfilling the goal of gaining food. The meaningfulness of the archetype becomes stronger the more difficulties there are in fulfilling that function, and thus the more energy has to be put into it. Cultural expressions of the archetype provide us with further support in meeting those challenges, for example in the shape of stories (in anecdote, mythology, art, or religion) where the hero defeats the shadow and comes to possess the attractive other.

---

9 This is discussed in greater detail in Ellis (2021) 1.c and d.

The problems arise as we get into the habit of applying the meaning of an archetype *in general* to a specific person or thing. This is another way of saying that we act in a biased and prejudiced fashion, making sweeping generalisations or denying reasonable ones. This is when an archetype is *projected*, usually onto ourselves or someone else who is not distinguished from the archetype, because it is so powerful and we are insufficiently aware to separate it from the more complex person behind our projection. Thus we may project the hero by really believing that our hopeless business will still succeed against the odds. We may project the anima/animus by falling in love – attributing mysterious positive qualities to a person, probably of the opposite sex, who largely lacks them. We may project the shadow by thinking of a politician we oppose as thoroughly evil, rather than containing a much more likely mixture of good and bad qualities. Even if the mixture is 99% bad and 1% good, we need to acknowledge that 1%. Projection is a form of absolutisation, because projection is problematic primarily because we are unaware of alternatives to the projected reality we are creating. We think we have got the final story.

We can avoid this projection of the archetype by separating the person from the archetype itself, both by reflecting on the difference and by cultivating appreciation of the archetype in itself. For Jung, much of the work of distinguishing archetypes from the people or things we project them onto was done in the process of psychoanalysis, but there are also a variety of types of personal practice that can facilitate it. Jung's huge body of writings about traditional symbols can all be read as celebrating the archetypes in themselves, so that we also feel less need to project them.

These three basic archetypes as they appear in the *Red Book* (the hero, anima, and shadow) will be the subject of later chapters, so I won't go into them any further here. However, I have not yet mentioned the God archetype. As the archetype of integration, the God archetype unites the other three basic archetypes. To fulfil our potential and to grow into something fuller than we are now, we need to fulfil our goals, but also choose the right goals – ones that are consistent, achievable, and beneficial; we also need to possess the attractive other, but not so much that it loses its power and benefit as other; and we need to gain an increasingly realistic view about how to distinguish genuine threats from other things that may vaguely remind us of threats. We need to avoid projection of

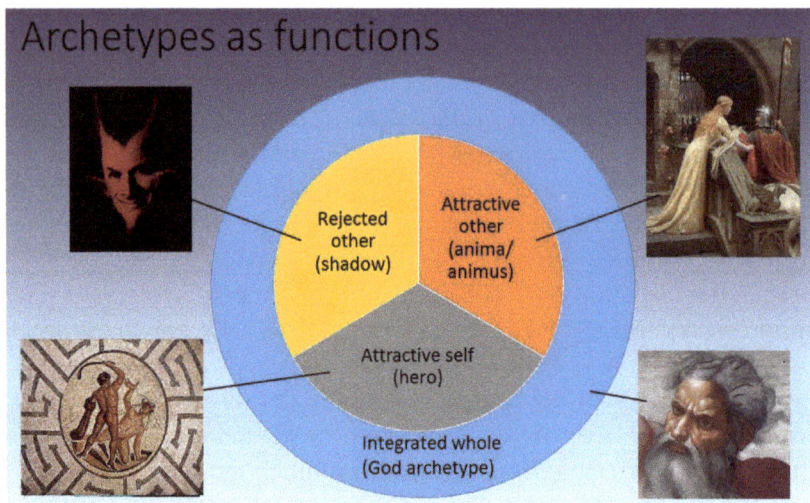

Illustration 2. Author's diagram of archetypes as functions, incorporating 'Devil Goat' by Rex Diablo (Wikimedia Commons), and other images that are public domain.

the archetypes in order to express them in more appropriate and adequate ways. The God archetype thus expresses the meaning and potential of integrating all the other archetypes, harmonising self and other, the attractive and the rejected. The diagram (**illustration 2**) shows this relationship between the God and other archetypes in visual form.

2.d. Integrating the God archetype

Now we can return to Jung's Old God and New God. In Jungian terms, both of the Gods are archetypal, but the New God is *consciously recognised* as archetypal – which is why, in the form of Izdubar, he can be carried home as light as a feather and then squashed into the size of an egg. The Old God, on the other hand, is a projected archetype: because there is a set of contradictory qualities that we would like to integrate, we assume that there is a being beyond ourselves who integrates them. We also project the activities of this God well beyond ourselves, into a universe that is also projected as an ultimate metaphysical reality. An acknowledged archetypal God, that is meaningful but not an object of metaphysical belief (which is the only kind of belief we could have in God due to his absolute features) is a *more adequate* kind of conception of God to have. If we can avoid projecting God we also avoid absolutising God, and being grossly deluded in our interpretation of divine experience.

The God archetype expresses the most crucial function because it is a moral function: that of living our lives effectively in relation to the conditions we encounter. If we *project* that moral function, it becomes inconsistent: we end up with a rule-giving tyrant whose rules are only right because they are given by him, somehow cohabiting with a loving God who saves us because we don't deserve it. These inconsistencies can only be glossed over, while belief in the absolute God continues, because we have reduced the worship of God to a set of 'dead' verbal formulae that we relate to overwhelmingly through the left brain, forming absolute beliefs that are also then beyond challenge because they are apparently immune to the effects of new information from the right hemisphere. We remain incentivised to accept these dead formulae only by the value of maintaining the approval of the religious group that uses them to create an easily manipulable shortcut to social power.

However, if, rather than projecting it, we recognise the God function as *our* moral function, we can begin to find it meaningful as a live symbol of integration. Instead of putting our energies into the constant challenge of believing and defending the unbelievable, we can start to put those energies into the actual practice of the path, and thus gradually overcome our conflicts and develop more meaningful lives.

This way of relating to the God archetype is an expression of the Middle Way that can also be illustrated in the stories about the Buddha. Shortly after his enlightenment, the Buddha is said to have encountered substantial doubts about whether it was appropriate to try to teach the insights he had gained. It would be very hard to communicate these insights, and he would be easily misunderstood. However, just as he became 'inclined to inaction' rather than teaching, his assumptions were challenged by a vision of God, in a form known as *Brahma Sahampati*.[10] Brahma offers something like a voice of conscience, broadening the Buddha's awareness so that he considers that there are some people 'with little dust in their eyes'

---

10 *Samyutta Nikaya* 6.2.561, Bodhi (2000) p. 234; *Majjhima Nikaya* 26:19 ff, Ñanamoli and Bodhi (1995) p. 260 ff.

who could benefit from his teaching.[11] He does not command, but is rather presented as pleading with the Buddha, and is thus clearly archetypal, either as a vision or as a personification of the Buddha's reflection processes. The crucial point is that he represents a glimpse of the Buddha's wider awareness, and is part of a process of development rather than a supposedly perfect or eternal point of view.

If in this way we identify God with a function of our own psyches, this also has the great advantage of identifying the *function* as universal rather than leading us to focus on the form it takes. I have already suggested that the meaning of God as an archetypal function is equivalent to that of Buddhist enlightenment and of enlightened beings such as Buddhas. I also suggested in chapter 1 that 'Truth' should be treated archetypally, where it would be another name for the God archetype, and I would also suggest similar interpretations of terms like 'Good', 'Nature', 'Beauty', 'Justice', and 'Liberty', all of which can have an absolute meaning that we can relate to archetypally, but which we should not claim absolute beliefs about if we are trying to follow the Middle Way.[12]

2.e. Varying names for the Self

Jung also uses a number of different names in different places in the *Red Book* for what remains, functionally, the God archetype: the Wise Old Man (which he recognises elsewhere as also potentially taking female form), Christ, the Tree of Life, and the Mandala (all of which will be discussed in subsequent chapters here). Jung later came to identify this archetype as 'the Self',[13] in the sense of the total potential self rather than the ego that we actually identify as ourselves, and this usage is foreshadowed in the *Red Book* in statements such as 'The God is behind the self, above the self, the self itself, when he appears.'[14]

It is thus entirely optional as to whether one uses the term 'God archetype' to describe this function. However, to do so has the advantage of connecting it readily to a large body of symbolism in a range of world religions. For some, the term 'God' immediately has

---

11 For a more detailed discussion of this episode, see Ellis (2019) 2.a.
12 See Ellis (2021) section 6.
13 Jung CW 6 §412.
14 LFT 338, RE 481.

negative connotations, and there may be a practical argument for them to initially engage with the God archetype in some other form – whether Buddhist, pagan or secularised – that does not conventionally have the term 'God' attached to it, and may be an impersonal symbol. However, if God is part of the set of meanings in our cultural background, we are most unlikely to succeed in eliminating the energy attached to the word 'God', and the integrative task of channelling that energy to helpful practical ends can only be put off temporarily.

2.f. Is the New God impotent?

The later part of the story of Izdubar, after Jung has brought him home squashed to the size of an egg, engages with some of the further issues potentially raised by the reduction of God to an archetype rather than a supernatural being. One anxiety that Jung seems to develop is that of the loss of God's power. Izdubar's loss of power is symbolised by his own destruction of his weapon. At first Jung seems to be accepting of this loss of divine power, and indeed to see its advantages:

> *He who conquers needs weapons. But what else do you want to conquer? You cannot conquer more than the earth.... You will not conquer anything for any length of time. Your power will turn into dust tomorrow.... So do not be a fool, throw down your weapon. God himself smashed his weapon. Armour is enough to protect you from fools who still suffer from the need to conquer. God's armour will make you invulnerable and invisible to the worst fools.*[15]

Jung seems confident at this stage that the practice of integration itself, making us more effective in our response to conditions, will make the use of power unnecessary. God's power is after all often abused, being appealed to to justify many human assertions of power. God is a dangerous weapon that humans will be better off without. Even the new archetypal God, Jung says, should be kept hidden:

> *The nearness of God makes people rave. They tremble with fear and fury and suddenly attack one another in fratricidal struggles, since each one senses the approaching God in the other. So conceal the God that you have taken with you.*[16]

15 LS 49, LFT 283, RE 297.
16 LS 49, LFT 283–4, RE 298.

If God's power consists only in the capacity for human absolutisation, leading to holy war, we are better off without it. However, the implication of this seems to be that God should be kept private.

Jung sings a series of incantations over the egg,[17] which celebrate the wonder of God despite this loss of power, but then suddenly anxiety strikes.

> *However, I am not ready, since I have still not accepted that which chokes my heart. That fearful thing is the enclosing of God in the egg.... I love and admire the powerful.... What is blasphemy compared to this? I would like to be able to blaspheme against the God. That way I would at least have a God whom I could insult, but it is not worth blaspheming against an egg that one carries in one's pocket.*[18]

Perhaps these reactions reflect an intuition many people will have at the idea of such a refashioning of the whole idea of God. Even atheists may feel such a nostalgia for a God they rejected. However, Jung then calms himself by recognising how much he loves God. Unlike God's power, his association with love need not be threatened at all by this new powerlessness.

Jung then opens the egg, an event that is dramatically captured in an accompanying picture (**illustration 3**). Izdubar dramatically emerges, and seems to be unharmed. Jung exclaims:

> *Oh Izdubar! Divine one! How wonderful! You are healed!*
>
> *'Healed? Was I ever sick? Who speaks of sickness? I was sun, completely sun. I am the sun.'*[19]

This suggests that, in principle, there is no loss of power for an archetypal God. After all, the religious experience of a non-theist (such as a Buddhist) can be just as intense as that of a theist, and the inspiration just as large. Jung's later comment that God had seized him beyond measure, already quoted in the previous chapter, suggests that this is also the case for Jung.

After this dramatic religious experience, however, Jung rapidly starts to feel a sense of anti-climax ('everything is as it has always been') and then starts to feel drained of energy:

17 LS 50–61, LFT 284–5, RE 200–304.
18 LS 62, LFT 285, RE 304.
19 LS 66, LFT 286, RE 308.

God as Integrative Archetype 51

Illustration 3. Jung's illustration of the opening of the egg (*Red Book* facsimile LS 64). Used by permission of W.W. Norton & Company, Inc.

> I did not know what was happening to me, since simply everything powerful, beautiful, blissful, and superhuman had leaked from my maternal womb; none of the radiant gold remained. Cruelly and unthinkably the sunbird spread its wings and flew up into infinite space. I was left with the broken shells and the miserable casing of his beginning, the emptiness of the depths opened beneath me.[20]

This experience seems to suggest that the transportation of God into the human world has not necessarily changed the basic repressive way in which absolutised belief operates, because the supernatural God is not the only source of absolutised belief. Jung's most basic psychological insight throughout the *Red Book* concerns the way in which our favoured ideals can only draw energy towards them by alienating another section of our energies. By creating a God and taking responsibility for it in this way, Jung seems to have set up a further conflict, excluding that part of himself that is not divinely-orientated and does not support this enterprise. He then feels drained of energy, because in order to bring about this new birth he has had to spend so much internally-focused energy holding his opposed feelings in check.

Jung's flip-flopping here is a further indication of his conflicted state. But ambivalent feelings can also precede breakthroughs. I do not interpret Jung as merely flip-flopping, but as gradually refining his underlying position as he becomes aware of each new turn of his feelings. We are not left with an undignified retreat back to a supernatural God, but rather with a realisation that recognising God as an archetype is only one necessary step on the path for many, not a panacea. One major reason for this is that God is not the only absolutising concept by a long way. Those who get rid of 'God' only to replace him with another projected absolutisation – such as the enlightened Buddha, the inevitable Communist revolution, the ultimate facts of Nature, or the coming Age of Aquarius – have really not made any particular progress. The genuine transformation of God into a symbol of integrative practice is also dependent on that integrative practice over a period of time, engaging with the shadows left by our ideals. It does not just depend on a sudden recognition that God is a human construction.

---

20 LS 67, LFT 287, RE 309.

2.g. Is the New God solipsistic?

Those used to the traditional theistic God may still nevertheless dismiss Jung's New God as 'individualistic' or even 'solipsistic', because it only appears in individual experience. Thus, for example, Drob writes 'It is...Jung's general *self-absorption* in this work that treads dangerously close to a solipsistic point of view.'[21] It is understandable that those unfamiliar with Jung's way of thinking may fall into this misunderstanding, but I find it concerning that someone who writes a whole commentary on the *Red Book* can do so. Solipsism is a metaphysical position that involves the denial of the existence of other people in the universe: one that almost nobody holds except a few schizophrenics,[22] but that for some reason offers a hugely exaggerated threat for some Western thinkers (particularly Wittgenstein, who appears to be constantly anxious about it). At no point in the *Red Book* does Jung deny the presence of other people. It is correct that the *Red Book* barely mentions other people in the 'external' world, but why should it, given that that is not its subject? We don't blame a book on Antarctic wildlife for telling us nothing about tropical wildlife. What this intellectual panic about 'solipsism' fails to take into account is that the *Red Book* is full of interactions with other people, namely the characters of Jung's visions, and that the underlying moral motive of the Middle Way with which Jung interprets those visions is overwhelmingly supportive of a more adequate engagement with others due to the separation of archetypes from their projections. If 'solipsism' is being reduced here to a mere lack of interest in other people, it is those who go round treating their boss as the devil, their lover as an angel, and themselves as a superhero who are uninterested in other people, because they are only interested in projected archetypes, not in what lies behind them. Jung's self-work as recorded in the *Red Book* potentially prepared him to avoid a much more dangerous type of 'solipsism'.

Jung addresses such concerns in relation to God in this passage:

> *We think that there is singleness within us, and communality outside us.... But if we are outside of ourselves, then we are single and selfish in the communal. Our self suffers privation if we are outside ourselves, and thus it satisfies its needs with communality. Consequently, communality is distorted*

21 Drob (2012) p. 61.
22 Sass (1994).

> *into singleness. If we are in ourselves, we fulfil the need of the self, we prosper, and through this we become aware of the needs of the communal and can fulfil them.*
>
> *If we set a God outside of ourselves, he tears us loose from the self, since the God is more powerful than we are. Our self falls into privation. But if the God moves into the self, he snatches us from what is outside us. We arrive at singleness in ourselves. So the God becomes communal in reference to what is outside us, but single in relation to us. No one has my God, but my God has everyone, including myself. So it is always only one God despite his multiplicity.*[23]

The unreflective assumption that we are single selves underlies so much unhelpful thinking! As Jung argues here, if we are 'outside our selves' in the sense of being in a state of conflict in which one part of us is pitched against another, we go into society with others to distract ourselves but simply project that conflict onto others. We are more likely to benefit society by becoming more whole first, which we can only do by recognising that we are not single in the first place. The projection of God as something external to us simply creates another such conflict. However, if God becomes identified with becoming more single and whole in oneself rather than with an external entity, this not only enables us to relate better to others, but also enables God to be shared with others. The absolutisation of God creates conflict with others, because we each believe that we have the correct 'truth' about God and his will, but the internalisation of God enables us to find common ground with others that did not exist before.

Jung has a similar answer for the traditional Christian concern with the God of love, which may be tied in with the concern that Jung is too self-absorbed.

> *Unequivocalness is simplicity, and leads to death. But ambiguity is the way of life. If the left foot does not move, then the right one does, and you move. The God wills this.*
>
> *You say: the Christian God is unequivocal, he is love. But what is more ambiguous than love? Love is the way of life, but your love is only on the way of life if you have a left and a right.*[24]

---

23 LP v(r), LFT 245, RE 172–3.
24 LP v(r), LFT 244, RE 170.

In other words, it is easy enough to talk about 'love', and appeal to it as a concept. However, to put it into practice requires one to constantly make choices as to how to act lovingly in an ambiguous context. For example, is it more loving to reprimand a child for an action that may become damaging if it turns into a habit, or to avoid over-reaction, set an example of calm, and be tolerant? In practice you will have to make choices between 'left' and 'right' in a state of uncertainty. A projected absolute God who offers us supposed certainties is not going to help us simply by telling us to be 'loving' in this kind of situation. What is required is that we become integrated enough to autonomously make a more adequate, though still uncertain, decision in applying the love that we already feel.

The *Red Book* is practically-orientated as well as inspiring, but often takes the form of intuitively-packed and somewhat opaque passages like the two quoted above. Yet when interpreted carefully in the light of the Middle Way, these passages yield a great deal that is relevant to the immediate practice of our lives as well as revolutionary in its implications. God is only one of the many areas where this is the case. We will find in the next few chapters that there is a lot more of this kind of material even in relation to different versions of the God archetype, even before we get on to the other archetypes.

3. The Wise: Elijah and Philemon

3.a. The Wise Old Man

On the night when I considered the essence of the God, I became aware of an image. I lay in a dark depth. An old man stood before me. He looked like one of the old prophets. A black serpent lay at his feet. Some distance away I saw a house with columns.[1]

Thus does Jung introduce his first vision involving a Wise Old Man figure. This figure is Elijah, the Old Testament prophet, and he is accompanied by Salome, the seductive daughter of Herod who demanded the head of John the Baptist. Jung encounters this pair in three successive visions at the end of the *Liber Primus*, then again twice later on. At first he is shocked by their pairing, and still coming to terms with the idea of an inner character, but the tone rapidly changes to one of instruction, with Jung seeking the wisdom of Elijah with the respectfulness of a disciple. Elijah also shows the confidence of the teacher, showing Jung visions for his instruction and rebuking him. By the time of the final encounter, in *Scrutinies*, the role of the Wise Old Man has been taken over by Philemon (of whom more later), and Elijah is a much diminished figure being instructed by Jung.

It is no coincidence that this vision arrives on the same night that Jung is considering the nature of the New God. For the Wise Old Man is an aspect of the God archetype. God the Father as depicted in the Christian tradition of art is generally in the form of a Wise Old Man, and we encounter the same archetype in our images not only of prophets but of wizards, saints, philosophers, Buddhas, and gurus. The female equivalent, the Wise Old Woman, is less commonly appreciated in traditionally patriarchal cultures, but the priestess and female oracle was an established figure in classical antiquity. When we try to think of God in human form, we tend to think of a figure who is old and wise. However, we cannot rule out

1 LP v(v), LFT 245, RE 174.

the possibility of seeing other kinds of figures that play the same role.

Age is associated with having had the opportunity to acquire wisdom from experience rather than with necessarily having done so, whilst wisdom is here equivalent to integration. The term that Jung most commonly uses for integration is actually *individuation*, and he tended to link individuation to the process of life, maturity and age. There is a case for distinguishing the two terms, though, because individuation is the integrative process of an individual over the period of their life, whereas integration refers more generally to the reconciliation of opposed forces. Integration can happen at any moment of judgement, and can happen to groups as well as individuals. Individuation is the result of an accumulation of integrations over a period of time. The Wise Old figure is individuated, which means they will have followed their own distinctive path of integration.

In Jung's own commentary on the initial scenes with Elijah and Salome (given in Appendix B of the published *Red Book*), he stresses the way in which Elijah represents *Logos* (a term which is associated with God in the opening of John's Gospel, and was also used by the Stoic philosophers to indicate the idea of supreme reason in Nature).

> *A descendent of Logos is Nous, the intellect, which has done away with the commingling of feeling, presentiment, and sensation. In contrast, the Logos contains this commingling. But it is not the product of such blending, or else it would be a lower animalistic psychic activity, yet it masters the blend, so that the four lower activities of the soul become subordinate to its principle. It is an independent principle of form that means understanding, insight, foresight, legislation and wisdom. The figure of an old prophet is therefore a fitting allegory for this principle, since the prophetic spirit unites in itself all these qualities.*[2]

Jung thus obviously wants to emphasise the integrative role of 'reason' in a broad sense: presumably one that is not necessarily about reasoning, but about wider awareness that can bring together other faculties and see them in relation to each other. The Wise Old Man figure is rich in these qualities, which are also the qualities of the archetypal God. Jung later differentiates this Wise Old Man figure

2 LFT 365, RE 563.

from the scholar figure who is a 'distorted likeness' of him,[3] presumably representing Nous rather than Logos – intellect disconnected from other qualities.

Like the supernatural God, however, the Wise Old Man is a projection. The person on whom the projection is placed is likely to have a degree of wisdom, Logos, or individuation, but cannot have an absolute integration, since (as already argued in chapter 1) this is incompatible with imperfect human life. Not only will Wise Old Men still not be aware of a large range of conditions, but even the judgement they apply to the conditions they are aware of will still be subject to biases and projections. The specific status given by various religious and philosophical traditions to wise religious teachers, such as the Buddha in Buddhism, or the Wise Man in Stoicism who has achieved eudaimonia, are thus projected discontinuities foisted by social requirements on the complex diversity of human development. There are no completely Wise Old Men or Wise Old Women, and if you think you have met a person who fulfils this archetype, the first necessary step is to differentiate the archetype from the person. That need not prevent us from appreciating wisdom in people – but wisdom is always a matter of degree.

Though this principle applies to people we meet in the world, we are in less charted terrain when we consider whether it applies to Elijah and Philemon in *The Red Book*, who are inner figures representing parts of Jung's own psyche. Are these figures infallible because they are internal, and thus not subject to the complex imperfections of the external? The answer to this will be clear when we consider that they are aspects of Jung himself. Is Jung himself infallible? Obviously not. Therefore, his inner figures, however much they represent a *more* integrated perspective than Jung's own habitual one, cannot be wiser than he is, but merely represent the best of his available wisdom.

3.b. Jung and Elijah

In his first vision with Elijah, Jung largely just utters incredulous questions and exclamations that show his difficulties in adjusting to the context of the vision. In the second, however, Jung's words

---

3   LS 8, LFT 263, RE 226.

towards Elijah seem to show a strong projection. He has effectively decided that Elijah can tell him 'truths' about the way to the integration that he craves, but is also awestruck, and confusion remains about how he should behave and what he really wants.

> *Forgive me, it is not obtrusiveness or arrogance that leads me here. I am here perchance, not knowing what I want. A longing that stayed behind in your house yesterday has brought me here. You see, prophet, I am tired, my head is heavy as lead. I am lost in my ignorance. I have toyed with myself enough.*[4]

Elijah then shows Jung a series of visions, to which Jung responds:

> *These visions are full of torment, and the meaning of these images is dark to me. Elijah, please shed some light.*[5]

At this stage, then, it is clear that Jung believes that Elijah offers an infallible source of wisdom. Projection is in full swing.

Typically of Wise Old Men, however, Elijah is evasive and often does not answer questions directly. He does not attempt to explain the visions, instead discussing Jung's motives and his reasons for being there. He asks awkward questions and tells Jung confidently that he is 'evasive', or 'lying'. In the third vision Elijah tells Jung that he 'wanted to come here far too much' and rebukes him for being impetuous. He reveals things to Jung about his own psychic states. However, he offers no 'truths', whether about facts, values, or methods. The nearest Elijah comes to this is what he says about his own status, thus implicitly offering the same argument I gave in the previous chapter against 'solipsism'.

> *You may call us symbols for the same reason that you can also call your fellow men symbols, if you wish to. But we are just as real as your fellow men. You invalidate nothing and solve nothing by calling us symbols.*[6]

Being an internal Wise Old Man, then, is much more about style than substance. A dignified setting is important, and you must be accompanied by mysterious symbols. However, you cannot actually tell the disciple anything he does not already know, but only bring emotions, beliefs and assumptions to light and ask probing questions. Your authority will also be reinforced by stinging rebukes.

---

4   LP vi(r), LFT 248, RE 184.
5   LP vi(r), LFT 248, RE 185.
6   LP vi(r), LFT 249, RE 187.

When I first read the *Red Book*, I was expecting all these classic archetypal projections to simply be reproduced all the way through, so that I could just enjoy the archetypal atmosphere – rather like a slightly more episodic version of J.R.R. Tolkien. So it came as a shock when, soon after the beginning of *Liber Secundus*, Jung started talking back to his inner figures, debating with them, disagreeing with them, and ultimately even defying them and instructing them. But then I realised that Jung is illustrating his own integrative process, which consists in critically considering and overcoming his projections without diminishing the archetypes themselves.

Jung's relationship with Elijah changes substantially later in the *Red Book*. This change is symbolised by Jung having stolen the serpent that Elijah always had with him in the earlier visions.

> *E: You have changed since I last saw you. You speak another language, one that sounds foreign to me.*
>
> *I: My dear old man, I'd like to believe that you find me changed. But you too seem to have changed. Where is your serpent?*
>
> *E: She has gone astray. I believe she was stolen. Since then things have been somewhat gloomy with us....*
>
> *I: I know where your serpent is. I have her. We fetched her from the underworld. She gave me hardness, wisdom and magic power. We need her here in the upperworld, since otherwise the underworld would have had the advantage, to our detriment.*
>
> *E: Away with you, accursed robber, may God punish you.*
>
> *I: Your curse is powerless. Whoever possesses the serpent cannot be touched by curses. No, be sensible, old man: whoever possesses wisdom is not greedy for power. Only the man who has power declines to use it.*[7]

The serpent represents that aspect of wisdom that offers power, and is unpredictable and devious. By stealing the serpent, Jung is integrating that wisdom into himself rather than seeing it as other, and his possession of the serpent reveals itself in much greater confidence than Jung showed in his first encounter with Elijah. He now addresses him with a touch of patronage as 'my dear old man', and gives him moral instruction. The tables are turned, because Elijah's role of representing Jung's wisdom is no longer necessary.

---

7   LS 186–7, LFT 324, RE 439.

In Jung's final encounter with Elijah and Salome, in *Scrutinies*, Elijah is presented as behind the times, because he still thinks in terms of one God whilst Jung has moved on to thinking of many gods. Elijah has become that aspect of Jung that is still rigidly attached to old thinking, and thus presented as even less wise. However, it is possible that Jung is to some extent deceiving himself, and that Elijah still represents wisdom of a kind he is no longer prepared to recognise. Elijah's decline is obviously closely related to the rise of his rival in the Wise Old Man stakes, namely Philemon.

3.c. Jung and Philemon

Jung first goes to see Philemon to seek magical instruction. Philemon is here presented as a retired magician, who has put away his magic books and now humbly cultivates his garden with his wife Baucis. When Jung requests magical instruction from him, he is quite off-hand and dismissive at first, but Jung is very persistent. Philemon then tells him that magic is not rational or a matter of the intellect, that it is 'the negative of what one can know', and that it 'eludes comprehension'. It is thus impossible to learn, and arises with the decline of reason in old age.[8]

Following this conversation, Jung enters into a paean of praise for Philemon. His name, together with that of his wife Baucis, comes from a classical story in which he hosts two visiting gods in disguise, offering hospitality that all his neighbours declined. Hosting the gods thus becomes a symbol for hosting integration. 'Philemon' means lover, but he is a lover of his soul rather than of others, following the argument mentioned in the last chapter as to the importance of integration in making love effective. Jung praises him for *not* acting like a saviour and for leaving others to work out the truth.[9] He is what Buddhists would refer to as a Tantric guru: a teacher who points to wisdom in contradictory ways and breaks social rules so as to challenge the assumptions of disciples. In the modern jargon of education and training you could call him a supreme facilitator, who never needs any recourse to 'chalk and talk', but who educates merely by manipulating the student's expectations to ensure that they learn.

---

8 LS 140–2, LFT 312–14, RE 398–402.
9 LS 146–52, LFT 315–16, RE 407–12.

A further passage provides a hint as to why Philemon has now supplanted Elijah. Elijah was a prophet of the old school who, even if he did not actually know very much, arrogated supreme authority. But this, it seems, is no longer Jung's view about how Wise Old Men should behave.

> *Killing off would-be prophets is a gain for the people. If they want murder, then they may kill off their false prophets. If the mouth of the Gods remains silent, then each can listen to his own speech. He who loves the people remains silent. If only false teachers teach, the people will kill the false teachers, and will fall into the truth even in the way of their sins. Only after the darkest night will it be day. So cover the lights and remain silent so that the night will become dark and noiseless. The sun rises without our help. Only he who knows the darkest error knows what light is.*[10]

This suggests that, as part of his integration process, Jung has now come to understand a further vital element of the Middle Way in association with Philemon. The Middle Way is largely found, not by receiving 'truths', but by the process of tacking between errors suggested by the hot-cold path in the Izdubar story. This is an implication both of the individuality of the path, and of our tendency to constantly separate ourselves from a shadow with which we need to reintegrate. The Middle Way thus proceeds by recognising errors, and this also has implications for what kind of teaching, and what kind of teacher, will help one to learn it. A prophet who delivers supposed revelations from God and then rebukes you for not following his rules will be much less helpful than a teacher who lets you make your own mistakes.

This aspect of the Middle Way is also reflected in the Buddha's methods of teaching, for the Buddha's relationship to his disciples seems to be much more that of Philemon than that of Elijah to Jung. When questioned by a group of villagers called the Kalamas about whom to believe amongst competing teachers, the Buddha laid the emphasis on the villagers' own autonomous judgement of what would be practically helpful.[11] There are also many stories of the ways in which the Buddha led disciples on to develop their own autonomous understanding of the better course, rather than simply instructing them in it. For example, he encouraged a lovelorn monk called Nanda to recognise that his practice offered more profound

---

10 LS 153, LFT 316–17, RE 412.
11 *Anguttara Nikaya* 3.65, Nyanaponika and Bodhi (1999) pp. 65–6.

The Wise: Elijah and Philemon

Illustration 4. Jung's picture of Philemon (*Red Book* facsimile LS 154). Used by permission of W.W. Norton & Company, Inc.

satisfactions than distracting sexual obsession, by showing him visions of 'dove-footed nymphs' that could lead him towards sublimation of his desires.[12] He also aided a woman called Kisagotami in accepting the death of her baby by sending her on an educative search to find a grain of mustard-seed from a house that had had no deaths.[13]

A gentle symbolisation of the transition from Elijah is suggested in Jung's picture of Philemon in the *Red Book* (**illustration 4**), where a text in Greek at the top reads 'Father of the Prophet: Beloved Philemon'. If Philemon is seen as the father of Elijah, he presumably represents a higher and more basic wisdom from which Elijah's is a less effective offshoot. The temple under Philemon's feet here is the humble house of Philemon and Baucis, that was turned into a temple by the gods. On his right is probably the Tree of Knowledge and on his left the Tree of Life, which seems to have many trunks,

---

12 *Udana* 3.2, Ireland (1990) p. 35.
13 *Therigatha* 10:1, Olendzki (2013). Also see Ellis (2019) 2.c.

perhaps representing the individuality of the path, along with the serpent, given a positive interpretation in Jung's mythology.

3.d. Does Philemon become dogmatic?

Though Philemon may start off as a symbol of higher wisdom in Jung, we need to bear in mind that the whole relationship is still one of projection. If Jung is not infallible, neither is Philemon, because Philemon is Jung. Philemon may deserve some of the praise that Jung gives him because he represents a far more effective wisdom than Elijah did, but I still worry that this praise is too unconditional and one-sided, and thus that having adopted Philemon as his inner Wise Old Man, Jung may start to project the God archetype onto him in its entirety. There is a danger of complacency at any point of the path, even after (or perhaps because of) many prior breakthroughs and achievements.

Philemon's nature changes as we go on from the *Liber Secundus* into *Scrutinies*, representing Jung's experiences after April 1914. His first words there could hardly be more different in tone from those attributed to him as an elusive retired magician, being apparently highly instrumental, even though they are highly ambiguous:

> *I want to turn you around. I want to master you. I want to emboss you like a coin. I want to do business with you. One should buy and sell you.*[14]

Shortly after this, Jung explicitly comments on this change:

> *Since the God has ascended to the upper realms, ΦΙΛΗΜΩΝ [Philemon] also has become different. He first appeared to me as a magician who lived in a different land, but then I felt his nearness, and, since the God has ascended, I knew that ΦΙΛΗΜΩΝ had intoxicated me and given me a language that was foreign to me and of a different sensitivity. All this faded when the God arose and only ΦΙΛΗΜΩΝ kept that language. But I felt that he went on other ways than I did. Probably the most part of what I have written in the earlier part of this book was given to me by ΦΙΛΗΜΩΝ. Consequently I was as if intoxicated. But now I noticed that ΦΙΛΗΜΩΝ assumed a form distinct from me.*[15]

---

14 LFT 337, RE 475.
15 LFT 339, RE 483.

The Wise: Elijah and Philemon

Though this is not entirely clear, it does not sound as though Jung is integrating Philemon in the way that he integrated Elijah. Instead, he remains under the delusion that Philemon is separate from him. Although he sometimes seems to be talking as Philemon, when he does so he seems different ('intoxicated').

After this, Philemon intervenes twice in ways that seem extremely helpful, providing a voice of integration. Firstly he intervenes to release Jung from the influence of 'three shades' who seem to want him to devote himself to their welfare rather than that of the living.[16] Philemon points out that these shades are motivated by power.[17] Secondly, he soothes a quarrel between Jung and his soul, by being extremely polite and appreciative to his soul.[18]

However, from that point begin the 'Seven Sermons to the Dead', delivered by Philemon in a completely didactic fashion as a set of metaphysical dogmas taken from Gnosticism. The dead apparently expect either truth or falsity from Philemon, though they are very resistant and grumbling between most of the sermons. However, by the end of the seventh sermon they are apparently satisfied and 'ascended like smoke',[19] presumably to eternal rest. The dead have been given, and have accepted, an 'answer' to their questions which does not involve integration, and is in striking conflict with the gradual and imperfect progress made in the rest of the book.

I will discuss the content of the 'Seven Sermons to the Dead' and their relationship to the dead later in this book (chapter 11). However, for the moment I just want to remark on the way that they represent a complete departure from the integrative process of the Wise Old Man archetype as it has been occurring in the rest of the *Red Book* up to that point. The Wise Old Man seems to be completely projected, and just stands there uttering 'truths' rather than facilitating anyone's understanding or showing any degree of fallibility. Jung also seems to have returned to an extremely respectful and insufficiently challenging mode, resembling his approach to Elijah in the earlier visions. Jung does ask questions of Philemon after many of the sermons, but, as I shall discuss later, Philemon's answers to those questions are so completely inadequate that one

16 LFT 339–42, RE 483–94.
17 LFT 342, RE 495.
18 LFT 345, RE 500–1.
19 LFT 354, RE 535.

can only assume that Jung, by letting him get away with them, has suspended the critical faculties that are elsewhere in evidence.

The history of modern religious movements offers many cautionary stories concerning the projection of the Wise Old Man archetype. In particular, people can be attracted to cult-like movements by genuine insights, helpful practices, and support for integrative development, but nevertheless find that the wise guru figure either becomes dogmatic, or complacent in other ways, and abuses his authority. Rajneesh (later called Osho) offers one well-known example, but there are many others. In many cases, the guru may be genuinely highly integrated, sincere, and subtle in his teachings, yet even so, the expectations of disciples gradually lead him into an accustomed position of authority in which he loses much capacity to critically question his own beliefs, and then tends to transmit that tendency to his followers.[20]

The development of Philemon, though obviously free of the social pressures associated with external gurus, seems to me to also follow this pattern, shaped primarily by Jung's expectations. It is not surprising if his transition from balanced guru to dogmatic guru is gradual and involves lapses followed by returns, since this obviously follows the gradual emergence of a conflict in Jung in which different voices may emerge at different times. However, the evidence is clear that we see a more absolutist Philemon emerging some time before the Seven Sermons, even if he then reverts. After this, my main argument is that the Seven Sermons themselves are dogmatic and out of harmony with the rest of the text – an argument on which this point about Philemon depends. That argument is a complex and controversial one that will have to wait until chapter 11.

3.e. The Middle Way of authority

The most important issues I want to highlight here are not biographical ones to do with Jung, but epistemological and psychological ones concerning our attitude to authority. If we absolutise authority, then we accept or reject claims simply because of their source. This is the *genetic fallacy*, whereby we assume that a claim is true

---

[20] I discuss this process in the case of Sangharakshita, founder of the Triratna Buddhist Order, in Ellis (2020).

or false, regardless of its merits in other respects, because it does or does not come from an authoritative person or text. This fallacy needs to be distinguished from the mere use of credibility criteria, whereby we apply certain tests such as those of reputation, expertise, evident bias, vested interest, or ability to access relevant information in order to conclude whether a source is likely enough to be reliable to be worth investigating more closely. Thus, for example, if you want to find out about an issue in physics you are likely to consult a physicist because she has relevant expertise, and you would be justified in listening to the physicist more than a columnist in the *Daily Mail*. However, it is possible, though relatively unlikely, that where they disagreed, the columnist could be right and the physicist wrong. If we were subject to the genetic fallacy, we would miss this point, either because we have accepted the physicist as necessarily correct to begin with, or because we have perversely ruled her out as an 'expert' whom we distrust on principle.

Our tendency to indulge in the genetic fallacy is underlined psychologically by the *authority bias*, which was demonstrated in a famous experiment by Milgram in 1961. Milgram found that 65% of people were willing to administer what they knew to be a potentially fatal electric shock to an innocent person when under the instructions of an authority figure.[21] Even though some debates continue about his methods, this result is by any standards an astonishing figure.

Why did so many people obey an authority figure, against their better judgement? One potential answer lies in the projection of the Wise Old Man archetype, interdependent with our experience of parental and social authority from infancy. If we come to believe (whether from genetic or environmental causes) that certain kinds of people are likely to be able to meet all our needs and can guide our total development, we are likely to set up a shortcut function to trust them automatically, thus absolutising our responses to them. Freud talked here about projection of the father-figure giving rise to the superego and belief in God, but we can appreciate a similar point more fully if we broaden the role of the father to authorities in general, and avoid getting bogged down in speculations about its origins. The opposite shortcut function can also operate if we *reject*

---

21 Milgram (1974). For more on the general question of our tendency to absolutise sources, also see Ellis (2015) 3.e.

someone who is put in a social position of authority but doesn't sufficiently fit the archetype (think for example of school pupils 'playing up' with a student teacher). Whether the wise authority figure is internal or external, then, we are less likely to weigh up the justification of what they say and more likely to absolutely accept or reject it without further reflection.

To avoid this type of authority projection interfering with our judgement, the Middle Way will need to be a practically essential part of our strategy. It will consist in a moment of reflection at each non-urgent moment when we are confronted with authoritative claims, enabling us to be aware of the possibility of alternatives, so that we don't absolutise the archetype by automatically assuming either that it is true or that it is false.

At the same time, the conscious recognition of the archetype in its own right can help us to be more aware of why we are likely to project it, and of how it may reflect a helpful part of ourselves. We can start with the obvious mythical, religious, or fantasy figures: God the father, Guru Nanak, Gandalf. However, the practical application of our awareness of the Wise Old Man (or Woman) archetype may need to take us further than that into less obvious figures, including female ones. Why, for example, is one teacher or politician authoritative in a way that another is not?

In this type of reflection process, Jung for the most part offers an example of inspiration. Not only does he offer us striking examples of the Wise Old Man archetype in operation from his personal experience, but also (for the most part) an inspiring example of how to work with that archetype so as to make use of its wisdom but avoid absolutising it.

4. Christ as the Middle Way

4.a. The Christ archetype

Christ is mentioned and discussed many times in the *Red Book*, but it is only towards the end that he actually appears in person.

> *When night fell, ΦΙΛΗΜΩΝ approached me in an earth-coloured robe, holding a silver fish: 'Look, my son,' he said, 'I was fishing and caught this fish; I bring it to you, so that you may be comforted.' And as I looked at him astonishedly and questioningly, I saw that a shade stood in darkness at the door, bearing a robe of grandeur. His face was pale and blood had flowed into the furrows of his brow. But ΦΙΛΗΜΩΝ knelt down, touched the earth, and said to the shade, 'My master and my brother, praised be your name....'*[1]

In his later works, Jung has a great deal to say about the fish as a symbol of Christ, most of which is not about Christ but about astrology, and the coincidence of the astrological aeon ruled by Pisces (the fish sign) with the coming of Christ.[2] Jung rejects as incomplete the normal Christian explanation of the fish as derived from a Greek acronym,[3] and instead points out the way that baptism immerses the Christian in water, where their souls are then said to swim like fishes. The fish lives in the (unconscious) depths but can also be hauled out of them and used as food to sustain the self. As a universal symbol dependent on our immediate and embodied relationship with fish, the fish can stand for the universal function of Christ as an archetype, rather than just an allegory of Christian doctrine about him.

The Christ archetype is in some respects another version of the God archetype, but the human element of Christ also connects to the hero archetype. We identify with Christ in his struggles in a way that we do not need to identify with a Wise Old Man. So Christ

---

1 LFT 356, RE 541.
2 Jung CW 9ii §127 ff.
3 The initial letters of Ιησους Χριστος Θεου Υιος Σωτήρ ('Jesus Christ, Son of God, Saviour') spelling ΙΧΘΥΣ ('fish').

could be seen as the hero archetype developing into the God archetype by absorbing the other archetypes, including the shadow. That is why Jung often talks about the importance of the Antichrist as being part of the Christ, saying that Christ 'became Hell' during his traditional descent there between his crucifixion and resurrection.[4] By developing in this way he bridges the gap between the human and the divine.

It is in that sense that we can also identify the Christ archetype with the Middle Way. One set of absolute attributes are associated with God and his values, and the opposite with human beings: for example perfect/imperfect, good/evil, omniscient/ignorant. Christ takes the meaning of the perfect values as an ideal, but makes them compatible with human imperfection through a dialectical process of engagement. In my recent book about the Christian Middle Way that is very much inspired by Jung's approach to Christ,[5] I argue that to make a practical difference to our judgements, the divine standards in connection with the human ones have to make us break our confirmation bias and re-examine our current assumptions: something that Jesus tries to impel by the shock tactics of the crucifixion. However, there are lots of ways that they can fail to do so: if we assume that it is simply a matter of heroic effort, if we leave it all to God, if we flip between God and hero, or if we turn the mediation into a mere abstraction or a piece of magic.

To do this, Christ clearly has to be recognised as an archetype rather than projected, so he has to be part of us. That this is so is reflected at a variety of points in the *Red Book*. For example, Salome says to Jung 'You are Christ',[6] and that she is his sister, because both of them are born from Mary.[7] Jung also unfavourably contrasts 'being Christ' with 'carrying Christ', using the image of St Christopher, who is supposed to have carried the Christ child (which is where he got his name):

> *The Christ child became an easy burden for the giant Christopher, since Christ himself said 'My yoke is sweet, and my burden is light'. We should not bear Christ as he is unbearable, but we should be Christs, for then our yoke is sweet and our burden easy.... The God outside us increases the weight*

---

4 LP iv(v), LFT 242, RE 164.
5 Ellis (2018).
6 LP vi(v), LFT 252, RE 197.
7 LP vi(r), LFT 249, RE 187.

Christ as the Middle Way 71

> *of everything heavy while the God within us lightens everything heavy. Hence all Christophers have stooped backs and short breath, since the world is heavy.*[8]

Jung clearly sees *being* Christ as an unavoidable aspect of the way, presumably in the sense that to follow the way we have to engage with the functions of the hero archetype in relation to the God archetype. For someone from a Christian background (and Jung evidently assumes that this is his audience), those archetypes will come in the form of Christ:

> *You can certainly leave Christianity behind but it does not leave you. Your liberation from it is a delusion. Christ is the way. You can certainly run away, but you are no longer on the way.*[9]

This perspective is part of what makes it supremely puzzling when Jung later adopts Gnosticism instead: not because he was previously an orthodox Christian, or that he then even formally converted to orthodox Gnosticism, but because he so obviously recognises the importance of working with the religious symbols that you find most deeply rooted in your experience and interpreting them in terms of the Middle Way. That's one reason why I think the Gnostic Jung was running away from his own earlier insights, and thus, to use his own words, why he was then no longer on the way (see chapter 11). In the very final scene of *Scrutinies*, Philemon, now identified with the historical Gnostic Simon Magus, welcomes Christ in his garden. Rather like the dead, Christ is then miraculously and discontinuously converted to Philemon's Gnostic viewpoint, saying 'You speak the truth'.[10] The scene is evidently intended to synthesise Christ into the new Gnostic dispensation, but the synthesis is premature, as there is no attempt at all to probe whether Gnosticism can as effectively represent the integrative process that Christ previously represented for Jung.

4.b. Suffering for creativity

The symbolic importance of Christ for Jung is closely tied into the importance of recognising and accepting suffering, because

---

8 LS 48, LFT 283, RE 296–7.
9 LS 99, LFT 293, RE 331.
10 LFT 359, RE 549–51.

suffering may force us out of previous assumptions and limitations and enable us to integrate new ones. This perspective is closely related to the Middle Way, because we need a negative stimulus to force us out of the absolutisation of closed feedback loops discussed in chapter 1, in which anxiety or craving from the back of the brain constantly motivates a view of the world in the front of the brain that enables us to fulfil them and reinforces the drives. It's only by finding a perspective beyond these feedback loops that we can hope to change the cycle, and the suffering of new difficult conditions is often the only thing that will do this. In the *Red Book*, the crucifixion, the mockery accepted by Christ, and the eucharist are all interpreted in terms that support the way.

In two places Jung directly links this acceptance of suffering or its symbols with the Middle Way, suggesting that he had an intuitive understanding of the role of feedback loops:

> *Just as Christ was crucified between the two thieves, our lowest lies on either side of our way.*[11]

> *To deliver the men of his time from the stretched hanging, Christ effectively took the torment on himself and taught them: 'Be crafty like serpents and guileless like doves.' For craftiness counsels against chaos, and guilelessness veils its terrible aspect. Thus men could take the safe middle path, hedged both upward and downward.*[12]

This second quotation introduces the role of chaos in negative feedback loops, which can also be seen as a process of order being disrupted. We need to embrace that disruption in order to make spiritual progress, avoiding the extremes of positive or negative rigidity (represented by the two thieves) in order to do so. To genuinely counsel against chaos, you have to incorporate suffering and change into your view of the world. On the other hand, you will also need a degree of continuity deriving from a 'guileless' confidence in the process of the path to make the degree of chaos manageable.

Jung even expressed this point about suffering visually, in the form of what might be called a mandala of suffering (**illustration 5**). Four quarters of the mandala depict, first, a person lying on spikes and having what is presumably a roller (though it looks rather like the mandala as a whole) run over him; second, the crucifixion; third,

---

11 LS 112, LFT 300, RE 356.
12 LS 112, LFT 300-1, RE 357.

Christ as the Middle Way

Illustration 5. Jung's 'mandala of suffering' (*Red Book* facsimile LS 127). Used by permission of W.W. Norton & Company, Inc.

animal suffering; and fourth, the suffering of plants. The heading 'amor triumphat' (love triumphs), however, suggests the positive wider role that these forms of suffering may possibly play. In his note underneath the picture, Jung says that it 'expresses I know not what kind of grief', and identifies the four pictures with the 'functions' found in *Psychological Types*: thinking, feeling, sensation, and intuition.[13]

The acceptance of suffering is heroic in one sense, but when taken to the point of death requires us to abandon the egoistic basis of the hero archetype. Jung sees the acceptance of the shadow as essential to moving beyond the limitations of the hero archetype into the God

---

13 LS 127, LFT 307 n. 240, RE 381 n. 240.

archetype, so the crucifixion could be seen as an attempt to jolt us into a recognition of the shadow and hence into a wider awareness. The God, from a state of integration, also represents that part of us that suffers from our lack of integration:

> *The God suffers when man does not accept his darkness. Consequently men must have a suffering God, so long as they suffer from evil. To suffer from evil means: you still love evil yet love it no longer. You still hope to gain something, but you do not want to look too closely for fear that you might discover you love evil. The God suffers because you continue to suffer from loving evil.*[14]

Jung dramatises the agonies involved in accepting a change in one's perspective in terms of a death and resurrection of his own that reflects that of Christ. He perishes 'on a dung heap' and is then born again in three days.[15] 'For if the wretchedness and poverty of this life ends, another life begins in what is opposed to me.'[16]

4.c. Eating flesh and drinking blood

Jung clearly has a strong feeling for the significance of the eucharist (which he later wrote extensively about[17]), based as it is on symbolically drinking the blood and eating the flesh of Christ, in memory of the suffering he underwent. The power of this can be metaphorically transferred from a formal religious context to a symbolic private practice where the Christ that one is eating is one's own.

> *Your God should not be a man of mockery, rather you yourself will be a man of mockery. You should mock yourself and rise above this. If you have still not learned this from the old holy books, then go there, drink the blood and eat the flesh of him who was mocked for the sake of our sins, so that you totally become his nature, deny his being-apart-from-you: you should be he himself, not Christians but Christ, otherwise you will be of no use to the coming God.*[18]

There is further cannibalism, with similar implications, in the notorious scene of the *Red Book* where Jung, at the command of his

---

14 LS 67, LFT 287, RE 310.
15 LS 31, LFT 275, RE 268.
16 LS 31, LFT 275, RE 267.
17 CW 11 §296 ff.
18 LP ii(v), LFT 234, RE 136–7.

soul, eats a piece of the liver of a murdered child. The scene is set in a way that would do justice to a well-made horror film:

> *A marionette with a broken head lies before me amidst the stones – a few steps further, a small apron – and then behind the bush, the body of a small girl – covered with terrible wounds – smeared with blood. One foot is clad with a stocking and shoe, the other is naked and gorily crushed – the head – where is the head?*[19]

His soul stands beside the body and instructs Jung to first cut out the liver from the body, and then 'perform the healing act with it' by eating part of it. In the face of Jung's protests his soul goes on

> *You have devised the most horrible torment for the murderer, which could atone for his act. There is only one atonement: abase yourself and eat.*[20]

It is probably only at this point, if you have managed to drag yourself out of the frame of a horror film and remember that this is Jung's fantasy, that you might realise that Jung is the murderer – in the sense that it is he who imagined all this. The soul gives him the reason that he shares the guilt because he is a man, presumably on the grounds that all men (or even women) might well imagine this scene or find it within them somewhere. To heal, we need to perform an act of atonement that simply involves the acceptance of the most extreme elements of our psyche. Only thus can we integrate these elements of ourselves.

The link to the eucharist is also subsequently made explicit:

> *A God who is no stronger than man – what is he? You should still taste holy dread. How would you be worthy of enjoying the wine and the bread if you have not touched the black bottom of human nature?*[21]

By ritually eating pieces of human flesh or drinking human blood, we are potentially integrating the murderers and cannibals within ourselves, by giving them a recognition that we would normally deny them. At the same time we shake our absolute moral assumption that we are essentially not that sort of person. Of course, everything depends on the ritual context, namely the framing and the particular attention given to the act. The ritual is made far more effective if we really feel that the disgusting, shadowy thing is what

---

19 LS 76, LFT 290, RE 320.
20 LS 76, LFT 290, RE 321.
21 LS 78, LFT 291, RE 324.

we are doing, rather than going through a highly conventionalised process that distances us from the impact and moves its meaning wholly into the left hemisphere.

4.d. The imitation of Christ

The eucharist is a process of 'imitating' Christ, who told his disciples to 'do this in memory of me' when he drank the wine and ate the bread, and the imitation of Christ is also an important theme in the *Red Book*, especially of the sequence of four visions narrated in 'Divine Folly' and the ensuing three nights. Much light can be cast on this by considering the distinction between the two forms of 'imitation', typical of the specialisations between the brain hemispheres mentioned in chapter 1. The left hemisphere, which assumes a represented linguistic world, imitates 'literally', assuming that the actions of one person can be turned into instructions that can then be turned back into actions by another person. This, of course, involves ignoring both the contextual differences between the people concerned and the ambiguities of language, which can only be compensated to a limited extent by greater conception precision. The right hemisphere's 'imitation', on the other hand, is a creative and imperfect process that Erich Auerbach called *mimesis*. Here there is no expectation that imitation is or can be precise – rather the introduction of new adaptive variants by another strengthens the adequacy of the imitation.[22]

In the first of Jung's visions on this theme, he borrows a copy of Thomas à Kempis's *Imitation of Christ* from a library, and the scholarly librarian shows disapproving surprise, especially when Jung says that he wants it for prayer rather than scholarly study. The librarian says that the book is 'old-fashioned' (not in what Jung would call *the spirit of this time*, which he sees as scientific). The librarian goes on:

> 'We can no longer get involved in Christian dogmatics these days, surely.'
>
> 'We haven't come to an end with Christianity just by putting it aside.' [replies Jung] 'It seems to me that there's more to it than we see.'
>
> 'What is there about it? It's just a religion.'[23]

22 McGilchrist (2009) p. 247 ff.
23 LS 98, LFT 292, RE 529.

Christ as the Middle Way

The librarian's attitude here is very typical of a heavily left-hemisphere, 'literal' understanding of imitation. For him 'religion' is a matter of dogma, and the imitation of Christ could only possibly mean trying to act in the same way Christ did. He does not consider the huge ambiguities involved in the very idea of acting in the 'same' way Christ did when you are not in his context.

The library is interestingly on the *right* hand side of an ante-room, and in the following vision Jung instead opens a door on the *left*-hand side that leads him into a world that allows a much more creative interpretation of the imitation of Christ. The left hemisphere of the brain is linked to the right side of the body and the right hemisphere to the left side of the body, so we are actually more inclined to associate left-hemisphere dominant attitudes symbolically with our right, and more right-hemisphere influenced attitudes with our left.

Through the left-hand door he encounters a cook, who recognises the book, which was left to her by her mother. She obviously gains an immediate personal inspiration from it. Whilst sitting at the kitchen table he randomly opens the book and reads 'The righteous base their intentions more on the mercy of God, which in whatever they undertake they trust more than their own wisdom.'[24] This Jung refers to as Thomas à Kempis's 'intuitive method'. This very much suggests a creative interpretation of the 'imitation of Christ'. Our sense of God is a matter of wider awareness and synthesis, coming from the right hemisphere, which will present us with symbols rather than instructions. We find those symbols inspiring in the way the cook found the book inspiring, so they may actually have the power to change our judgements in experience, as well as being adaptable to our own context, very different from Christ's. In past ages, it seems, 'God' may often have just been the term that people used for their wider intuitive awareness.

Though many of us may intuitively welcome this emphasis, and sympathise with the cook more than the librarian, more recent research suggests that intuition is only an effective way to support our *beliefs* in fairly limited and predictable circumstances. Daniel Kahneman sees intuition as an unconscious method through which we get information from our environment, and notes that it can be

24 LS 101, LFT 294, RE 334.

very helpful and reliable where there are a limited range of conditions we have experienced in the past.[25] He quotes the example of firefighters, who can have excellent intuitions about when a burning building is about to collapse, based on lots of unconsciously processed previous experience. However, using your intuitions to decide which stocks are going to do better on a market is likely to be far less successful, because the conditions are far more unpredictable. The cook's use of Thomas à Kempis, however, is not only for 'good counsel' but also for comfort.[26] Given her intuitive approach to it, it may not necessarily provide her with very helpful beliefs, but it will provide her with a motivating and flexible source of meaning that may provide her both with motivation and with symbolic resources.

Jung's sense of the imitation of Christ, however, is clearly in the realm of meaning rather than that of belief. As often, his initially contradictory language masks an underlying sense.

> *If I thus truly imitate Christ, I do not imitate anyone. I emulate no-one, but go my own way, and I will also no longer call myself a Christian.*[27]

To 'truly imitate' seems obviously to mean *mimesis* or creative, imperfect inspiration, whilst the second 'imitate' here is the precise copying form. This ability to 'truly imitate' Christ clearly follows from *being* Christ, recognising his archetype in ourselves, rather than imagining Christ to be someone separate, whether historically or supernaturally. It also follows from the individuality of the path, since Christ's path cannot possibly be the same as mine except in its pattern of finding the Middle Way at each moment.

Once again, we can also make parallels with the Buddha's practice of the Middle Way. To imitate the Buddha in a deeper sense, like imitating Christ, means developing the archetype of the Buddha within ourselves, rather than doing exactly what the Buddha did in his context. In the stories of the Buddha, this point becomes most important just before his death, when the Buddha explicitly urged the same kind of autonomy in his followers, simultaneously stressing the ways that such autonomy depends on wider awareness that can be built up from awareness of the body.

---

25 Kahneman (2010).
26 LS 101, LFT 294, RE 334.
27 LS 99, LFT 293, RE 332.

Christ as the Middle Way 79

> *You should live as islands unto yourselves, being your own refuge, with no-one else as your refuge, with the Dhamma [teaching] as an island, with the Dhamma as your refuge, with no other refuge. And how does a monk live as an island unto himself...with no other refuge? And how does a monk live... with no other refuge? Here, Ananda, a monk abides contemplating the body as body, earnestly, clearly aware, mindful and having put away all hankering and fretting for the world....*[28]

For Jung, the individuality of Christ and his path also has profound moral implications, for literal 'imitation' is an instance of absolutisation and the use of power.

> *What suffering must be brought upon humanity, until man gives up satisfying his longing for power over his fellow man and forever wanting others to be the same. How much blood will go on flowing until man opens his eyes and sees the way to his own path and himself as the enemy, and becomes aware of his own success.*[29]

The following passage, finally, makes it clear just how difficult the mimetic imitation of Christ is. It is very much easier to follow the pre-driven shortcuts of imitation than to authentically take responsibility for our path in our circumstances, with the courage of Christ in trying to shock the world into changing its assumptions.

> *Truly, the way leads through the crucified, that means through him to whom it was no small thing to live his own life, and who was therefore raised to magnificence. He did not simply teach what was knowable and worth knowing, he lived it. It is unclear how great one's humility must be to take it upon oneself to live one's own life. The disgust of whoever wants to enter into his own life can hardly be measured. Aversion will sicken him. He makes himself vomit. His bowels pain him and his brain sinks into lassitude. He would rather devise any trick to help him escape, since nothing matches the torment of his own way.*[30]

Those who have tried meditation may well have experienced directly what Jung is talking about here, which can be psychologically referred to as 'resistance'. If you sit down to meditate, sometimes your reluctance to confronting your own wider state with awareness can result not only in galloping thoughts, but quite commonly in drowsiness on the one hand or restless itchiness on the

---

28 *Digha Nikaya* 16.2.26, Walshe (1995) p. 245.
29 LS 137, LFT 310, RE 391.
30 LS 136, LFT 310, RE 389.

other. In extreme cases 'psychosomatic' pains and nausea might even play the same role.

The way of Christ as Jung sees it is the way of authenticity, and also the Middle Way. If we are ourselves inclined to turn Jung into Christ we might also need to bear in mind that the implications of this apply to him as well. If you are impressed by Jung, try to *be* Jung at his best rather than *copying* Jung. To do this we will need to avoid the extremes of uncritical acceptance or rejection and work out the Middle Way in our own lives.

5. The Tree of Life and the Mandala

5.a. The Tree of Life

The symbol of the Tree of Life, though it is developed only relatively briefly in the text, is a profound symbol of the Middle Way and of the New God in the *Red Book*. Jung finds it and develops it symbolically from the Tree of Life in Genesis and from the Norse world-tree, Yggdrasil, as well as from wider 'vegetation myths' around the world. Its central meaning is well explained in a passage from 'Nox Tertia'.

> *He sees the tree of life, whose roots reach into Hell and whose top touches Heaven. He also no longer knows differences: who is right? What is holy? What is genuine? What is good? What is correct? He knows only one difference: the difference between below and above. For he sees that the tree of life grows from below to above, and that it has its crown at the top, clearly differentiated from the roots. To him this is unquestionable. Hence he knows the way to salvation.*[1]

This makes a crucial point about the values of the Middle Way and symbolically encompasses them. The Middle Way has a direction rather than a final goal, as I argued in chapter 1, but this direction does provide us with a basis of value. What is *better* in the terms of the Middle Way is growth, synthesising and integrating the nutrients on which we draw in the shape of past conditions. All other distinctions must be laid aside in the sense that their value is far more contingent. Growth as a value, however, is universal, not because of any abstract reasoning, but because we constantly experience it in our embodiment and thus can make a reasonable generalisation about it.

Jung also makes an important distinction between the ways in which the tree relates to hell and heaven. Its roots *reach into* hell, because the prior conditions from which we grow include even those

1 LS 114, LFT 301, RE 359-60.

conditions we reject. The tree grows up away from hell because it feels the limitations of the earth, when it needs sun and air, even though it also needs the earth. Its top *touches* heaven. It does not have heaven as a goal, but rather grows up away from the limitations of hell, with heaven only as a vague possibility, until it stumbles against it. This reflects the way in which the Middle Way needs to be about *avoidance* of the absolute extremes of evil, in the process of which one finds one's own alternative way to grow, rather than imitation of an idea of a positive goal. If we had an idea of a positive goal that was too precise, we would undermine it by copying it in too left-brained a fashion and thus create an absolute.

This is why the Middle Way is not relativist.[2] Though it makes all values questionable, it does not remove right value as a justifiable basis of judgement. There is still such a thing as objectivity, in an embodied sense where some judgements involve facing up to conditions more than others. The tree does not know the right way to grow before it starts, but at each moment responds to the conditions around it so as to judge whether to grow in one direction or another. If it grows in a less helpful direction, by ignoring where the light is, it will be a less 'objective' tree.

Jung's first sentence also makes the point that we cannot experience this value if we only 'see' the Tree of Life as something separate from us. We have to *be* the Tree of Life, just as we have to acknowledge the other archetypes within us. They have to be *our* roots in hell and *our* crown brushing heaven.

A similar tree, with a similarly significant relationship to the Middle Way, occurs in the story of the Buddha's life. Four significant events in the Buddha's life – his birth, early experience of inspiration, enlightenment, and death – are all said to have occurred under trees. The one of these episodes with the biggest symbolic significance, however, is the Buddha's achievement of enlightenment, which is represented as occurring under the Bodhi tree. Like the tree itself, the Buddha sits down and vows to grow into enlightenment, rooted in one spot as he does so.

---

2 At least, not relativist in the ways that practically matter as defined here. If you want to adopt a different philosophical definition of relativism that makes the Middle Way 'relativist', then so be it. But you will be appealing to philosophical tradition rather than using a practical basis of judgement.

> *Then he took up the supreme, immoveable cross-legged posture with his limbs massed together like the coils of a sleeping serpent, saying 'I will not rise from this position on the ground till I achieve the completion of my task.'*[3]

That rootedness can symbolise the Buddha's full acceptance of the previous conditions that formed him, as well as his embodied awareness as a basis of more abstract types of awareness. When he sits down, like the tree, he does not know in exactly what direction he will grow, but only that he will meet the buffeting of new conditions in a way that maintains his rootedness whilst responding to them.

If we were to absolutise the tree by turning it into an abstract principle that does not merely develop from the experience of growing at each point of judgement, there is a danger that we might miss the point of it altogether. The Tree of Life, for example, does not represent a principle of 'Nature' or 'Natural Law'. There you would be taking a prior concept, that of 'Nature', and making the experience of growth at each moment fit that concept, rather than letting your idea of what is 'natural' develop from a fresh assessment of integral judgement at each moment. The Tree of Life symbol should thus not be appropriated by Naturalism, Natural Law, Deep Ecology, or any other value system that superficially appears to resemble it by top-down deduction of the right direction from concepts of growth and nature. All these systems end up by telling the tree where it ought to grow, and setting up a heaven as its goal. They might even require it to pull up its roots out of disgust at where it came from.

The process of the tree's growth might also be interpreted as evolutionary, as long as, again, we do not turn evolution into a new absolute. Evolution operates by mutation with a slight degree of randomness (though skewed towards what went before), followed by natural selection as unsuccessful innovations die out. We do not need to know exactly what *causes* each new moment of growth in the tree in order to judge that some moments of growth are better adapted than others. The addressing of conditions through growth may be seen as adaptation, as long as we do not make absolutising assumptions that limit what 'adaptation' means. We do not have to see successful adaptation of the Tree of Life only in terms of survival and reproduction, for there might be many unexpected forms

---

3   Ashvaghosha, *Buddhacarita*, xii.20, Johnston (1972).

of creativity. A successful development is sustainable and enters into a relatively stable, homeostatic relationship with its environment. However, that environment may be a social and cultural one rather than only a biological one, making creativity in arts, sciences, relationships, or construction successful in a human context.

All of these points about the Tree of Life flow from the basic uncertainty in which we make judgements from moment to moment. We cannot make prior judgements about what would make one growth 'good' or another 'bad' too far ahead, but we can experience a balanced relationship with the environment where new adaptation is always going to maintain that balance. Because of uncertainty, what is good is not just what we think will *lead* to growth, but rather what *is itself* growth by taking a new condition into account. We ourselves are the tree. On the other hand, failing to grow confidently in a direction well supported by experience can also be problematic. For example, we cannot simply ignore the evidence of global warming because there is still a degree of uncertainty attached to it. The challenge and stretch lies in responding to that new condition in our lives, and we are obliged to do this *without* certainty.

Jung's continuing discussion of the Tree of Life in 'Nox Tertia' particularly draws on the Biblical story, and compares it to the Tree of Knowledge of Good and Evil.

> *To unlearn all distinctions save that concerning direction is part of your salvation. Hence you free yourself from the old curse of the knowledge of good and evil. Because you separated good from evil according to your best appraisal and aspired only to the good and denied the evil that you committed nevertheless and failed to accept, your roots no longer suckled the dark nourishment of the depths and your tree became sick and withered. Therefore the ancients said that after Adam had eaten the apple, the tree of paradise withered.*[4]

It is the absolutising nature of the knowledge of good and evil as it was often applied that I take to be the 'curse' here. Jung cannot be telling us that we are cursed just because we can make practical distinctions, as he has just exempted one distinction, 'that concerning direction', for praise. So it cannot be our ability to separate good from evil in general that is the curse, but rather the dogmatic or absolute way in which we often do so, preventing integration of the shadow. The eating of the forbidden fruit was a mixed blessing,

---

4 Ibid.

Tree of Life and Mandala

that enabled both 'good' and 'evil' in the larger terms defined by the Tree of Life.[5]

5.b. The bidirectional tree

Lest we should get too attached to the symbol of a unidirectional tree, however, Jung also includes in the *Red Book* an image of a bidirectional tree, which grows in both directions at once (**illustration 6**). This tree has its roots *both* in hell and in heaven, with apparently leaves in between. Though this image is less effective at showing us

Illustration 6. Jung's illustration of a bidirectional tree (*Red Book* facsimile LS 22). Used by permission of W.W. Norton & Company, Inc.

---

5   See Ellis (2018) section 4.

the basis of moral judgement in the Middle Way than the unidirectional Tree of Life described above, it does work well as a way of illustrating the relationship between meaning and the Middle Way. The Middle Way avoids absolutising either heaven and hell (which in turn represent opposed absolutes in general), but nevertheless depends upon them for meaning.

As I suggested in chapter 2, truth can be regarded as an archetype similar to the God archetype – with falsehood being similarly allied with the shadow. We obviously still need to be able to think meaningfully about the possibility of truth in order to make judgements, even if those judgements involve holding back from the belief that we possess absolute truth. We could thus suggest that the meanings of all the symbols we use in judgements when trying to follow the Middle Way are still rooted in heaven and hell, in the sense that they are dependent on the *idea* of absolutes.

This image is put at the head of the chapter in which Jung debates the meaning of language with Ammonius, so it makes immediate sense to interpret it as being primarily about meaning. The diagrams to the left and right of the bidirectional tree seem to illustrate two different opposed views of language that arise in the discussion with Ammonius (a theme I shall return to in chapter 9). The scarab, which Jung was observing rolling dung in his vision,[6] seems to represent an example object to be related to its meaning. On the left-hand side, the experience of a scarab is made the basis of a word that means only 'scarab'. The practically-led way of understanding meaning leads from hell to heaven, and is also suggested by the human figures amongst the runes at the bottom. On the right-hand side, though, we start with a crossed circle, that Jung often uses to signify a mandala, but that here seems to mean the infinite potential of meaning in any word, even 'scarab'. That infinite potentiality includes the scarab itself, but also lots of other things – a huge context in which to place the scarab. This is the position that Ammonius was taking, that from the divine perspective language has an infinite amount of possible meanings, though from the worldly perspective we limit these meanings to one.[7] The Middle Way here involves recognising that both particular representation and the infinite potential of ambiguous meaning are found in human experience and are

---

6   LS 23, LFT 271, RE 253-4.
7   LS 17, LFT 268, RE 244.

rooted in the two extremes. It is good to be as open about meaning as possible, but whenever we make a judgement we have to assume a particular state of affairs in which words mean one thing.

5.c. Destruction and regeneration

The Norse world tree, Yggdrasil, which was another of the sources for the Tree of Life symbol, appears in another of Jung's images in the *Red Book* (**illustration 7**). This depicts a fire in the world tree

Illustration 7. Jung's illustration of a fire in the world tree (*Red Book* facsimile LS 135). Used by permission of W.W. Norton & Company, Inc.

spread from Muspelheim, the abode of the Fire Giants. The fire destroys life, but new creatures are depicted emerging from the smoke and ash at the bottom. All this destruction is part of a cycle that will create new life, symbolised by the fact that it is all in an egg that is being incubated by a God.

This cycle of destruction and regeneration is part of the big picture represented by the Tree of Life, as it is only by destruction that the conditions for growth can occur. The roots of the Tree of Life can be said to feed on the ashes of destruction and the soil of decayed life. It is only by accepting this destruction, rather than repressing our awareness of it, that integration can occur.

Another version of this point occurs when Jung is resistant to passing on power to his 'son' (who may represent his work, or the Gnostic system he adopts late in the *Red Book*) who is stronger than him. His position is likened to a king in a fairy tale who receives his powerful son by magical means, reverses this by more magic when he is dismayed at his son wanting to supplant him, but then feels remorseful so gets the son again.[8] Here the message seems to be that if we are growing on the Tree of Life, in addition to growing as individuals we must expect to be surpassed as individuals.

5.d. The meaning of mandalas

The other impersonal symbol of the God archetype I want to consider here is the mandala. Jung seems to have started drawing mandalas before he related them to the Buddhist symbols or applied that name to them, and his earliest sketches are included in Appendix A of the *Red Book*. The first inspirations seem to have been the natural forms reproduced by Ernst Haeckel[9] and city plans, especially after a formative 'Liverpool' dream that Jung recounts in *Memories, Dreams, Reflections*.

> *I found myself in a dirty, sooty city. It was night, and dark, and winter, and raining. I was in Liverpool. With a number of Swiss – say, half a dozen – I walked through the dark streets…. When we reached the plateau [we had been walking towards] we found a broad square illuminated by street lights, into which many streets converged. The various quarters of the city were arranged radially around the square. In the centre was a round pool, and in the middle*

---

8 LFT 327-8, RE 450-3.
9 Cambray (2014).

of it a small island. While everything round about was obscured by rain, fog, smoke, and dimly lit darkness, the little island blazed with sunlight. On it stood a single tree, a magnolia, in a shower of reddish blossoms. It was as though the tree stood in the sunlight and was at the same time the source of light.[10]

Jung commented on this dream:

This dream brought with it a sense of finality, I saw that here the goal had been revealed. One could not go beyond the centre. The centre is the goal, and everything is directed towards that centre. Through that dream I understood that the self is the principle and archetype of orientation and meaning.... For me, this insight signified an approach to the centre and therefore to the goal.[11]

Mandalas can thus be understood as symbolic diagrams of integration. What they have in common is a circularity, or rough circularity, of form (the original term 'mandala' being the Sanskrit for 'circle'), with the centre representing a point of integration and the periphery of the circle, by comparison, lacking that integration. Buddhist mandalas also often symbolise the different qualities that have to be unified in different quarters or segments of the circle, and also symbolise the path through the changes that take place between the periphery and the centre of the circle, though many of Jung's early mandalas do not do this.

The *Red Book* contains a stunning collection of Jung's mandalas, showing both the potential varieties of the form and the various relationships these could have with other symbols used by Jung. Here I shall only be able to discuss a selection of these in order to illustrate that symbolic variety and its relationship to the Jungian Middle Way.

5.e. Combining mandala and tree symbols

Some of Jung's mandalas have obvious links to the Tree of Life symbol. Jung regarded the two symbols as closely related. In his essay on the tree symbolism, *The Philosophical Tree*, he writes

If a mandala may be described as a symbol of the self seen in cross-section, then the tree would represent a profile view of it: the self depicted as a process of growth.[12]

10 Jung (1989) p. 223.
11 Ibid. p. 224.
12 CW 13 §304.

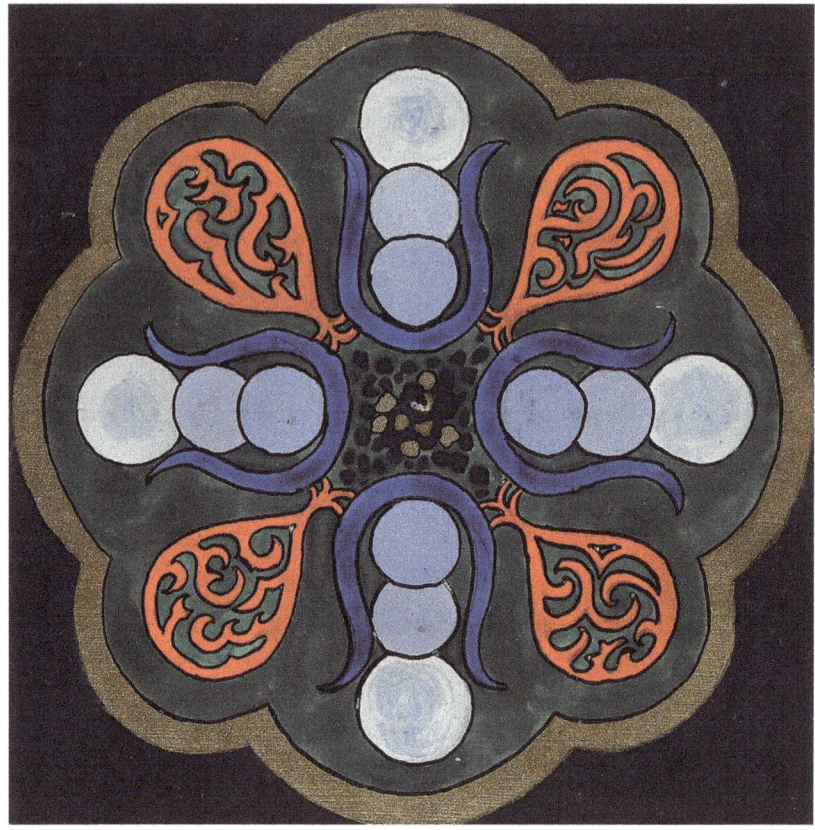

Illustration 8. One of Jung's 'seed case' mandalas (*Red Book* facsimile LS 80). Used by permission of W.W. Norton & Company, Inc.

Some of the earliest mandalas included in the *Red Book* are influenced by Haeckel, and seem to have a pronounced vegetable quality, resembling seed-cases or cross-sections of a stem (**illustration 8**). Perhaps we can associate them with cross-sections or seeds of the Tree of Life? The relationship between the seed and the centre-point of integration also suggests the importance of the acceptance of destruction and re-creation, as in the previous image of the fire in the world tree. Some of these 'biological' mandalas are disrupted but are shown releasing seeds from their disruption, again reinforcing this point (**illustration 9**).[13]

---

13 Illustration 9 shows LS 84, but this could also be illustrated by 85, 86 or 89.

Illustration 9. Jung's 'disrupted seed case' mandala (*Red Book* facsimile LS 84). Used by permission of W.W. Norton & Company, Inc.

A number of Jung's mandalas also illustrate the Middle Way by putting a brighter or sun-like form at the top (representing heaven), and a darker form at the bottom to represent hell. Sometimes the mandala hovers in between these two poles, but sometimes it is placed on a wavy line that apparently shows the point of balance of the Middle Way between the two extremes.[14]

The mandala in *Liber Secundus* 96 is unique in combining three major types of symbolism: the mandala, the Middle Way, and the Tree of Life (**illustration 10**). The brightly-coloured curved form at the top represents the positive absolute (heaven/sun), and the black form at the bottom with the red circle within it the negative absolute. In the centre is a mandala form, representing the integration of the extremes, including concentric circles, a quartered form and a star (all of which Jung uses to represent integration in different places). The vertical wavy lines bisecting the picture and linking the extremes with the mandala may well indicate the meaning that needs to come from the extremes despite the Middle Way needing to avoid beliefs on each side. Running horizontally across and bisecting the picture again are more wavy lines following the balancing point of the Middle Way, and at each end of these lines are roots representing the Tree of Life.

Once again we have a bidirectional tree, but this time the roots are not in heaven and hell but at either end of the Middle Way. This is possibly a more direct symbolism than either of the other two variations on the Tree of Life we have seen so far: the uni-directional tree growing out of hell and the bi-directional tree growing out of heaven and hell. The uni-directional tree depicts the moral vision of the Middle Way, and the bi-directional tree the sources of meaning, but a tree rooted in the Middle Way itself represents the conditions for the tree to flourish in terms of the avoidance of extreme *beliefs* that are required. Of course, if we are imagining a tree, the beliefs would be implicit: but you could say, for example, that a tree that leaned over to the left *believed* that this was the best way to grow so as to limit the negative impact of prevailing wind conditions. A tree that continued to grow only in that direction even long after the prevailing wind changed, thus limiting its access to light, would be adopting an absolute belief to its own detriment. The tree that has

---

14 LS 91, 92, 93, 95 and 96 all illustrate this.

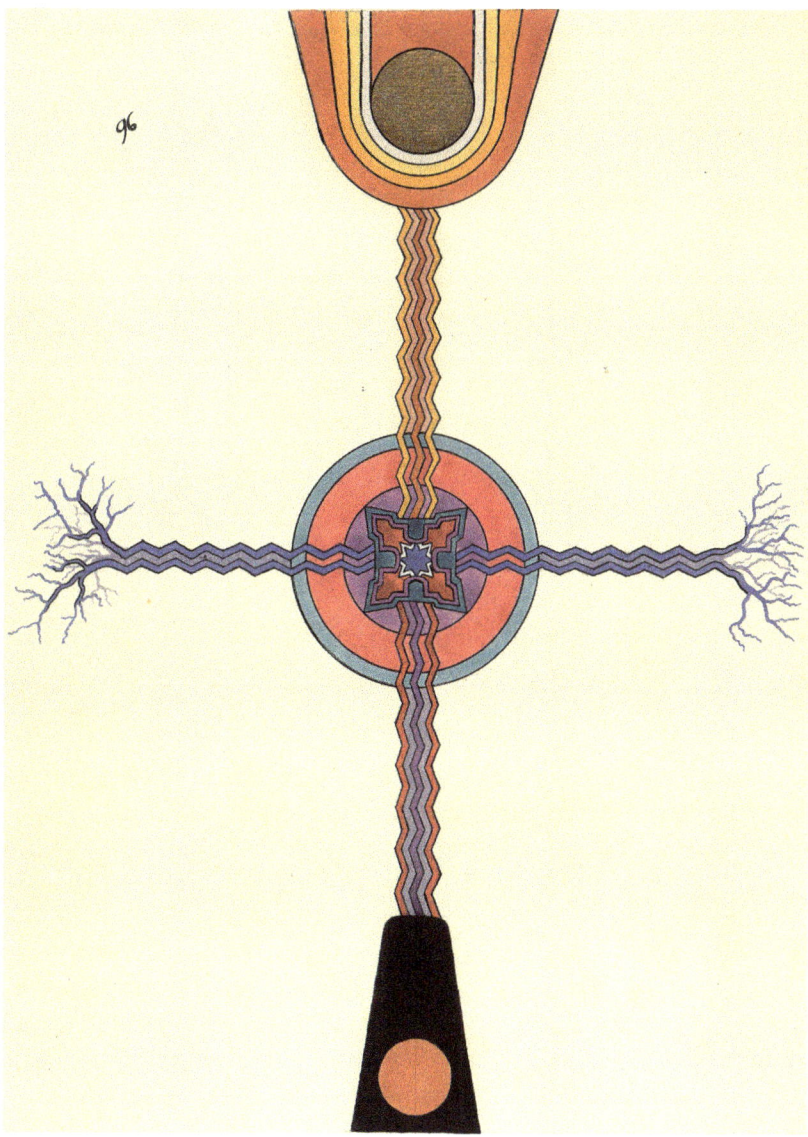

Illustration 10. Jung's mandala, incorporating Middle Way and bidirectional tree motifs (*Red Book* facsimile LS 96). Used by permission of W.W. Norton & Company, Inc.

its roots in the Middle Way grows in a way that is as balanced and flexible as is feasible for a tree.

Perhaps others of Jung's mandalas are more visually striking and less abstract, but none is more symbolically comprehensive than this one. It is rich because it can visually show us *the relationships between symbols* rather than just one symbol. The more we can imagine the relationships between different symbols, the more flexible we can become in the models we use and the metaphors they depend on, rather than assuming that one metaphor tells us the whole story, which carries the danger of absolutising it.

5.f. Mandala as city

The idea of a mandala as a city, as Jung found it in his 'Liverpool' dream, is also realised in two mandalas included in the *Red Book*,[15] with a third in which a mandala appears in the sky *above* a town.[16] The mandala in *Liber Secundus* 163 resembles a city-fortress with a moat, but also a flower (**illustration 11**). Jung reproduced this image twice, in both *Commentary on 'The Secret of the Golden Flower'* and *Concerning Mandala Symbolism,* in the latter making comparisons with the Imperial City in Beijing, the Heavenly City of Jerusalem, and the City of Brahma on Mount Meru in Indian mythology.[17]

This brings out a further aspect of integration that in my view is insufficiently explored in Jung's theory, even though it is implicitly symbolised in the *Red* Book: namely that integration can also be understood at a social and political rather than only an individual level.[18] It is hardly surprising if our socially-formed structures resemble our individual ones, because much the same forces apply to each. There is a division of energy and belief in any given social group, which can be absolutised or integrated just like the division of energy and belief in an individual psyche. Though the image of a fortress-city has the unfortunate connotation of absolute opposition to what lies beyond it, within that fortress there is a designed unity that at least ideally reflects a unity within the city. There is a

---

15 LS 159 and 163.
16 LS 125.
17 LS 163, LFT 320 n. 307, RE 422–3 n. 307.
18 See Ellis (2012b) for further discussion of the relationship between psychological and socio-political integration.

Illustration 11. Jung's 'city' or 'fortress' mandala (*Red Book* facsimile LS 163). Used by permission of W.W. Norton & Company, Inc.

transcendent centre in Jung's fortress-mandala to reflect the meaning that integrates the population, but beyond this there is no division, no East End and West End, but rather a citizenry all having equal access to the centre. Within the city-mandala the God archetype is recognised as internal, rather than being projected into an external power that can then support power-hierarchies within the human population.

5.g. Mandala with archetypes

Jung seems to have produced only one mandala in the *Red Book* that tried to show the relationship between integration and another type of symbol that we have been discussing much – the archetype. That is the beautiful and complex mandala in *Liber Secundus* 105 (**illustration 12**). This apparently shows three archetypes in relation to each other: the Wise Old Man at the top, the shadow at the bottom, and two versions of the anima (positive and negative) in between. In his explanation of this image, however, Jung relates the 'Luciferian' figure at the bottom of this mandala to the trickster figure, which also has some of the functions of the hero as well as of the shadow.[19] This type of mandala can show graphically the ways in which each archetype can contribute positively to the integration of the whole. Because they are on the periphery of the mandala, however, this also reminds us that our view of them is partial and subject to projection.

This type of mandala is closest to the type we find in Buddhism, which often breaks down the *qualities* of the meaning of enlightenment (i.e. integration), as a prism breaks down the component colours in white light. For the purposes of comparison we could look at a Five-Buddha mandala from Buddhist tradition (**illustration 13**). Here the four Buddhas in the quarters again represent different qualities of integration, which in this case are associated with four different wisdoms: action (green), reflectivity (blue), sameness (yellow) and discrimination (red). Each of these qualities appears to potentially be in conflict with its opposite: if you recognise the ultimate sameness of everything and accept it equally (yellow), as Jung tried to do in the passage from the *Red Book* already mentioned,[20] it

---

19 LFT 297 n. 186, RE 344, n. 186.
20 LS 124, LFT 305–6, RE 374–5 (see chapter 1).

Tree of Life and Mandala 97

Illustration 12. Jung's mandala incorporating archetypes (*Red Book* facsimile LS 105). Used by permission of W.W. Norton & Company, Inc.

is impossible to make the discriminations between goals required to act (green), just as if you are endlessly reflective (blue) this will prevent you having the kind of discriminating passion towards particular things represented by the Red Buddha, that is required to act. To reach the integration represented by the White Buddha, these contradictions have to be dialectically engaged with each other using the Middle Way.

The mandalas of the *Red Book* are not only an aesthetic feast, but also a visual and diagrammatic source of understanding for the various kinds of concepts surrounding integration and the relationships between them. Some are austerely abstract, but others provide strong evocations of aspects of wider experience that can be linked

Illustration 13. *Mandala of the Five Buddhas* by Dharmachari Aloka. Reproduced by permission of Ian Linn.

to the concepts. However, mandalas are not necessarily only objects for passive appreciation. We can also make our own. This can be an integrative exercise, whether or not you possess Jung's artistic skills and whether or not you ever show them to anyone else.

The creation of a personal mandala can be a helpful way of reflecting on the desires and beliefs in your experience and how much each contributes towards integration or drags you away from it. Although you could make a mandala with words, the process of producing visual symbols for these things often obliges you to think of them more experientially and intuitively. The symbols could be quite universal ones such as Jung used, but they could also be quite personal. For example, you could have a little icon of a wine bottle representing a disintegrative desire at the edge of your mandala, and a little picture of the *Red Book* further in towards the centre.

6. Integrating the Shadow

6.a. The nature of evil

I find myself in a gloomy vault, whose floor consists of damp stone slabs. In the middle there is a column from which ropes and axes hang. At the foot of the column there lies an awful serpent-like tangle of human bodies. At first I catch sight of the figure of a young maiden with wonderful red-gold hair – a man of devilish appearance is lying half under her – his head is bent backward – a thin streak of blood runs down his forehead – two similar daimons have thrown themselves over the maiden's feet and body. Their faces bear an inhuman expression – the living evil – their muscles are taut and hard, and their bodies sleek like serpents. They lie motionless. The maiden holds her hand over one eye of the man lying beneath her, who is the most powerful of the three – her hand firmly clasps a silver fishing rod that she has driven into the eye of the devil.

I break out in a profuse cold sweat. They wanted to torture the maiden to death, but she defended herself with the force of the most extreme despair, and succeeded in piercing the eye of the evil one with the little hook. If he moves, she will tear out his eye with a final jerk. The horror paralyses me: what will happen? A voice speaks:

'The evil one cannot make a sacrifice. He cannot sacrifice his eye. Victory is with the one who can sacrifice.'[1]

Jung takes evil extremely seriously, as this Dante-esque descent into hell shows. Most of us have met some people we didn't like, but few have met a devil. The most urbane forms of religion tend to pass over him. Jung was quite clear that there is a devil, and that all the rawness of evil could be experienced in earnest. However, this evil lies within ourselves in the form of the shadow archetype. To attribute pure evil to somebody else almost inevitably depends on a great deal of projection, but we should not confuse the archetype of evil itself with its delusory projection.

This passage dramatises some interesting aspects of evil. Why should a devil particularly value his eye, and be unable to sacrifice

---

1 LS 73, LFT 288–9, RE 315.

it? Jung explains that 'The devil knows what is beautiful, and hence he is the shadow of beauty and follows it everywhere,' but a fuller explanation is needed than he seems able to offer. The eye is the most predatory of the sense-organs, most linked to the goal-driven left hemisphere. Hearing, smell, touch, and taste are most often used for wider awareness, on the alert for unexpected conditions that may offer potential threats. Though scanning with the eyes can also be used for this purpose, our eyes are more often on our goal: the animal we are hunting, the tool we are making, the fire we are kindling, and the potential mate we want to procreate with. When we are predatory and goal-driven, our desires framed by the parts of the left pre-frontal cortex that are associated with goals and representations, we are most likely to interpret the world only in terms of our narrowly focused desires. Predatory and goal-driven states are most likely to be externally signalled by the use of the eyes. Sartre talked here about 'the look' and feminists talk about the 'male gaze'.

We all have goals, and thus predatory moments. However, it is the over-dominance and narrowness of such goal-driven states, closing us off to new information, that makes us evil. What is sinister about the demons in Jung's vision is that they were intent on torturing the innocent maiden (Jung's soul) with no possibility that they would turn aside in the light of new thoughts or experiences. They were closed to any sympathy with the maiden, closed to any other considerations from outside. The fitness of their bodies also becomes sinister rather than attractive when it just enables them to do their narrow, obsessive task more effectively, rather as a bigger monster is more frightening than a smaller one even if it is no more malicious.

It is not the devils themselves, but their mental state that makes them evil. That narrowly-focused, instrumental state is not confined to them, but also spreads. Those we regard as 'good' may be driven to 'evil' methods by the need to defend themselves against those who no longer play by any rules. Sticking a silver fishing rod in someone's eye is, after all, not a very nice thing to do. As Jung puts it 'The eye of the evil one sucked in all the force of my soul; only its will remained, which is just that small fish hook. I wanted evil, since I realised that I was not able to elude it.'[2] Evil thus tends to create a

---

2   LS 74, LFT 289, RE 318.

cyclic process in which opposing evil develops, and those whom we first thought of as 'good' compete in an egoistic race to the bottom.

Yet the voice that Jung hears asserts that there is a distinct difference between the maiden and the demons, despite the similarity in their tactics. The demon, it is suggested, cannot *sacrifice*, and it is implied that the maiden and her like will win in the end because they can. I take this to mean, not that sacrifice itself has any value (we cannot tip the scales of cosmic justice through sacrifice, as the five ascetics in the life of the Buddha wished to do), but that if we can have the wider perspective that sacrifice would require, we still have an advantage over the narrowly evil. To sacrifice something you really value (not somebody you don't value, which the evil do readily), you need to be able to think beyond your obsessive possession of the thing you value, and a degree of integration over time is needed for that. We can see this point demonstrated time and time again in stories about good and evil: that the villain loses in the end because he does not consider the possibility of the hero being motivated by love or self-sacrifice, or in any way not thinking like him. The weakness of the evil is that they are stuck in a dualistic paradigm and cannot reframe (or if they do, they cease to be evil).

6.b. Mara and the absorption of evil

It is interesting to compare the application of the Middle Way to evil in Jung and in Buddhist accounts, for at first sight they may seem rather different. In the life of the Buddha, evil is represented by the figure of *Mara*. Like Brahma Sahampati as the God archetype in the life of the Buddha, Mara can be easily understood to be an aspect of the Buddha's own psyche, an archetypal figure representing the shadow rather than an externalised supernatural entity. Mara's role is usually one of introducing conflict so as to disrupt the Buddha's more integrated desires and beliefs. That conflict is associated either with craving or with fear and anxiety, those responses coming from the 'reptilian' parts of our brains that disrupt our gradually acquired emotional and cognitive integration by creating closed feedback loops between narrowly focused beliefs and 'fight or flight' emotions.

In the life of the Buddha, Mara features in a fightback after the Buddha discovers the Middle Way, and has rooted himself beneath the Bodhi tree in determination to achieve enlightenment. Mara is then depicted as trying to undermine the Buddha's confidence, sending monstrous armies to attack him and induce fear, and sending his daughters as sexual temptation to induce craving. However, the Buddha remains immovable. The weapons thrown at him turn into lotus petals, and he remains indifferent to the charms of the seductive daughters.[3]

The Buddha can be seen at this point as practising the Middle Way that he has lately realised, indeed in the process showing dramatically the close relationship between the practice of the Middle Way, embodiment and integration. The base of his steadfastness is not abstract certainty, but bodily awareness of a kind that allows him to put these extreme reactions of anxiety and craving into a wider context. It is this that allows him to maintain confidence, despite the immense difficulties he is encountering. In the process he shows how the narrowly-focused, disruptive emotions associated with evil can be absorbed.

This steadfastness in the face of evil may well be the best response to it in many circumstances, where the evil is found in our own projected fear or craving. Evil is 'overcome' by being absorbed into a larger context that adopts its energy, not by being fought against. Very often we are only fighting against our own projections. However, Jung's demonic encounter as the maiden makes quite a different point. The maiden appears to be struggling against evil, but she does so by attacking something that is identified symbolically with the narrowness of our desires. In practice, we are unlikely to be satisfied by sweeping claims that evil is always part of our own projected assumptions, and we are very likely to continue to feel that evil is still to some measure present beyond us and that it needs fighting. There are some circumstances where we can simply remain steadfast, but there are also others where that rooted steadfastness needs to be expressed more actively so as to try to prevent further conflict and destruction. We may think of these circumstances as ones where the evil is in 'others' rather than 'oneself', but perhaps the division is not as neat as that. There may well be some occasions when we need either to absorb the evil of others or

---

[3] *Sutta Nipata* 3.2.426–43, Sadhatissa (1985) pp. 48–9; Ashvaghosha, *Buddhacarita* 13, Johnston (1972); *Samyutta Nikaya* 1.4.505–18, Bodhi (2000) pp. 217–20.

struggle with it in ourselves, in both cases in the service of a moral motive.

When should we use the maiden's response to evil rather than the Buddha's? As I will discuss in more detail in chapter 12, the Middle Way does not give us any absolute moral prescriptions, but it is precisely for that reason that it offers a more adequate moral model. The Buddha's rooted passivity and Jung's activity are both possible Middle Way responses to evil, but they are united by the developing recognition of the need to integrate the shadow in the long term, and implicitly by the need for awareness of the nature of the shadow that is not simply a projection of our reptilian emotions.

6.c. Good's dependence on evil

Jung's ever-recurrent theme in the *Red Book* is that evil is the flip side of good. You cannot have good without evil, he keeps telling us, because otherwise evil will be repressed and the energy that good needs from evil will be missing.

> *Because I wanted to give birth to my God, I also wanted evil.... You cannot undertake one without the other. But if you want to escape evil, you will create no God, everything you do is tepid and gray. I wanted my God at any cost. Hence I also wanted my evil.*[4]

We can also say more about this in the light of brain lateralisation. Those same left-hemisphere centres that can become obsessively dominant in states of evil are also necessary for those of good. The right hemisphere, which opens up and broadens the left through wider awareness, meaning, bodily connectedness and the senses, needs to have something to work on, and is helpless without the left as it has to re-learn how to use representational language and tools or to have goals. Jill Bolte Taylor reports her experience of a stroke disabling her left hemisphere, leaving her in states of impotent open egoless bliss.[5] So Jung's tepidness and grayness might not be our experience without evil, but it may be a way of talking about lack of goals to focus our energy.

Good needs desires, meaning and beliefs, otherwise it is unable to act. We cannot have integration – and thus God – without the

---

4   LS 73, LFT 289, RE 316.
5   Bolte Taylor (2006),

ego, which creates the nucleus of the integrated psyche. We cannot have a God archetype without the integration *of* the hero, anima, and shadow archetypes.

Jung thus objects to the traditional Christian conception of evil as *'privatio boni'*, the privation or absence of good, because he stresses that good actually needs evil. I would go further than him here and suggest that in practice we could turn this right around and describe good as *'privatio mali'* or the absence of evil. We have no non-dogmatic ways of identifying good in a pure form, since it consists experientially in the gradual integration of evil. As argued in chapter 1, we cannot assume the integration process to have a final destination, even though we find such a destination meaningful. Evil, however, is readily identifiable in our experience (at least when it becomes sufficiently aware) from its narrow obsessiveness, its assumption that we have the whole story. The more we integrate that evil into a larger context, the more we move beyond that evil, without ever losing it entirely.

An integrative understanding of evil also undermines other common but unhelpful assumptions about it. In many traditional religious contexts, evil is identified with desire and with the body, and there is also a Western tradition going back to Plato that treats evil as irrationality. Both of these approaches immediately create a difficulty with actually identifying good and evil in experience, as all human experience contains desires and beliefs in dependence on our bodies, and the beliefs are nearly always justified in some way. Very often the solution is to separate good desire from bad desire[6] and good ('rational') belief from bad belief, but this approach is usually dogmatic, and it is often difficult to tell from our experience which is which. The integrative model solves this problem at a stroke: all desires become good to some extent, dependent on how integrated they are. All beliefs also become incrementally good, apart from absolutising ones that block the process of integration. Good can be tested in each judgement according to the extent of its avoidance of the evil of absolutisation.

---

6 E.g. in Buddhism, the distinction between *dhamma-chanda* and *tanha* (Payutto 1992 pp. 33–6).

6.d. The Cabiri and the sword

Jung talks about the 'golden seed' or 'eggs of the gods' to be found within the devil, that makes us value him despite our hatred of him.[7] Out of these eggs spring the Cabiri, little gnome-like creatures that perform valuable integrative services at the roots of embodied processes. The Cabiri seem to represent the way that the 'natural' is still subject to the deliberate, or the ways that we can still influence apparently slow and inflexible processes. They come from the seed of the devil, because they are little instrumental engineers, but their field of expertise is the processes we might otherwise think of as determined. The Cabiri are at Jung's command to do things that he cannot do for himself: 'We carry up what slumbers in the earthly, what is dead and yet enters into the living. We do this slowly and easily, what you do in vain in your human way. We complete what is impossible for you.'[8]

The Cabiri then present Jung with the entanglement of his own brain, plus a sword specially sharpened to be able to cut through that entanglement. 'The entanglement is your madness, the sword is the overcoming of madness' say the Cabiri. But it turns out that the Cabiri themselves are the root-fibres of Jung's brain, and will be destroyed if he cuts. Nevertheless, they urge him to do so, because he is 'master of the lower nature'. He strikes.[9] This should not be taken literally as a representation of how we should destroy our brain, or even part of it, but nevertheless it tells us about how it may *feel* like self-destruction to actually free ourselves from the entanglements of left-hemisphere dominated obsession, and that we will need a great deal of confidence and a willingness to be decisive to do it. It also seems to convey the very process of 'sacrifice' that the evil are unable to perform. To the evil, giving up their current entanglements may feel like impossible self-destruction. To the Cabiri, though, despite the fact that they are sprung from the devil's seeds, the sacrifice of what seems to be indispensable at the moment is understood not to be so indispensable from the integrated perspective.

In some ways, though, this metaphor is one-sided. In practice, as I have already argued, we depend on our 'entangled' left

---

7 LS 165, LFT 320, RE 424.
8 LS 166, LFT 320-1, RE 426.
9 LS 167-8, LFT 321, RE 426-8.

hemispheres completely for good as well as evil. What makes them 'entangled' is absolutisation. Jung's sword might be best interpreted as a sword of wisdom cutting through entangling delusion rather than through any of our brain. We need to be kind to our brains, but our delusions, on the other hand, need firm rejection. The idea of a sword of wisdom cutting through entanglements is also found in Buddhist mythology, in the figure of Manjushri.

6.e. The shadow of destitution

In the chapter called 'One of the Lowly', Jung also acknowledges that the shadow has a social side. Jung finds himself on the road with a tramp, who turns out to be an out-of-work locksmith and ex-convict. Jung buys him a meal at an inn, but during the night the tramp dies in Jung's arms, apparently of tuberculosis or something similar.[10]

Given that we are in a slightly more familiar world than hell, we might need to be reminded that the tramp is also Jung. As Jung puts it, 'A destitute joins me and wants admittance into my soul, and I am thus not destitute enough.'[11] Jung is surprised that the destitute resembles him in wanting stimulating work, and that the cinema that the tramp admires oddly seems to consist of scenes from medieval literature (not so surprising when Jung confesses his dislike of cinema – the tramp has to draw on the same visual memories that Jung does!). Even the tramp's former trade as a locksmith is a more literal version of Jung's specialisation in unlocking symbols.[12]

Jung appreciates the tramp as his shadow, representing his 'depths' that are essential to his 'heights'. Without awareness of these 'depths', he also cannot appreciate the 'heights': 'If I am always on the heights, I wear them out and the best becomes atrocious to me.'[13] At the low point, he also says, 'you are no longer distinct from your fellow beings'.[14] This is a point of moral importance, suggesting that our capacity for human solidarity is dependent on our ability to integrate the shadow. Jung does not draw out the political

---

10 LS 11–13, LFT 265–6, RE 232–6.
11 LS 13, LFT 266, RE 236.
12 LS 12, LFT 265, RE 233–4.
13 LS 13, LFT 266, RE 237.
14 Ibid.

implications of this, but it seems clear that if we want a more just society, the more privileged need to learn to integrate their shadows. Jung effectively admits that he rarely thinks about the poor, but if those in a position with any degree of power fail to recognise that they are also the poor, they are likely to maintain policies that fail to respect the poor's full human interests.

6.f. How to talk to the devil

However, for inspiration in the practice of integrating the shadow, we should look to Jung's discussion with the Red One.[15] Here we no longer have a nasty devil in the pits of hell, but an urbane, sophisticated devil – Mephistopheles rather than Satan. To add to the practicality, there is a degree of creative doubt, as Jung merely *thinks* he is the devil during the process of the discussion, rather than being quite sure. The uncertainty is related to the individuality: 'Surely this red one was the devil, but my devil.'[16]

The vision begins with Jung standing on a high tower and watching a distant red horseman approach. The horseman eventually arrives, as a tall figure entirely clothed in red, and comes up the tower to see Jung, saying 'Your waiting has called me.'

The Red One knows what Jung is thinking, because, of course, he is Jung. He knows that Jung thinks he is the devil, and cannot explicitly deny it. However, he immediately takes advantage of this to adopt a pained innocence, and put in a pre-emptive strike as though Jung has accused him of being the devil.

> I: Who are you?
>
> T.R.: Who am I? You think I am the devil. Do not pass judgement. Perhaps you can also talk to me without knowing who I am. What sort of a superstitious fellow are you, that you immediately think of the devil?[17]

The Red One is thus immediately defensive and ad hominem, attacking Jung as a person as a distracting move rather than answering his question. He is also hypocritical, telling Jung 'not to pass judgement', but then immediately doing so himself.

---

15 LS 2–5, LFT 259–61, RE 212–19.
16 LS 4, LFT 260, RE 217.
17 LS 2, LFT 259, RE 212.

Integrating the Shadow 109

How does one respond to such defensiveness? Jung tries introducing a little evidence:

> I: *If you have no supernatural ability, how could you feel that I stood looking on my tower, looking out for the unknown and the new?*[18]

However, The Red One does not answer this. Instead he moves into flattery ('You hit your nail on the head'; ' You're truly a good diviner of riddles'), and now Jung begins to move into the same narrow, devilish form of communication ('You sound cool and sneering'). The Red One then aims straight below the belt in another ad hominem, and Jung responds primly.

> T.R.: *You're an unbelievably ponderous and serious person. Are you always so urgent?*
>
> I: *I would before God always like to be as serious and true to myself as I try to be. However, that certainly becomes difficult in your presence.*[19]

Those of us used to the perils of internet discussion might by now be seeing the Red One as a bit of a troll. Jung is struggling not to feed the troll. The conversation goes on in a similar vein, with the Red One going back to flattery, fake sincerity, and barely veiled mockery, accusing Jung of fulfilling Christian stereotypes. Jung fails to be granted even the possibility of finding value in Christianity without fulfilling those stereotypes.

> T.R.: *Your solemnity smells of fanaticism. You have an ethical air and a simplicity that smacks of stale bread and water.*
>
> I: *I can say neither yes nor no: you speak as one trapped in the spirit of this time. It seems to me that you lack the terms of comparison.*[20]

Having started off in the Middle Way defying the Red One's false dualism, though, Jung ends up starting to fulfil the Red One's stereotyping by sounding even primmer and a bit dogmatic.

> *I repeat: he whose heart has not been broken over the Lord Jesus Christ drags a pagan around in himself, who holds him back from the best.... What I mean is that it's hardly a coincidence that the whole world has become Christian. I also believe that it was the task of Western man to carry Christ in his heart and to grow with his suffering, death, and resurrection.*[21]

18 LS 2, LFT 259, RE 213.
19 Ibid.
20 LS 3, LFT 260, RE 214.
21 LS 3, LFT 260, RE 215.

One can see that Jung is still referring to his archetypal interpretation of religion here, but the Red One can be forgiven for not picking that up and hearing only standard evangelism. The Red One then manages to polarise the conversation even more by introducing the Jews, and again Jung does not respond entirely creditably:

> T.R.: *Well here are also Jews who are good people and yet have no need for your solemn gospels.*
>
> I: *You are, it seems to me, no good reader of people: have you never noticed that the Jew himself lacks something – one in his head, another in his heart, and he himself feels that he lacks something?*
>
> T.R.: *Indeed I'm no Jew, but I must come to the Jew's defense: you seem to be a Jew-hater.*
>
> I: *Well, now you speak like all those Jews who accuse anyone of Jew hating who does not have a completely favourable judgement, while they themselves make the bloodiest jokes about their own kind. Since the Jews themselves only too clearly feel that particular lack and yet do not want to admit it, they are extremely sensitive to criticism.*[22]

By modern standards, Jung seems, if not actually anti-semitic, at the very least rather patronising towards Jews here, and apparently unable to imagine other authentic ways by which Jews could engage in the path without being Christians. But this may be a narrower Jung than usual, stimulated by the Red One's narrow attitudes in turn. It is the Red One who again plays the crude ad hominem card, responding to a claim by making an accusation against the person making the claim as a distraction, rather than addressing the claim itself. A polarised discussion framed only in terms of 'Anti-Semitism' vs. 'Jewish Paranoia' is obviously heading nowhere and needs to be reframed. It is doubtful whether Jung is really trying hard enough to reframe it.

Most of us are unlikely to end up in a pit watching a red-haired maiden being tortured by demons (or if we do experience this, we may recognise its symbolic nature). However, the kind of conversation that Jung has with the *Red One* is everyday fare: on internet chat, in bars, in kitchens, and in parliaments. The devils slip into these conversations all the time in the form of narrowed awareness. The devil offers only two options when there are more, or assumes

---

22 LS 3, LFT 260, RE 215-16.

it is the other person who is at fault without addressing their reasons for thinking as they do, or stereotypes people or things that form a varied and complex category, by uses distracting tactics to avoid answering critical questions. Sometimes the devil says something positive, but this is always of questionable sincerity.

Jung's responses do not offer textbook ways of reframing these devilish terms of reference. For these you will need to study critical thinking so as to become aware of common fallacies, cognitive psychology so as to become aware of biases, and disciplines such as Non-Violent Communication or other mediation methods so as to have the skills to defuse heated disputes. What they offer, instead, is an illustration of how easily we can get drawn into them despite an intuition of the Middle Way. We are usually not independent of the tone of discussion set by the other person, and there are myriad subtle ways in which they can quickly get you talking in their polarised frame of reference rather than yours. Opposition is easy, but reframing is relatively complex by comparison. Jung illustrates very effectively how if you want hell on earth, all you need to do is keep fighting the devil.

In his comments after the vision, Jung summarises rather well a Middle Way approach to evil, though apparently fails to recognise that he did not live up to it very well:

> *If ever you have the opportunity to speak with the devil, then do not forget to confront him in all seriousness. He is your devil after all. The devil as the adversary is your own other standpoint: he tempts you and sets a stone in your path where you least want it.*

> *Taking the devil seriously does not mean going over to his side, or else one becomes the devil. Rather it means coming to an understanding. Thereby you accept your other standpoint. With that the devil fundamentally loses ground, and so do you. And that may be well and good.*[23]

---

23 LS 4, LFT 261, RE 218.

7. The Soul and the Anima

7.a. Jung's view of the soul

On the second night I called out to my soul:

I am weary, my soul, my wandering has lasted too long, my search for myself outside of myself. Now I have gone through events and find you behind all of them. For I have made discoveries on my erring through events, humanity, and the world. I found men. And you, my soul, I found again, first in images within men and then you yourself. I found you where I least expected you. You climbed out of a dark shaft. You announced yourself to me in advance in dreams....

I wandered for many years, so long that I forgot that I possessed a soul. Where were you all this time? Which Beyond sheltered you and gave you sanctuary?[1]

Christian literature has a long tradition of these kinds of addresses to one's soul. The soul addressed was taken to be one's true self, the eternal self beyond the limitations of worldly temptation and delusion. Hence it was closely attached to a metaphysics going back to Plato, in which the soul was taken to be an immaterial personal essence, possessing reason but not the contingent features of one's physical nature. The soul could hence be reborn or resurrected when the body perished.

Jung's genius is to take the meaning of this tradition and give it a new, relevant form, whilst leaving aside the metaphysical beliefs about the soul. His soul is compensatory rather than essential, consisting in those positive and attractive parts of him that are not recognised by his conscious ego as such. Whilst ancient philosophers absolutised the soul positively, and modern physicalist ones absolutised its absence, Jung found a Middle Way by reframing the meaning of 'soul'. It is not one's 'true' self, but rather the neglected other half of oneself. Because of that it is encountered in unexpected, intuitive ways beyond one's normal frames of assumption.

1   LP ii(r), LFT 233, RE 130–1.

Soul and Anima

The soul is also an archetype, otherwise known as the anima (which is simply the Latin for 'soul'). Like any other archetype it can be projected or integrated, and Jung's useless search for his soul in the world was due to seeking it outwardly in projected form. As discussed in chapter 2, the anima archetype is the psychological function of the attractive other, so it seems to me that we can project it onto any attractive other: an animal, a landscape, or an artwork, for instance. All of these things have some life of their own that may be vitiated by too much possession, yet at the same time we wish them to be ours. Most strongly, though, of course, we project the anima onto the opposite sex (or those we find sexually attractive) and onto children. That is what led Jung to coin the term *Animus* to refer to a male form of the soul in women.

For Jung, however, as a mature heterosexual man, the soul took an overwhelmingly female form, usually a young female: a maiden. He stresses that the soul has all his potential qualities, and thus also other compensating features. So, if we are clever, the soul is simple-minded, and vice-versa.[2] If we are authoritative, the soul is a servant, and vice-versa.[3] To become attuned to the soul and listen to it we must get in touch with our opposite qualities, which for Jung meant swallowing his pride and being a servant, leaving aside his cleverness and becoming simple-minded, as well as getting in touch with feminine and childlike qualities.

The core function of the anima/animus is thus compensation, which makes me dissatisfied with some aspects of Jung's later discussions of it, for example in the chapter 'The Syzygy: Anima and Animus' in *Aion*, his 1951 monograph.[4] Here Jung theorises about anima and animus in terms of the principles of logos and eros rather than in terms of a compensatory psychological function, and engages in a good deal of sexual stereotyping that will look suspicious to many modern readers. However, in the context of the *Red Book*, we do not have to worry too much about the defects of this later theory, because the basic insights are very clearly and dramatically explored in relation to Jung's specific experience. I am not sure that it is necessary to separate anima from animus at all, since both refer to the same function – and this is a function that could also

---

2 LP iii(r), LFT 237, RE 145.
3 LP iii(r), LFT 235, RE 140.
4 CW 9ii, ch. 3.

be applied to the attractive other and its projection in the context of homosexual, trans-sexual, and non-sexual drives as well as the heterosexual ones that Jung adopted as the norm.

This process of compensation is also, of course, a process of integration and of questioning absolutisations about our own essential nature. By becoming more attuned to the feminine, for example, a man does not cease to be a man, but seeks a Middle Way between one set of rigid absolutisations about what being a man means, and their negation on the other hand. This helps him to make more adequate judgements as a man, because he can also appreciate other perspectives and thus understand more about his ignorance. As Jung puts it:

> *Without balance you transgress your limits without noticing what has happened to you. You achieve balance, however, only if you nurture your opposite.*[5]

From the rebalancing of gender identity, too, a wider vision of human wholeness emerges:

> *What about masculinity? Do you know how much femininity man lacks for completeness? Do you know how much masculinity woman lacks for completeness? You seek the feminine in women and the masculine in men. And thus there are only men and women. But where are people? You, man, should not seek the feminine in women, but seek and recognise it in yourself, as you possess it from the beginning. It pleases you, however, to play at manliness, because it travels on a well-worn track. You, woman, should not seek the masculine in men, but assume the masculine in yourself, since you possess it from the beginning. But it amuses you and is easy to play at femininity, consequently man despises you because he despises his femininity. But humankind is masculine and feminine, not just man or woman.*[6]

Not only views about oneself, but also many social and political beliefs have absolutised the identities of men and women, particularly those of traditional patriarchal culture. Jung's separation of masculinity from men and femininity from women has provided a key concept that has helped to undermine those absolutisations and contributed to the shift towards the development of new, more adequate gender roles in many areas of Western society.

---

5   LS 8, LFT 263, RE 226.
6   LS 8–9, LFT 263, RE 226–7.

This wider human wholeness also helps to fulfil the God archetype, as it integrates both individuals and societies that were previously placed in institutionalised conflict by the repression of all exceptions to fixed gender identities. As long as the anima/animus archetype is integrated enough for us to recognise that it is ourselves rather than others, it can lead us towards the integration of the God archetype: 'My God in my soul is a child'[7] as Jung puts it. Along the way, however, it will also need to integrate the hero and the shadow.

7.b. Salome

However, Jung's responses to the anima at different points in the *Red Book* seem to vary between the integrated and the projected. At some points he recognises the soul as part of himself, and is able to work impressively in the ambiguity that is created by him conceiving the soul at one and the same time as something separate and as part of him. At other times, though, he seems to forget that this feminine projection is part of himself. He is puzzled by her contradictory nature, falls in love with her, challenges her, and even has rows with her in the intimate but merciless way people sometimes do with their spouses.

The figure of Salome is a particular focus for these projections. Jung often seems to differentiate Salome from his soul in a way that gives her a different, projected status. Jung first encounters Salome in an early vision of the *Red Book*, in which she is inseparable from Elijah (who is discussed in chapter 3 above). At first Jung is horrified by the close association between Salome and Elijah:

> E: ...*Consider this, I and my daughter have been one since eternity.*
>
> I: *You pose dreadful riddles. How could it be that this unholy woman and you, the prophet of God, could be one?*
>
> E: *Why are you amazed? But you see it, we are together.*
>
> I: *What my eyes see is exactly what I cannot grasp. You, Elijah, who are a prophet, the mouth of God, and she, a bloodthirsty horror. You are the symbol of the most extreme contradiction.*
>
> E: *We are real and not symbols.*[8]

---

7 LP ii(v), LFT 234, RE 135.
8 LP v(v), LFT 246, RE 176.

Salome never provides any evidence of being 'bloodthirsty' within Jung's visions, but only of being an attractive young woman who declares her love for Jung. Nevertheless, the name Salome provides him with a whole set of associations by which Jung links her with manipulative and unscrupulous female behaviour. He seems to desire and fear her at the same time, saying later that 'A thinker should fear Salome, since she wants his head, especially if he is a holy man. A thinker cannot be a holy person, otherwise he loses his head.'[9] Salome suggests the close association of the anima with the shadow and the Wise Old Man, the ways in which the genuine acceptance of the other that we are most drawn to also involves the acceptance of our fears. Amongst those fears, for those who most value their 'head' – i.e. their left-hemisphere goal-oriented representations – is the fear of 'losing one's head',[10] or of losing the control and goal-orientation that tends to accompany this 'rational', 'thinking' self. To become a holy person (or more integrated person), however, does require that we are able to 'lose our heads' in the sense, not of ceasing to use this part of ourselves, but of putting its self-protective obsessions into a wider perspective.

Salome reappears later in a striking scene in which she offers herself in marriage to Jung (and is also offered by Elijah), but Jung reluctantly rejects her.[11] Here she is a personification of self-giving love, but Jung responds to her 'beautiful gift' with somewhat tormented circumspection. 'Your sweet words wind around me and I stand like someone crucified.'[12] It seems that he rejects the temptations of this projected love, like many a religious ascetic, on the grounds that it is an illusion that will stand in the way of his integration of the love that Salome represents. Jung tries to offer a Middle Way solution:

Sal: Are you sending me away?

I: I'm not sending you away. You must not be far from me. But give to me out of your fullness, not your longing. I cannot satisfy your poverty just as

---

9   LP vi(r), LFT 248, RE 182.

10 According to German speakers that I have consulted, Jung's original German 'verfällt sein Kopf', does also imply confusion and loss of control in the same way that the English 'loses his head' does. This seems to be a pun, because the literal loss of St John the Baptist's head at the wish of Salome is also being referred to.

11 LS 180-6, LFT 323-4, RE 435-9.

12 LS 183, LFT 324, RE 436.

you cannot still my longing. If your harvest is rich, send me some fruit from your garden.[13]

However, Salome cannot understand or accept such an integrative way of challenging the fragility of Romantic love, and seems to interpret it simply as a rejection: 'What a hard and incomprehensible man you are.' This seems to fit Jung's general recognition that his projected figures did not share all his understanding, but tended to stay stuck in the limited terms of their projection.

Jung's struggle with Salome at different points in the *Red Book* seems to be a struggle with the projection of the anima. As long as he desires Salome in a way that relates to her as something external, he also fears her. However, by the time of their later meeting, he has become more integrated, and thus no longer simply subject to the overwhelming power of projected sexual love. Both his love and his fear have been placed in a wider field of awareness that enables him to make more adequate responses – even if we can still debate whether or not these were the best possible responses. As we will see later in this chapter, Jung's attitude to love still raises questions even in his later and more integrated phase.

7.c. The serpent and the bird

The wider and more integrated anima is represented more directly by Jung's soul, who appears to him in the form of a bird or a serpent. As mentioned in chapter 3, by the time of their later encounter Jung has stolen the serpent from Elijah, indicating the ways that he has internalised the wisdom that was previously projected onto the powerful Wise Old Man figure. The serpent constantly challenges him and remains beyond his grasp, in contrast to the behaviour of Salome. Just before Elijah and Salome reappear, indeed, the serpent warns 'Just don't assume that somehow you could ever grasp me and embody me.'[14] The rejection of Salome thus appears to be a way of keeping faith with the integrated anima and rejecting the delusions offered by the projected anima. Earlier Jung has put this distinction in relation to his desire:

---

13 LS 185, LFT 324, RE 438.
14 LS 180, LFT 323, RE 435.

> *He could find his soul in desire itself, but not in the objects of desire. If he possessed his desire, and his desire did not possess him, he would lay a hand on his soul, since his desire is the image and expression of his soul.*[15]

This symbolisation of compensatory desire is also beautifully realised in Philip Pullman's series of fantasy novels, the *His Dark Materials* trilogy.[16] In one of the alternative fantasy worlds that these novels are set in, every person has a 'daemon' who takes the form of an animal who accompanies them everywhere, and cannot be detached without at least the loss of vital motives and energies, usually death. The daemon can be of various types, but tends to reflect the personality type of the person, and is always of the opposite sex. Crucially, the daemon is able to change its animal form during childhood, but becomes fixed in one form at adolescence. The daemon exhibits repressed emotions of the human, so watching the daemon becomes a way of gaining awareness of those emotions in oneself or another.

7.d. The hidden daughter in the castle

Jung's encounter with a scholarly old man and his daughter in 'The Castle in the Forest' provides further ways of understanding the role of the anima, in relation to embodied meaning and Jung's preoccupation with banality. In Jung's vision, he loses his way in a dark forest but takes refuge in a remote castle. There he finds an old scholar in charge of the castle, who is unable to tear himself from his work and is 'absent and defensive' in his response to the newcomer,[17] but distractedly offers him a bed. In bed but unable to sleep, Jung imagines that the scholar is hiding a young and beautiful daughter in the castle – and then she appears. 'I am the old man's daughter. He holds me here in unbearable captivity,'[18] she explains.

The repressed maiden harboured in the castle of the distracted scholar is a powerful symbol, not only of the unrecognised role of the anima as the feminine in man, but also of the related relationship between embodied and representational meaning. The theme of embodied meaning will be explored more fully in chapter 9, but

---

15 LP ii(r), LFT 232, RE 129.
16 Pullman (2011).
17 LS 6, LFT 261, RE 220-1.
18 LS 7, LFT 262, RE 223.

Soul and Anima

for the moment let us note a whole series of false dichotomies that can be associated with this symbolism. The scholar stands for facts as identified in theory and recorded in language, separated from values, emotions, practice, and wider meaning. He is narrowly goal-oriented, which means he lacks awareness of wider conditions beyond these goals. He is caught up in the feedback loop mentioned in chapter 1, in which the goal-oriented and representational centres of the pre-frontal cortex of the left hemisphere of the brain become obsessed with certain beliefs, reinforced by obsession and anxiety from the 'reptilian' brain. In contrast, it is the wider awareness of the body and imagination, associated with the front of the right hemisphere, that can provide wider meaning and wider attention, in the process imparting life and value to the dead, artificial, over-controlled world of the scholar.

The maiden in the castle, then, represents not just the 'feminine' in the male psyche, but an even more profound compensatory source of human integration that cuts across all associations with gender. After all, women can become desiccated scholars as much as men can, even if they do so less frequently. The 'slim girl, pale as death' who represents this wider embodied meaning in Jung's psyche might well take a different form, including a male form, in another psyche. But the hiding of the girl in the castle is significant. Where the castle is the psyche, it suggests the unacknowledged dependence of representational meaning on embodied meaning, of the left hemisphere's cognitive meaning on the right hemisphere's bodily awareness. This will be discussed further in chapter 9.

Jung, however, has difficulty in believing in the reality of the maiden, because he is so obsessed by the banality of the story, which he describes as 'pulp fiction from the lending library'.[19] His concern both with her 'reality' and with the artistic originality of the story she appears in seem to be products of the same way of thinking as the scholar, namely a narrowly left-hemisphere, factual and literalistic way of thinking, that might allow stories as a diversion only as long as they meet high social expectations of originality. The girl herself has to point out to Jung how inappropriate his worries about 'banality' are:

> *'Do not stumble now over the fabulous, since the fairy tale is the grandmother of the novel, and has even more universal validity than the most avidly read*

19 Ibid.

> *novel of your time. And you know that what has been on everyone's lips for millennia, though repeated endlessly, still comes nearest the ultimate human truth…. Only what is human and what you call banal and hackneyed contains the wisdom you seek.'*[20]

Jung's worries about banality are obviously part of his worries about the other, and are a product of his class and high level of education. However, given the compensatory nature of the anima, if Jung has refined aesthetic tastes his anima will have banal ones. Jung's class-consciousness, and the value of looking beyond it to more universal human experience, is also shown at other points in the *Red Book,* such as his encounter with the tramp (already discussed in chapter 6) and with the cook with a direct and intuitive sense of 'the imitation of Christ' (already discussed in chapter 4).

What is human can indeed be mistaken for the banal and hackneyed, because it is simple. That simplicity is another aspect of the resistance of the highly-educated scholar to the girl. Yet complexity is always built up from simpler elements, in meaning as in construction. The scholar's complex concepts depend for their meaningfulness on the simple *gestalt* symbols that become meaningful to us in childhood as we first interact with the world around us, through the process explained by George Lakoff[21] (see chapter 9). Elaboration, as Lakoff explains, depends on a process of metaphorical extension from these more basic holistic meanings, but these metaphors have a tendency to become dead, as we forget that dependence on metaphorical structures and start to process what started off in the right hemisphere only in the left.[22] This is when the scholar represses the maiden and starts to think that her simple stories are 'banal', even though her life-force remains entirely necessary for the scholar.

But there are other ways of interpreting the idea of 'banality' that are not so much dependent on the equation of banality with simplicity or lack of highly-educated sophistication. The banal can alternatively be interpreted as the false: the unreflectively reproduced, the artificial, the sentimental, the performance driven by social expectation and power-relationships. In this sense of 'banal', the maiden in the castle is the very opposite of banal. It is not the commonality or popularity of her story that makes it sentimental, but the easily

---

20 LS 7–8, LFT 262, RE 224.
21 Lakoff (1987).
22 McGilchrist (2009) pp. 115 ff.

manufactured socially acceptable emotions that might accompany it. Every time her story occurs, however, we can alternatively think of it, not as 'hackneyed', but as deepened in significance by each iteration. The more we recognise our own and others' genuine experience in it, the more important and the less banal it becomes. Jung thus turns out to misjudge the very meaning of 'banal' – or at least its most useful and integrative meaning. If we let go of the expectations associated with social prejudice, it becomes easier to see why a more important sort of banality in the artistic sphere is worth avoiding. To do this we have to integrate our 'banal' anima.

7.e. The proposal of marriage

The climax of Jung's struggle with the anima occurs after Salome's offer of marriage and Jung's rejection of it, in the form of a moral crisis over the importance of love. Jung seems to wish to preserve his independence and authenticity in the face of Salome's endless giving, asking her to also maintain her authenticity and 'give to me out of your fullness, not your longing'. This response is also consistent with Jung's attitude to the maiden in the castle – he wants to avoid sentimentality. However, after his dismissal of Salome, Jung starts to be tormented by second thoughts, because he begins to recognise that this attitude, too, may be a projection. Salome is, after all, part of him, not an external woman. Could autonomy be appropriate in such a case? Perhaps the love of Salome is actually a profound expression of integration through self-acceptance.

> I accepted Salome as pleasure, and reject her as love. But she wants to be with me. How, then, should I also have love for myself? Love, I believe, responds to others. But my love wants to be with me. I dread it. May the power of my thinking push it from me, into the world, into things, into men. For something should join men together.[23]

Here Jung expresses an attitude that has become common in Christian (perhaps particularly Protestant) culture, whether or not it is necessarily Christian – namely the belief that love is intrinsically external, that it should be focused on its objects in the shape of others rather than cultivated as an emotion experienced within oneself. For example, the liberal Christian ethicist and originator

---

23 LS 188, LFT 324–5, RE 440.

of Situation Ethics, Joseph Fletcher, argued that true Christian love (*agape*) should be *conative* – a matter of effort rather than an emotion.[24] On the other hand we have the mystical tradition in Christianity, in which love is often experienced as an overwhelming emotion in the context of vision or meditation, separated from its object. This separation is an unfortunate aspect of the fact-value and reason-emotion distinctions that have become so dominant in much Western thought. Jung's thought here seems to be the typical externalising one, that love that is merely felt within, towards internal objects that are ultimately parts of oneself, is somehow false.

However, this externalising view of love relies too much on the ego, and underestimates the authentic sources of emotional energy in the parts of oneself that seem other. Salome seems other, and seems to be an object of desire, but when integrated, as Jung seems to be gradually understanding, she can be the source of *his* energy, whether directed towards himself or others. We cannot summon up a love we do not feel by an 'act of will', but rather can only gain access to it by meeting our Salomes and learning how to return the love they freely give us.

7.f. Hanging on the tree of life

After the beginning of these reflections, Jung hears Salome still crying. 'What does she want, or what do I still want?' he asks himself, perhaps realising that these amount to the same question. But it is the integrated anima, the serpent, who then offers another voice challenging him.

> *Serpent: Do you mean to live without sacrifice? Life must cost you something, mustn't it?*
>
> *I: I have, I believe, already paid. I have rejected Salome. Is that not sacrifice enough?*
>
> *Se: Too little for you. As has been said, you are allowed to make demands of yourself.*[25]

Jung is thus confronted with the demand for sacrifice, the endless demand of the other. His soul in the form of a bird goes up to

---

24 Fletcher (1966) ch. 6.
25 LS 188, LFT 325, RE 440.

heaven and comes back down with a crown that is inscribed with the words 'Love never ends', apparently symbolising that endless demand.[26] Salome is ecstatic when she sees this: 'The crown – you are to be crowned! What blessedness for me and you!'[27] However, Jung can neither wholly accept nor wholly reject this endless demand. Paralysed by the contradictions between the infinite demands of the anima and the wise recognition of human limitations, he is left hanging on the Tree of Life, in an image reminiscent of both Christ and Odin.

> *I remain silent and hang high above the ground on the swaying branch of the divine tree, for whose sake the original ancestors could not avoid sin, my hands are bound and I am completely helpless. So I hang for three days and three nights.*[28]

Jung's hanging is a wonderful symbol for the tormented state we are left in without the Middle Way, pursued by ideals that we are unable to live up to. The pressures of human reasoning are also represented. A philosophical raven drops by and tells Jung that his hanging depends 'on your notion of love and the other'. And blames him for being an ideologue when he says 'I've set my mind on being a complete and fully-fledged man.'[29] Then Satan comes and mocks him: 'See what comes of the reconciliation of opposites! Recant, and in a flash you'll be down on the greening earth.'[30]

Jung is finally released from his hanging by his soul in the form of a bird, who reminds him of the projection.

> *'You see, Salome is what you are. Fly, and she will grow wings.'*
>
> *The clouds part, the sky is full of the crimson sunset of the completed third day. The sun sinks into the sea, and I glide with it from the top of the tree towards the earth. Softly and peacefully night falls.*[31]

It seems that the spell of the projection needs to be broken again and again for Jung to be able to integrate the demands of love with the limitations of embodied humanity, to see that the most loving thing to do needs to lie within the path of human possibility rather than

---

26 LS Draft, LFT 325, RE 441.
27 LS Draft, LFT 325, RE 443.
28 LS Draft, LFT 326, RE 443.
29 LS Draft, LFT 326, RE 444.
30 LS Draft, LFT 326, RE 445.
31 LS Draft, LFT 326, RE 446.

in the idealisation of the mere idea of love. As Jung then puts it 'Not the power of the flesh, but of love, should be broken for the sake of life, since life stands above love.'[32] 'Life' here seems to stand for the whole set of conditions in which we operate, addressing which creates the requirement for wisdom that works in a dialectical relationship with love.

Jung rightly saw working with the anima as a profound challenge, going far beyond that of reconciliation with the shadow. Hatred can be dissolved into a wider compassionate awareness, but love is much trickier because it is stickier, and the anima as the attractive other is the embodiment of love. How can we love the representations of other in ourselves, without losing the balance and integration that we require to keep addressing conditions? There is no single answer to this central ethical question, but rather a series of answers as we resolve our priorities in each different situation. However, we can say that the Middle Way answer in each case involves the recognition and acceptance of the Salome figure without its projection and absolutisation. Jung's journey in relation to the anima records a sequence of such projections and their integration, an ongoing and never wholly completed process.

7.g. The abodes of Brahma

I have been pursuing Jung's exploration of the Middle Way in relation to the anima here without any mention of Buddhist parallels, because there is no similar explicit discussion known to me in the Buddha's life and teaching of how the feminine can be integrated into the experience of men, let alone of how the masculine can be integrated into the experience of women. Yet, at the same time, the Buddhist tradition does engage with the profound difficulty posed by the anima/animus symbolised by Jung's hanging on the Tree of Life. That issue could be posed as this question: 'How can I integrate love, rather than projecting it onto one desirable person?' To integrate love is not to deny its power in relation to a specific attractive other, nor to deny the sexual instincts that often boost that power, but it is to reconcile that power with the conditions that surround it – the conditions of limited energy and attention for any individual,

---

32 LS Draft, LFT 327, RE 448.

the conditions of self-love or self-hatred, and the conditions of love for others that we find less immediately attractive. A more integrated love is one that is both applied within the bounds of practicality, and stretched so as to focus less obsessively solely on the attractive other.

The Buddhist tradition offers well-established ways of cultivating that more integrated love, in the form of the *brahmavihara* practices, attributed to the teachings of the Buddha in the Pali Canon.[33] The Four Brahmaviharas consist of loving-kindness (*metta*), compassion (*karuna*), sympathetic joy (*mudita*), and equanimity (*upekkha*). They are all open positive emotions without expectation of recompense, taught by the Buddha as the ways to Brahma (in other words, one could say, ways of integrating with the God archetype). The differences between them depend on our responses to the situation of a person: loving-kindness being general positive emotion, compassion a response to suffering, sympathetic joy a response to happiness, and equanimity a response to variations between suffering and happiness. It is easy for us to feel positive emotion towards what we find attractive, but the challenge lies in making such emotion both authentic and non-possessive (as Jung discovered), so that it does not create exclusivity and thus conflict. The brahmavihara practices can be seen as ways of working with our response to the attractive so as to find a Middle Way that avoids projection. Our views of what we love tend towards absolute love or absolute hate, but the art of love is that of constantly surfing the engaged, authentic edge of our emotions that tries to see the object of our perceptions (or of our hatreds) without those interfering projections.

Buddhist tradition offers meditation practices for the cultivation of each of the brahmaviharas, of which the best known is the *metta-bhavana* or cultivation of loving-kindness.[34] This practice begins with a connection to bodily and emotional awareness, to ensure that one remains rooted in one's actual emotions rather than pursuing an abstract idea of an emotional state. However, one then focuses on the positive and expansive elements of one's emotional state, so as to develop goodwill whilst reflecting upon or visualising objects of goodwill. In a series of prescribed stages, one begins by focusing

---

33 *Tevijja Sutta, Digha Nikaya* 13.76–8: Walshe (1995) p. 194. *Anguttara Nikaya* 10.208: Nyanaponika and Bodhi (1999) pp. 269–70.
34 For more details see Kamalashila (1992) ch. 2, or Salzberg (1997).

that goodwill on oneself, then on a good friend, then on a neutral person, then on an enemy, and finally the whole universe.

The danger in such a practice, as I have found myself in the past, is that we can nevertheless remain hanging, still obsessed by our 'notion of love and the other' as Jung's raven puts it. We can be obsessed with an idea of radiating love to all that remains just an idealisation, or we can get stuck in our projected emotional responses to others, whether those are possessive ones, emotions of hatred or mere indifference. To make progress in this practice is difficult, but it nevertheless offers one of our best opportunities to break down the mere projection of the anima/animus and liberate some of the energy that is bound up with it. To make an impression, it needs to be used repeatedly over a period of time, and to be tied in to practising other aspects of the Middle Way. In the process we might possibly somewhat speed up the cycle of projection and integration that Jung describes, and aid our mature development of a balanced but positive approach to others relatively free of projections.

8. Death of the Hero

8.a. The murder

I was with a youth in high mountains. It was before daybreak, the Eastern sky was already light. Then Siegfried's horn resounded over the mountains with a jubilant sound. We knew that our mortal enemy was coming. We were armed and lurked beside a narrow rocky path to murder him. Then we saw him coming across the mountains on a chariot made of the bones of the dead. He drove boldly and magnificently over the steep rocks and arrived at the narrow path where we waited in hiding. As he came around the bend ahead of us, we fired at the same time and he fell slain. Thereupon I turned to flee, and a terrible rain swept down. But after this, I went through a torment unto death and I felt certain that I must kill myself, if I could not solve the riddle of the murder of the hero.[1]

Thus Jung introduces another crucial archetypal event in the *Red Book*. As mentioned in chapter 2, the hero archetype represents the function of attraction towards what is identified with as 'mine'. It is the ego archetype. Whenever I fantasise about something I might achieve, the version of myself that I create in that fantasy is a projection of the hero archetype. If I identify with another person and their success in gaining the things they want despite difficulties, I am also projecting the hero archetype. Parents may identify with 'their' children's achievements in this way, and thus we may identify directly with the hero of a story. While the hero struggles in a film, it means my struggle, and when the hero succeeds, it means my success and satisfaction too, experienced directly in my body's responses. Why else do we leave cinemas with the tears drying on our cheeks?

Why should the ego have a vision of killing itself? There is something profoundly contradictory about the very idea of doing so - not in a merely logical sense, but in terms of the psychic conflict it creates. This inherent contradiction is presumably reflected in Jung's

---

1   LP iv(v), LFT 241-2, RE 160-1.

'torment unto death', and his feeling that by killing the hero he was killing himself. However, the fantasy of killing the ego is a common one, and is especially found in religious traditions of asceticism. An ascetic assumes that because the ego is the source of obsessive or unhelpful desire, it should therefore be exterminated, despite the fact that the desire to exterminate it comes from the ego. Many interpretations of 'enlightenment' in ascetic traditions include egolessness. However, egolessness can only ever be an abstract and absolute goal, not one that is capable of fulfilment in meaningful embodied experience, because the goal of egolessness is one that is maintained by an ego. We cannot achieve the satisfaction of achieving a goal of egolessness because such satisfaction requires an ego. Indeed, we need a brain with a functioning striatum, producing dopamine rewards to motivate our actions, as well as a functioning amygdala to stimulate avoidance of danger through fear. These parts of our brain, by interacting with the representational pre-frontal areas of the left hemisphere, produce the tendency to identify with what we desire – namely the ego. A functioning brain needs all these parts to be operating and thus could not be egoless.

So how can we 'solve the riddle of the murder of the hero', with the torment that this riddle gives to Jung? What does the murder of the hero mean, if it does not mean the eradication of the ego? The answer to this, as with all the other archetypes, lies in the distinction between the projected and integrated archetype. The hero who is murdered in Jung's vision is a *projected* hero – representing an absolutised belief in the value of achievement against resistance, which Jung identifies with in the form of a person who makes these achievements. Jung can only murder his own drive in the sense that he can dramatically renounce his own identification with idealisations of himself. At the time that might feel in some respects like killing oneself, but it is only identifications that one is killing, not any embodied entity.

Rather than a destruction of the ego, Jung's symbolic murder of the hero presumably represents an integration of it. Where there was formerly a conflict between one identification and another, it has been implicitly recognised that one of these identifications addresses conditions better than the other, and that the less effective identification needs to be discarded, so that Jung's energies can be unified only on the more effective identification. However, this

Death of the Hero

process can still trigger a sense of loss, because the figure we formerly identified with seems to have disappeared.

The relief of killing the hero, of letting go of the overstressed position, is experienced in Jung's vision as rain. At first this is 'a terrible rain', but when Jung recognises that 'The highest truth is one and the same with the absurd' his relief becomes 'like rain after a long hot spell, it swept away everything in me which was too highly tensed'.

8.b. The motif of sacrifice

Jung conveys the significance of the murder in a variety of ways in his discussion before and after the vision in which the hero is slain. The ineffectiveness of the projected hero is conveyed as incapacity in the face of new challenging conditions:

> The hero wants to open up everything he can. But the nameless spirit of the depths evokes everything that man cannot. Incapacity prevents further ascent. Greater height requires greater virtue. We do not possess it. We must first create it by learning to live with our incapacity. We must give it life. For how else shall it develop into ability?[2]

The need to sacrifice inadequate capacity in order to create new and more adequate capacity can also be thought of in terms of the mythic trope of sacrifice for renewal.

> The blond hero lay slain. The black beetle is the death that is necessary for renewal.[3]

This mythic trope also encompasses the death of the king for the renewal of the land, suffering for creativity – a trope that is also closely linked to the role of Christ and his sacrifice as used in the *Red Book*, already discussed in chapter 4 above. Jung also amplifies this into the theme of the death of Gods. The 'Gods' here presumably have a similar psychological function to heroes, in that they represent idealisations or projections of particular desires rather than the potential for integration itself. The hero is always a limited conception of the God, just as the unintegrated prematurely represents itself as having reached the goal of integration, and we need to kill

---

2 LP iv(r), LFT 240, RE 155.
3 LP iii(v), LFT 239, RE 151.

the Gods in the sense of cutting off our premature identifications with projected versions of God.

> *Our Gods want to be overcome, since they require renewal. If men kill their princes, they do so because they cannot kill their Gods, and because they do not know that they should kill their Gods in themselves.*[4]

The role of sacrifice in improving our addressing of conditions has been interestingly explored by Nassim Nicholas Taleb.[5] To operate in that way it needs to be accompanied by *optionality*, namely having a range of alternative options to make use of in appropriate conditions. Sacrifice by itself may achieve nothing but loss, and does not magically create a recompense, but when new conditions arise and we have alternative options that are better adapted to the new conditions than old options, we need to be prepared to sacrifice the old options in order to take advantage of the new ones. The capacity for sacrifice is thus an element of adaptability, whether we are discussing it in the context of evolutionary patterns in animals (where ill-adapted individuals are 'sacrificed' for the species) or a human having a Plan B for a career that requires the sacrifice of costs that have been sunk into Plan A. If you put all your heart into the ambition to be a lawyer, but then realise you're not going to make it, you have to murder that lawyer within you at the point where you start training to be a hypnotherapist instead.

The theme of sacrifice recurs in a number of ways in the *Red Book*. As Drob puts it:

> *In the Red Book, sacrifice is the path of individuation: sacrifice of the 'hero within', sacrifice of one's egoistic aspirations and desires, sacrifice of the belief that certain things are essentially good and necessary and must be attained or achieved, and finally...sacrifice of the quest for complete fulfilment.*[6]

Perhaps the most intense experience of sacrifice in the *Red Book* is the 'sacrificial murder' of the child whose liver Jung eats, already discussed in chapter 4. Apart from the acceptance of the shadow in this situation, it also demands both heroic resolution and the abandonment of a particular projection of heroism. One has to be even more heroic than before to renounce heroism – but in a way that demands a more integrated form of heroism.

---

4 LP iv(v), LFT 242, RE 162.
5 Taleb (2012).
6 Drob (2012) p. 123.

Death of the Hero

The Buddhist tradition also offers a version of the murder of the hero in the shape of the popularised Zen ko'an 'If you meet the Buddha on the road, kill him.'[7] Here, as in Jung's version, there is a strong suggestion in context that the heroic individual, with which we usually identify, is a projection, and that more integrative progress requires the painful abandonment of that projection. A parallel truism making the same point in literary composition is the instruction to 'murder your darlings' – in other words, the fact that you are deeply attached to particular words or sections in your composition may suggest the need to remove them for the sake of the whole, however painful that process may be.

8.c. The hero as an object of imitation

Elsewhere in the *Red Book*, Jung brings out a further dimension of the projected hero's limitations.

> *The image of the hero was set up for all in every age through the appetite for imitation. Therefore the hero was murdered, since we have all been aping him. Do you know why you cannot abandon apishness? For fear of loneliness and defeat.*[8]

The heroic action itself may be creative, but the projected archetype of the hero has little to do with the experience of heroic action, but rather with dwelling on a particular representation of the hero. Our representation of the hero can easily become an obsessive substitute for the heroic action itself, and this has quite a different psychological function for us from the one that the heroic action had for the original hero. Instead of doing, we may merely retell, but even when we emulate the hero we are no longer in the context where the hero's actions were a fresh and integrated response to the conditions. For example, to imitate a warrior one continues fighting the same old battles even after peace has been declared, and the moral imitator of Jesus is reduced to cherry-picking from scriptural accounts to find actions of Jesus that can offer ad hoc confirmations of her attitudes.

---

7 This appears to be a version of a ko'an attributed to Linji: 'If you meet a Buddha, kill the Buddha. If you meet a Ghost, kill the Ghost.'
8 LP vi(r), LFT 249, RE 188.

Iain McGilchrist explains the relationship between two forms of imitation and the brain hemispheres.[9] Left-hemisphere dominated imitation consists of precise copying, whether that copying is understood as copying an idea or a model. The value of the imitation is seen entirely in terms of its degree of reproduction of the idea or model. Right-hemisphere dominated imitation (or mimesis), on the other hand, introduces creative variation: one is stimulated or inspired by a model to respond to conditions in a more living and authentic fashion. 'There is a continual tendency for the authenticity of right hemisphere "presencing" to be transformed into an inauthentic "representing" in the left; in essence, what was living becomes a cliché.'[10] This appears to explain the process by which living heroism becomes dead copying of beliefs about heroes – or indeed how the inspiration of heroism may turn into what Jung calls 'apishness', with not only representation but also obsessive goals being associated with the linguistic centres in the front of the brain's left hemisphere. Closely associated with this obsession is also fear of alternatives, associated again with a closed loop between the motivations from the back of the brain and the representations of the left front.

Jung's discussion makes this relationship especially clear in relation to the God archetype:

> I must say that the God could not come into being before the hero had been slain. The hero as we understand him has become an enemy of the God, since the hero is perfection. The Gods envy the perfection of man, because perfection has no need of the Gods. But since no one is perfect, we need the Gods. The Gods love perfection because it is a total way of life. But the Gods are not with him who wishes to be perfect, because he is an imitation of perfection.[11]

This relationship with the God archetype shows the close relationship between the symbolic murder of the projected hero and the Middle Way. Each of the absolutes avoided by the Middle Way, whether negative or positive, involves an assumption of perfection, and it is the belief in perfection that separates God from human beings. When the idea of the hero becomes perfect, that idea usurps the role of God as a meaningful archetype of integration. However, the absolutised hero is not distanced in the same way as God, not

---

9   McGilchrist (2009) ch. 7.
10 Ibid. p. 244.
11 LP v(r), LFT 244–5, RE 171.

regarded as holy and beyond human knowledge – so we might well end up absolutising the hero more easily than we absolutise God. I think that's what Jung can be taken to mean when he says that perfection has no need of the Gods. At the same time, though, 'the Gods are not with him who wishes to be perfect, because he is an imitation of perfection': in other words, the mere idea of perfection has been taken as a basis of left-hemisphere imitation, and a genuine process of integration (in which the limitations of such ideas are recognised) has not been engaged in.

We do not become more integrated, in the way represented by God, through substituting a hero as a model for imitation, implicitly imagining the hero to be absolute and perfect in the process. It is only if the hero is given a more appropriate place, as a *fallible* and *partial* model embodying some of our ambitions, that the hero can take his place in the larger integrative function of archetypes as discussed in chapter 2. Given that the problem with the ego is not its positive function but rather its overweening claims of omniscience and supremacy, the hero always has a role for us in inspiring new development, and he can successfully guide us towards integration as long as he does not claim an absolute status for himself. St George needs to be reconciled with the dragon and to recognise the independence of the maiden, whilst putting all his endeavours in the wider context of God.

8.d. Magic and the heroic

Although the death of the hero takes place early on in the *Red Book*, in its later stages Jung often refers to the same underlying themes in a slightly different guise. The process by which one's identification with the hero can be integrated is the avoidance of projection and the development of more integrated desires that stretch the ego – but this, of course, does not remove the power of the ego. Rather than disappearing through integration, the ego merely tends to develop more powerful forms. The better we can address conditions, the more effective we can be in getting what we want, so the ego remains just as much of a potential trap for the partially integrated (which is most of us) as it is for the very unintegrated.

Jung's developing ability to get what he wants – and his capacity to balance love with a relatively integrated will of a powerful sort – is reflected by the theme of magic as it appears later in the *Red Book*. Jung's attitude to Philemon, who initially appears as a magician, has already been discussed in chapter 3. However, it is Jung's attitude to magic itself that is potentially a matter of more integrated heroism. Magic, in Jung's thought, seems to be a method of getting what one wants – except that the self that wants it and the object of desire have gone through a process of integration, making the whole process of success against resistance a more subtle and effective one.

> *Magic is a way of living. If one has done one's best to steer the chariot, and one then notices that a greater other is actually steering it, then magical operation takes place.*[12]

The use of magic can also be associated with cleverness and the use of knowledge – sometimes known in political terms today as 'soft power'. The heroism of the softly powerful is that of Odysseus rather than that of Achilles, incorporating craft and forethought. This type of heroism is particularly represented for Jung in what he later came to call the *trickster* archetype, and here its power is represented by the serpent, who is simultaneously an appearance of the anima or soul and a kind of powerful tool. Jung enchants the serpent through his own magical skill learned from Philemon, but wearing the trappings of heroism:

> *I continue on my way, accompanied by a finely polished piece of steel, hardened in ten fires, stowed safely in my robe. Secretly, I wear chain mail under my coat. Overnight I became fond of serpents, and I solved their riddle. I sat down next to them on the hot stones lying by the wayside. I know how to catch them cunningly and cruelly, those cold devils that prick the heel of the unsuspecting. I became their friend and played a softly toned flute. But I decorate my cave with their dazzling skins. As I walked on my way, I came to a red rock on which a great iridescent serpent lay. Since I had now learned magic from ΦΙΛΗΜΩΝ, I took out my flute again and played a sweet magical song to make her believe that she was my soul.*[13]

There is an interesting reversal here. Rather than an outward symbol being recognised as part of his soul, Jung enchants an apparently separate creature, in an instrumental way, to *become* part of his soul. This is ironic, because, of course, as part of his vision it already

12 LS 144, LFT 314, RE 405.
13 LS 154, LFT 317, RE 413.

is. The significance of the process seems to be more one of making the powers that are already latent in him more serviceable, using what appears to be separate instrumentally. Yet at the same time this instrumentality is not a narrow or unintegrated instrumentality. By this stage in the *Red Book* Jung has progressed a long way from the naïve character we find in the initial encounter with Elijah and Salome. He is becoming a magician himself and thus beginning to inhabit some of the Wise Old Man archetype that he has previously projected as beyond himself. As he does this, the hero in him also grows up and becomes more sophisticated.

To address conditions effectively, we need this sophistication. This is recognised when Jung acknowledges to Elijah the theft of the serpent that had previously accompanied him, in a conversation already quoted and discussed in chapter 3. Here Jung says that the serpent gave him 'hardness, wisdom and magical power', and also claims that 'We need her in the upperworld, since otherwise the underworld would have had the advantage, to our detriment.'[14] If we are not clever and prepared to think in relatively integrated instrumental ways, it seems, we are likely to be undermined by unconscious processes that interfere with our wishes.

Jung's thinking about the necessity of integrated uses of power here of course makes no reference to politics or to the shadow of the First World War that formed the wider context of both the experience and its expression. However, when considered in terms of such a wider political context, Jung's reflections on power here have immense ethical importance. How can we justify the uses of power against others? If we adopt any kind of revelatory religious justification, or any kind of appeal to tradition, the authority we invoke is likely to be arbitrary and based, in the end, only on a limited egoistic assertion of the superiority of our wishes over those of others, supported by the rationalising selection of authorities that support our narrow wishes. If we appeal to utilitarian calculation as to the benefits of our use of power, we will nevertheless depend on our own judgements as to those benefits, even if those judgements are psychologically narrow and unintegrated. It is only if we have worked through the earlier stages of integration, represented by Jung in the *Red Book* in relation to projected archetypal figures, that we will be

14 LS 187, LFT 324, RE 439.

in a better position to use power in a way that addresses conditions and can thus be justified.

However wise we may become, there is always the danger of the conditions for wise judgement being undermined by the foolish and narrow-minded, whether in the extreme outward forms of war or political totalitarianism or in the internal forms of repression and self-censorship. It seems unavoidable that the conditions of integration (which are dependent in turn on peace, stability, social and political openness, and prosperity) must be defended, and to defend them we will need the guile and instrumentality of the serpent. Jung's work provides us with the moral insight that only integration can justify the use of power – an insight still in need of much discussion and refinement before it can be effectively applied in any political realm.[15]

8.e. The rebirth of the hero

However, the furthest development of the hero motif in the *Red Book* takes us back once again from the fruits of integration to the pain of loss. Towards the end of the lengthy 'Magician' section, Jung encounters the difficulties of succession – namely that he will be supplanted by his 'son'. The son seems not to be a literal son, but another way of engaging with the difficulties of identification with one's goals. Those goals are, in the end, best not pursued by oneself and what one most closely identifies with, but rather passed on – whether to parts of oneself that are bigger than one is now, or indeed to others.

The serpent tells Jung a fairy story about a king who created a son with the help of magic, but when the son grew up found that the son demanded his crown. The king then had his son killed, but subsequently regretted this action. So he went back to the witch who had helped him create the first son, and she told him how to create his son again by magic. The same son was born again, grew up and again demanded the crown. This time the king, made wiser by experience, yielded the crown and came to terms with the usurpation.[16]

---

15 See Ellis (2012b) section 6 for further discussion.
16 LS Draft, LFT 327-8, RE 450-2.

Death of the Hero

This story in some ways replays the death of the hero, with the king, the first time round, standing for the person on the brink of a process of integration who finds it necessary to kill the idea of the hero that they had. However, the second time round, the hero is reborn and is integrated with the 'father' or 'king' who previously rejected him. The Groundhog-Day style repetition provides a reminder that conditions that we don't address are very likely to keep recurring until we address them.

In this case the condition that Jung finds so difficult to accept is that of being supplanted – whether we understand that supplanting in terms of actual descendants, works, or a developing self. As Wordsworth put it, 'the child is father to the man'[17]: the development of a more integrated state for one individual involves renouncing previous states with which one identifies, so that it feels as if one is surrendering oneself to a force beyond oneself, just as it might to produce a new generation separate from oneself. Jung's resistance to this is expressed in 'I thought and hoped that I could be a man in every way'[18] (which presumably means to correspond with a particular idea of what it means to be one particular man). The acceptance of renewal, however, involves that of becoming or remaining a child, which Jung finds 'unbearable', 'humiliating', and 'shattering'.[19] In a child-like state, new learning and new character become possible.

The rebirth of the hero obviously has a close relationship to the Christ theme discussed in chapter 4. Its relationship with the Tree of Life is also brought out by the serpent's words 'Let everything grow, let everything sprout; the son grows out of himself.' If we see the development of a 'son' as a new growth on a tree, continuity is maintained as opposed to the sole focus on loss that is expressed by Jung's reaction.

8.f. Integrating the hero

Overall, then, Jung's treatment of the hero in the *Red Book* is far more difficult and complex than the initial motif of the death of the hero might lead us to anticipate. The hero does not die, because the

---

17 From the poem 'My heart leaps up...' (1802).
18 LS Draft, LFT 328, RE 452.
19 LS Draft, LFT 328, RE 453.

ego does not die, within the psychological context of Jung's visions. Rather the death of the hero marks the letting go of a deluded perception of the hero, attached to a deluded perception of oneself as taking a final and fixed form.

To be able to grow and integrate, we need not just to be prepared to kill the hero, but also to tolerate his rebirth in new forms. We need to accept the inspiration of the hero without too close an imitation of him, to be creative and authentic in our response to heroism. To deal with the full challenges of conditions in our experience, too, we need to be able to employ all the hero's armoury, including the cunning of the trickster and the magic developed by the wise. In a wider sense, then, we should not give up heroism, but rather constantly develop new forms of it.

At the core of Jung's insights on this topic, it seems to me, is the recognition that there is no discontinuity between God and the hero, just as there is no absolute discontinuity between one stage of our development and another. God is simply the hero writ large – the human who has shed a whole set of successive views of herself. Even though the hero may never reach absolute divinity, we do not need to be afraid of his motivations in human desire. These desires can always be refined, but never extinguished or wholly abandoned.

In practice, the Middle Way is central to our judgements about heroism, whether it is our own or others'. On the one hand we can idealise, and try fruitlessly to imitate our idealisation. On the other hand, we can dismiss the value and inspiration of the hero, despite the fact that it is always present in our lives in one form or another, whether implicitly or explicitly. As long as there are desires and difficulties, there will always be heroism. As with the other archetypes, we can find a balanced response to the hero not by projecting, but by separating the meaning of the hero from our beliefs about heroes, and continuing to celebrate the inspiration offered by the hero himself without the dogmatic beliefs that may become associated with him.

9. Embodied Meaning and the Scholars

9.a. The scholars

Perhaps you think that a man who consecrates his life to research leads a spiritual life and that his soul lives in larger measure than anyone else's. But such a life is also external, just as external as the life of a man who lives for outer things. To be sure, such a scholar does not live for outer things but for outer thoughts – not for himself, but for his object. If you say of a man that he has totally lost himself to the outer and wasted his years in excess, you must also say the same of this old man. He has thrown himself away in all the books and thoughts of others. Consequently his soul is in great need, it must humiliate itself and run into every stranger's room to beg for the recognition that he fails to give her.

Therefore you see those old scholars running after recognition in a ridiculous and undignified manner. They are offended if their name is not mentioned, cast down if another one says the same thing in a better way, irreconcilable if someone alters their views in the least. Go to the meetings of scholars and you will see them, these lamentable old men with their great merits and their starved souls famished for recognition and their thirst which can never be slaked.[1]

Thus Jung portrays the state of mind associated with 'the scholar', a dry-as-dust type whom Jung encounters both in the castle in the forest[2] and later on in the library.[3] The scholar is not so much an archetype in its own right as a caricature of the traits that allow projection of all the other archetypes. The scholar might be mistaken for a type of hero, as an attractive other, as a shadowy threat, or as a Wise Old Man – but any of these would be a projection onto those traits. In this passage, Jung emphasises their negative effects in the shape of craving, repression, irritability, and pride. All these vices are associated with a certain narrow-mindedness, pusillanimity, literalness, and abstraction. We are all subject to these 'scholarly' traits

---

1 LS 9–10, LFT 264, RE 229–30.
2 LS 5, LFT 261, RE 220 ff.
3 LS 98, LFT 292, RE 328 ff.

to some degree, and, like all the other vision characters, the scholars are aspects of Jung himself.

Jung's idea that the scholar lives 'for outer thoughts' and 'has thrown himself away' needs careful interpretation, both in the light of the Middle Way as the *Red Book* presents it, and in the light of the many hints throughout it as to Jung's attitude to language and meaning. It would be too easy to interpret this in terms of an 'inner' v 'outer' dichotomy that is actually a distraction from Jung's insights. The thoughts of the scholarly are unhelpfully restricted to the 'outer', I suggest, in the sense that they are *representational*. The scholar is deeply invested in theories about how things *are* or *are not* that require language to be constantly appreciated only in terms of representations, and that attempt to systematically exclude ambiguity, metaphor, connotations, and emotional responses from consideration. All these other qualities of meaning must be rejected as 'subjective', and the longer the exclusion of the 'subjective' is practised over time, the narrower habitual appreciation of meaning becomes, and the more alienated the scholar becomes from emotional and physical experience. The missing 'inner' in Jung's language here involves a good deal of implicit experience that cannot be acknowledged in a scholarly representational world.

In the Castle in the Forest vision, as already discussed in chapter 7, this repressed 'subjective' meaning takes the form of the maiden, the anima figure who erupts 'into every stranger's room to beg for the recognition that he fails to give her'. The maiden is the flip side of the scholar, animated by a pressing need to be recognised as 'real' given the way in which the scholar has systematically excluded imaginative and emotive experience from 'reality'. However, 'reality' itself is the language of scholarly representation. The maiden does not have to be 'real', and thus compete on the scholar's terms: rather she only has to be meaningful. It is the recognition of the maiden that counts rather than the 'reality'.

8.b. Embodied meaning and the image

As in the rest of this book, I am going to offer here an interpretation that depends not only on the text or on our knowledge of Jung's thinking, but also on a pragmatic argument about what we can most helpfully do with what Jung is offering us. I am going to suggest that Jung's presentation of questions of meaning throughout the *Red Book* implicitly supports an embodied approach to the meaning of symbols including language. Jung did not have a developed embodied meaning theory available to him, and the nearest he seems to have developed in that direction is his theory of the image. The *Red Book* shows him struggling to articulate an intuitive understanding of the embodied nature of meaning that can be better articulated now, not only with reference to Jung's account of the image, but also using the embodied meaning theory of George Lakoff and Mark Johnson.

The 'image' in Jung consists most basically in a range of types of experienced stimuli that, when experienced as a gestalt, produce a certain type of response. Jung exemplifies this with a leaf-cutter ant:

> *Every instinct bears in itself the pattern of its situation. Always it fulfils an image, and the image has fixed qualities. The instinct of the leaf-cutting ant fulfils the image of ant, tree, leaf, cutting, transport, and the little ant-garden of fungi. If any of these conditions is lacking, the instinct does not function, because it cannot exist without its total pattern, without its image.*[4]

As explained by Hogenson,[5] this concept of the 'image' draws on the previous work of Jacob von Uexküll, founder of the science of ethology (the study of animal behaviour). Von Uexküll used the term *umwelt* to describe the specific environmental experience of an organism that would stimulate a specific behaviour. In human experience, this *umwelt* becomes what Lakoff and Johnson refer to as an *image schema* – namely, a set of habitual associations between embodied interactions with our environment and meaningful images.[6] Jung thought of the image as *a priori*, but we do not need to either assume or deny this in order to recognise the image as the basis of human meaning.

For the leaf-cutter ant, there is an implied or assumed 'image' of the circumstances of leaf-cutting that stimulates leaf-cutting behaviour. For a human, the unconscious schematic image of a container makes us aware of the possibility of placing other things within that container – a possibility that we have experienced in early childhood by experimenting with actively placing things inside other

---

4 CW 8, §398.
5 Hogenson (2014).
6 Johnson (2007) ch. 7; Lakoff (1987).

things that hold them. This forms the basis of what Lakoff and Johnson call the *container schema*, which then creates an underlying condition for the meaning of terms like *basin, field, area, perimeter, incorporation*, and *expulsion*. Unlike the leaf-cutter ant (because of the development of our pre-frontal cortex), we are able to experience these meanings in isolation from the environment that is associated with them.

Jung's split with Freud was partly dependent on his recognition of the image, which was accompanied by his rejection of the mechanistic reductionism and determinism of Freud. For Freud, it was possible to understand human behaviour as inevitably caused by physical and unconscious processes, because those processes could be fully described and represented in theoretical language which was assumed to gain its meaning from that representation. If, however, our relationship to the meaning of language is embodied, dependent on the interaction of gestalt associations, there can be no complete representation and thus no theoretical reduction. Our freedom of action remains an ambiguous product of our ability to reflect using images distinct from the environments that would most directly stimulate them. The 'meaning' of a word is a complex experience inextricably combining cognition with emotion, connotation with denotation, communicative function with deep unconscious association.

Lakoff and Johnson can supplement Jung's understanding of the image by offering a developed account of the nature of image schemas and the way these can be built up into meaning without reliance on representation or correspondence. Even the most abstract terms gain their meaning through layers of metaphorical extension of image schemas and basic categories. We build up cognitive models on the basis of metaphors – for example that of medicine as warfare or time as a resource – and then build up complex theories and arguments that take these metaphors for granted.[7] These image schemas can also be used as a basis on which to understand archetypes.[8] Though Jung does not need to do any of this in the *Red Book*, what he does do is explore the underlying insights that make such understanding of meaning possible, with its implicit challenge to the widespread and unhelpful belief that meaning is a mere

7 Lakoff and Johnson (1980).
8 Knox (2003).

representation of actual or potential states of affairs (as represented by the scholars).

9.c. Embodiment and the Buddha's breakthrough

The relationship between embodiment and the Middle Way is also made explicit in the accounts of the Buddha's early life that record his abandonment of asceticism and discovery of the Middle Way. Asceticism is the most extreme possible symbolisation of the traits that Jung represents as the scholar, consisting of the belief that 'mind' can conquer 'matter', the two being assumed wholly separate, and matter being rejected as an encumbrance and source of delusion to be conquered by the egoistic will. In the story of Siddhartha Gautama before his enlightenment, asceticism is taken to extreme lengths. Urged on by five companions, he attempts to hold his breath indefinitely, and starves himself. It is only by pushing himself to the brink of death that he comes to recognise that this is not the way towards a more integrated state.

> *Just as a strong man might seize a weaker man by the head or shoulders and beat him down, constrain him, and crush him, so too, with my teeth clenched and my tongue pressed against the roof of my mouth, I beat down, constrained, and crushed mind with mind, and sweat ran from my armpits. But although tireless energy was aroused in me and unremitting mindfulness was established, my body was overwrought and uncalm because I was exhausted by the painful striving.*[9]

> *Because of eating so little my backside became like a camel's hoof. Because of eating so little the projections on my spine stood out like corded beads. Because of eating so little my ribs jutted out as gaunt as the crazy rafters of an old roofless barn. Because of eating so little the gleam of my eyes sank far down in their sockets, looking like the gleam of water that has sunk far down in a deep well....*[10]

In this kind of state, the ascetic is caught in a state of endlessly looped confirmation bias, in which any amount of pain showing the conflict of the basic conditions of the body with these practices is merely an indication that the ascetic has not yet tried hard enough. Similarly, Jung's scholar, though not inflicting pain on his body, is

---

9 *Majjhima Nikaya* 36:20, Ñanamoli and Bodhi (1995) p. 337.
10 Ibid. 36:28, p. 339.

caught up in a loop where any difficulty requires a representational explanation, and all mystery is merely a sign that not enough effort has yet been exerted to find the right explanation. In both cases the resolution can only come from sufficient sympathetic awareness of the body, and in the Buddha's case the breakthrough to a Middle Way perspective arises from a memory of a childhood experience of a spontaneously integrated state, rooted calmly under a rose-apple tree:

> *I considered: 'I recall that when my father the Sakyan was occupied, while I was sitting in the cool shade of a rose-apple tree, quite secluded from sensual pleasures, secluded from unwholesome states, I entered upon and abided in the first jhana, which is accompanied by applied and sustained thought, with rapture and pleasure born of seclusion.'*[11]

The temporarily integrated state of *jhana* is one that can be reached through the practice of meditation, and combines intense awareness with a strongly rooted embodied contentment and a surge of positive emotion. Anyone who has experienced that state will be aware that it is one reached only by gradually working *with* one's body and the conditions it creates, rather than by solely focusing one's mind. Indeed, the meaning of that state is a bodily one, based in association of the body's experience in that situation with the words used later to describe it. The Middle Way, which the Buddha recognised at that moment, needs to be understood not just as another representational belief justified by an experience and challenging the previous one, but as a recognition that the very way in which our experience is formed through the body makes the absolutisation of representational beliefs delusory. We can only absolutise our beliefs by forgetting their rootedness in the meanings enabled by our bodies.

9.d. The hidden daughter and the right hemisphere

Embodied meaning also has a close relationship to the disjunction of functions between the two brain hemispheres discussed in chapter 1. It is the pre-frontal cortex of the left hemisphere that handles representational language, and thus creates the context where we might assume language to be solely representational – yet at the

---

11 Ibid. 36:31, p. 340.

same time the meaning of this language depends on the connections to the rest of the body offered by the right hemisphere. Iain McGilchrist, drawing on a wide range of neuroscientific and medical evidence, writes incisively about this:

> *The superiority [of the left hemisphere] for language stems from its nature as the hemisphere of representation, in which signs are substituted for experience.... It seems to be...actually less concerned about meaning than the right hemisphere, as long as it has control over the form and the system. In conditions of right-hemisphere damage, where the left hemisphere is no longer under constraint from the right, a meaningless hypertrophy of language may result.... The right hemisphere's particular strength is in understanding meaning as a whole and in context.*[12]

Lakoff and Johnson's work, when synthesised with McGilchrist's, provides a plausible explanation for how meaning depends on basic embodied processes that must take place largely in the right hemisphere, because they involve bodily and sensual awareness being associated with symbols through the development of new synaptic connections. Both Lakoff and Johnson's image schemas and Jung's images must thus primarily depend on the right hemisphere, however complex the processes involved. The process of metaphorical extension, by which we develop more complex and abstract language, also depends on the right hemisphere, as McGilchrist documents.[13] This process of metaphorical extension is the basis of the cognitive models that the left hemisphere then takes for granted, though by the time they are taken up habitually by the left hemisphere, the metaphors have become 'dead'. Our language is full of the corpses of past 'live' metaphors, from space being metaphorically applied to time that is 'before us' or 'behind us', to nouns like 'icing' (originally from ice).[14]

The left hemisphere, then, often maintains a self-reinforcing sense of the meaning of its signs, which it assumes to be meaningful because of its relationship to other signs and the realities that they are taken to represent – even though these signs have lost the full experiential meaningfulness they may once have possessed when the metaphors they were built on were newly-minted. The more abstract our language, the more removed it tends to become from

---

12 McGilchrist (2009) p. 70.
13 Ibid. pp. 115 ff.
14 See Lakoff and Johnson (1980) for a great many more examples.

embodied meaning, and thus also from new and challenging perspectives that might be meaningfully accessed by going back closer to the source of meaning. The imagination, together with our awareness of the changes in bodily states that we tend to call 'emotion', is neglected. This, of course, is the tendency portrayed by the scholar figures in the *Red Book*. McGilchrist, again, expresses this strikingly:

> Metaphoric thinking is fundamental to our understanding of the world, because it is the only way in which understanding can reach outside the system of signs to life itself. It is what links language to life.[15]

When the hidden daughter appears to Jung, then, she represents not just repressed femininity, but also the repression of 'life itself' as we experience it through the body and imagination via the right hemisphere. The hidden daughter has been repressed by the characteristic over-dominance of the left brain in her scholar father, as shown not only by his 'rationality' but also his abstraction and distraction. Without a sufficient connection to the sources of energy and inspiration accessed through the right brain, the left brain cannot even maintain consistent attention to its manipulation of signs: as any distracted high-school student obliged to write an essay will know.

The fact that the hidden daughter appears to Jung at night in his bedroom obviously carries a sexual *frisson*, but it is also significant in other ways that are related to the hemispheres. However ruthless our left-hemisphere focus on our constructed realities based on systems of signs during the daytime, it is the night-time that allows compensation, whether in the form of fantasies, dreams, or crowding anxieties. Our intuitions, if previously given no scope, may come out to play at night. Jung's failure to get to sleep is due to a thought that 'doesn't let go of me, namely that the old man has hidden his beautiful daughter here'.[16] His disapproval of his own uncontrolled thoughts offers a classic left-hemisphere response, but given that he is not just a left pre-frontal lobe, he cannot control them merely through moments of disapproval. Rather, his whole body comes into play: 'the romantic can be felt in every limb'.[17]

---

15 McGilchrist (2009) p. 115.
16 LS 6, LFT 262, RE 221.
17 Ibid.

Jung's responses to the hidden daughter also illustrate characteristic defence mechanisms of the mind over-dominated by the left hemisphere, when confronted with the alternatives of the right. One defence mechanism is class-based and dependent on a rigid view of himself as meeting certain standards of 'rationality'. He is afraid that the idea of the hidden daughter is 'a vulgar idea for a novel'[18] or a 'hellish banality'.[19] This snobbery is also allied to the rejection of emotion as 'sentiment', on the assumption that the privileged thinker is 'rational' and free of such 'sentiment'. Jung is also reluctant to believe that the hidden daughter is 'real', and suspects her of being 'simply some unfortunate product of my sleepless brain'.[20] This reflects the tendency of the left hemisphere to believe as a default position that its coherent constructions are true, and thus to assume that all alternatives experienced are likely to be false, imposing a false dichotomy of truth or falsehood between this represented world and all alternatives.

None of this should be interpreted as undermining recognition of the central role of the left hemisphere in all our activities. However, the left hemisphere's tendency to absolutise the meaning of the signs it uses is an important aspect of the limiting delusions of the ego which block the process of integration. The Middle Way, as a navigation between these absolutes, does not involve the complete abandonment of the representational aspect of language (if that were possible), but rather the development of a continuing awareness of the dependence of that representation on a depth of meaning contacted through the right hemisphere. With that awareness, we can avoid committing ourselves to the absolutes, and continue to explore the ambiguous experience between them without being blocked by them. Such awareness implies a sufficient interconnection between the hemispheres for wider awareness to broaden the limited perspective of left-hemisphere dominated representations.

By the end of the vision of the castle in the forest, Jung shows signs of this wider awareness, because he has engaged with and recognised the hidden daughter, and evidently begun to reconsider his prejudice against the 'banality' of human experience. His implicit awareness of the painful difference between the hemispheres, and

18 Ibid.
19 LS 7, LFT 262, RE 223.
20 Ibid.

hence the need to integrate them, is also reflected in the structure of his later vision, recorded in 'Divine Folly' and 'Nox Secunda', in which Jung stands in an ante-room and has to decide whether to turn right (towards the library with its over-confident scholarly librarian) or left (towards the kitchen with its intuitive cook). Since the left hemisphere is closely connected with the right side of the body and vice-versa, it is no surprise here to find the direction of the hemispheres reversed from the functions recognised by modern neuroscience.

> On the right is my thinking, on the left is my feeling. I enter the space of my feeling which was previously unknown to me, and see with astonishment the difference between the two rooms. I cannot help laughing – many laugh instead of crying. I have stepped from the right foot onto the left, and wince, struck by inner pain. The difference between hot and cold is too great.[21]

In McGilchrist's more precise terms, to regard 'thinking' as the left hemisphere and 'feeling' as the right hemisphere is an over-simplification, and the subject of brain lateralisation is bedevilled by a history of over-statements and over-simplifications that lead some to too quickly dismiss the whole area. But what Jung is powerfully communicating here is not the precise nature of the conflict between the two hemispheres so much as the pain of the raw experience of recognising their disjunction and its effects. The cook thinks as well as feeling, and the librarian feels as well as thinking, but it is the librarian's assumption that his intellectual beliefs offer an adequate representation that is refreshingly challenged by the intuitive cook. Jung's halting attempts to integrate their perspectives are symbolised by Christ, as discussed above in chapter 4, and result in the openness and provisionality of scepticism:

> One thing becomes dreadfully clear, namely that contrary to my earlier way and all its insights and intentions, henceforth all is error.[22]

9.e. The spirit of the depths

The opening words of the *Red Book* contrast the 'spirit of the time' with the 'spirit of the depths'.

---

21 LS 102, LFT 295, RE 338–9.
22 LS 103, LFT 295, RE 339.

> *I have learned that in addition to the spirit of this time there is still another spirit at work, namely that which rules the depths of everything contemporary. The spirit of this time would like to hear of use and value. I also thought this way, and my humanity still thinks this way. But that other spirit forces me nevertheless to speak, beyond justification, use and meaning. Filled with human pride and blinded by the presumptuous spirit of the times, I long sought to hold that other spirit away from me. But I did not consider that the spirit of the depths from time immemorial and for all the future possesses a greater power than the spirit of this time, who changes with the generations.*[23]

What is the spirit of the depths? What are the depths? We are dealing here with a metaphor that represents understanding in terms of bodily experience. When we feel something 'deeply', this is a way of communicating that it suffuses our bodily experience and thus feels important. Related metaphorical terms, like 'underlying', also show conditionality in terms of depth: if something is deep, it provides a prior condition for other things and so can help us to explain them. There is thus little doubt that the 'spirit of the depths' refers to embodied meaning mediated through the right hemisphere.

The contrasting 'spirit of the time' is distinguished here by its pride and presumption, and its insistence on justification in terms of clear and recognisable use or value: making it equally clear that the 'spirit of the time' involves over-dominant left-hemisphere thinking in which representations are taken to offer the whole story.

Later, in 'One of the Lowly', when he meets a destitute man, Jung discusses the depths in terms of the range of human experience, acknowledging that they have a social as well as an individual dimension. The body is the basis of common human experience that we share with all others, regardless of class or culture. The destitute 'leads to the depths'.

> *At your low point you are no longer distinct from your fellow beings. You are not ashamed and do not regret it, since insofar as you live the life of your fellow beings and descend to their lowliness you also climb into the holy stream of common life, where you are no longer an individual on a high mountain, but a fish among fish, a frog among frogs.*[24]

This offers a reminder of the relationship between the body and compassion. Compassion is highly dependent on experience of the

---

23 LP i(v), LFT 229, RE 119.
24 LS 13/14, LFT 266, RE 237.

body rather than just on an abstract idea of serving others. To actually be motivated to relate strongly to others and their interests we need to recognise their meaningfulness to us as creatures with similar bodies. The flow of oxytocin, which enables a positive embodied response to others, is dependent on our brain's mirroring functions and our awareness of others as persons like ourselves,[25] and it is the right hemisphere that offers that awareness of our own physicality in direct relation to another's physicality.[26] We find the resources for the most helpful relationships with others in the depths, which is why periods of withdrawal and introversion, or practices that involve internal body awareness, may actually make us better members of society than we would be through uninterrupted social interaction.

9.f. Symbols from the depths

Jung's distinction between signs and symbols is one that has gained wide acceptance. The key difference between them is that a sign has a clear denotative meaning whilst a symbol instead has a wide range of association. It may be that the whole idea of a 'sign' with a single meaning is actually an empty abstraction, since all meaningful symbols have connotations that go beyond such a single meaning, and the idea of such a single meaning is a product of representationalism. However, the distinction in principle helps to make us aware that symbols are not just signs. Symbols, in effect, depend on embodied meaning. In the *Red Book*, Jung uses the term 'symbol' to especially indicate an archetypal symbol with a wide range of association in our depths, and he stresses its intuitive aspects.

> *The symbol is the word that goes out of the mouth, that one does not simply speak, but that rises out of the depths of the self as a word of power and great need and places itself unexpectedly on the tongue. It is an astonishing and perhaps seemingly irrational word, but one recognises it as a symbol since it is alien to the conscious mind. If one accepts the symbol, it is as if a door opens leading into a new room whose existence one did not previously know.*[27]

This idea of the word of power placing itself unexpectedly on the tongue fits closely with the role of prophecy in religious tradition.

---

25 Zak (2012) p. 62.
26 McGilchrist (2009) pp. 57 ff.
27 LS 137, LFT 311, RE 392.

Muhammad, for example, was told by the angel to 'recite' and the words of the Qur'an were said to then come to him intuitively. Words 'come to us' and we are 'inspired' as previously weak synaptic paths are opened and developed. But they can only begin to do so when our awareness has in some way returned to the right hemisphere (and through it, the body and senses), interrupting the dominant self-fuelling flow of conceptual links in the left hemisphere (the 'conscious mind').

The relationship between such symbols and the Middle Way is also explicitly developed in the *Red Book*. The Middle Way can take the form of a new integration of meaning that is able to counterbalance the previous left-hemisphere dominated beliefs by opening new and more adequate possibilities. Jung explores the theme of 'the word' in the sense of a newly-minted fresh symbol, associated with the renewed perspective of the early morning. This 'word' needs to be adopted and invested in, instead of (as often) destroyed by the press of more accustomed thoughts.

> *In the morning, when the new sun rises, the word steps out of my mouth, but is murdered lovelessly, since I did not know that it was the saviour. The newborn child grows quickly, if I accept it. And immediately it becomes my charioteer. The word is the guide, the middle way which easily oscillates like the needle on the scales.*[28]

Jung was a pioneer in this regard. As embodied meaning theory makes clear,[29] it is symbols that are the basic elements of meaning, not signs. Signs, if they exist at all in any strict sense, are the secondary products of the dominance of the cognitive models they take for granted. Symbols can be linguistic, where they are not fixed as units (they could be morphemes, words, terms, sentences, or even whole texts), but they can also be non-linguistic, taking the form of visual images, sounds, musical structures (melodies, chords etc.), or significant objects. The tree encountered on a daily walk is a symbol because it has meaning for me, as does the word 'tree' or the tune of 'Tannenbaum'. It is symbolic *of* all the associations that may be linked to my experience of it, not just the 'meaning' I could look up in a reference book. Each new symbol adds to the store I can draw upon in developing new beliefs about the world, and thus adds imperceptibly to my adaptability.

28 LS 138, LFT 311, RE 393.
29 See Johnson (2007), esp. pp. 207 ff.

9.g. Conversations with Ammonius

However, the practice of the Middle Way in relation to language is not simply a matter of embracing meaningful symbols and avoiding representational literalism. The appreciation of symbols is, after all, an ancient cultural achievement, yet even the most culturally sophisticated can continue to fall into traps when they fail to find an experiential balance in the interpretation of meaning. Jung's two conversations with Ammonius, the desert hermit, are fascinating in this regard, because they chart Jung's rebalancing moves first one way and then the other to avoid absolutisations about language.

When Jung first meets Ammonius, he finds him reading the gospel texts over and over again in order to find more and more meanings in them. Ammonius explains the theory behind this approach:

> You must know one thing above all: a succession of words does not only have one meaning. But men strive to assign only a single meaning to a succession of words, in order to have an unambiguous language. This striving is worldly and constricted, and belongs to the deepest layers of the divine creative plan. On the higher layers of insight into divine thoughts, you recognise that the sequence of words has more than one valid meaning. Only to the all-knowing is given to know all the meanings of the sequences of words. Increasingly we try to grasp a few more meanings.[30]

Ammonius' multiple approach to meaning reflects Jung's stress on symbols, which have multiple meanings, rather than signs, which have a single meaning. His approach to the *logos*, the 'word' that begins John's gospel, also suggests a move in the direction of embodied meaning, as he suggests that the *logos* was not a word or a concept but rather 'a light, indeed a man, and lived among men', referring to Christ.[31] Ammonius also talks about the desirability but difficulty of unlearning the assumptions of the single-meaning approach.[32]

However, in his reflections following this first conversation with Ammonius, Jung begins to recognise the practical limitations of the emphasis on multiple meaning.

> The writing lies before you and always says the same, if you believe in words. But if you believe in things in whose places only words stand, you never come

---

30 LS 17, LFT 268, RE 244.
31 LS 17, LFT 269, RE 246.
32 LS 18. LFT 269, RE 247.

> to the end. And yet you must go an endless road, since life flows not only down a finite path but also an infinite one. But the unbounded makes you anxious since the unbounded is fearful and your humanity rebels against it. Consequently you seek limits and restraints so that you do not lose yourself, tumbling into infinity. Restraint becomes imperative for you. You cry out for the word which has one meaning and no other, so that you escape endless ambiguity.[33]

Despite the deeply ambiguous embodied basis from which meaning arises, we nevertheless rely on left-hemisphere representations, based on cognitive models that provide us with an assumed world in which to act. When we act, we are obliged to assume that the world is a certain way, and that our words represent it correctly, otherwise we would have no way of engaging with our goals or with the conditions we need to deal with to reach those goals. There is thus an important part of us that cannot cope with endless ambiguity: it makes us feel as though we have to abandon the goals that are so important to us, so we feel anxiety.

Engaging with this challenge to the standpoint of embodied meaning, Jung nevertheless manages to find an integrative way forward. He begins to see Ammonius as a 'murderer' because 'he calls up the daimons of the boundless', but then he goes on:

> And yet you cannot find the new words if you do not shatter the old words. But no one should shatter the old words, unless he finds the new word that is a firm rampart against the limitless and grasps more life in it than the old word.[34]

This is an important aspect of the Middle Way in practice. If we recognise that we are dependent on words as signs within a cognitive model for practical purposes, and yet that no cognitive model can be assumed to be finally 'real' or 'unreal', we are yet left with the ability to *improve* our cognitive models, just as we can *improve* the theories about the world that are created using them. The improvement must be pragmatic and comparative, not a deduction from any kind of assumed metaphysical truth. No model is absolute, but nevertheless should only undermine a religious belief when we have a better alternative that fulfils the same functions, and (as philosophers of science such as Lakatos and Kuhn have recognised[35])

---

33 LS 21, LFT 270, RE 250.
34 LS 21, LFT 270, RE 251.
35 Lakatos (1974); Kuhn (1996).

we should only abandon a scientific paradigm when we have a better alternative to put in its place. The mere destruction of beliefs or their basis because of abstract failings is negative absolutism.

When Jung returns to his second conversation with Ammonius the next day, then, Jung is in a better position to combine appreciation of his insights with recognition of his limitations. For, despite his appreciation of multiple meaning, Ammonius is stuck in a solitary contemplation of those meanings as an end in itself, rather than an exploration or development of those meanings in embodied practice. Ammonius confesses that he has not yet found the meaning of the gospels 'which is yet to come' – that is, in full practical experience (the 'way that is to come' being the Middle Way with which the *Red Book* begins). But when Jung suggests that he might be able to find this better if stimulated by others, Ammonius rejects him as a temptation of Satan.[36]

As Jung later reflects on Ammonius:

> *He wanted to find what he needed in the outer. But you find manifold meaning only in yourself, not in things, since the manifoldness of meaning is not something that is given at the same time, but is a succession of meanings. The meanings that follow one another do not lie in things, but lie in you, who are subject to many changes, insofar as you take part in life.*[37]

As in Jung's treatment of the scholar in the castle in the forest, the 'outer' here refers to the basis of meaning: that is the assumption that meaning comes only from a representational relationship with states of affairs in the world. Ammonius had abandoned sole representational meaning, but not representational meaning itself. He needed to recognise that it is his experience that gives meaning, and that experience depends on practical judgements and interactions forming a process of development, not just on waiting for an insightful cascade of meaning to reach him from a text.

Taken as a whole, then, the conversations with Ammonius take us some way further towards establishing a Jungian Middle Way approach to meaning. Recognising embodied meaning is an important first step towards a more adequate response to the conditions of our lives, but as often when there has been an absolutisation, it is too easy to over-react by negatively absolutising the other way, which in this case would mean denying the ways we need to accept

---

36 LS 25, LFT 272, RE 258.
37 LS 28, LFT 273, RE 262.

Embodied Meaning and Scholars

representational frames for meaning for practical reasons. To use embodied meaning in a fully helpful way it needs to be interpreted using the Middle Way as part of a process of integrating opposed views about it. The bi-directional tree already discussed in chapter 5, which accompanies the conversation with Ammonius, can form a fit symbol of the Middle Way in relation to meaning.

9.h. The tower of confidence

As embodied meaning has sceptical implications, it may seem superficially to undermine our confidence, but when confidence is an *experience* rather than a dogmatic stance it grows out of embodiment. We find such confidence when we are prepared to question what we previously believed on the basis of new evidence, showing in the process that confidence is not a matter of certainty about beliefs, but on the contrary being prepared to question them without being emotionally undermined – because our sense of security comes from bodily experience rather than deductions from absolutes. Later in the *Red Book*, Jung offers a striking image for this embodied confidence – namely the tower.

> *My tower grew for several thousand years, imperishable. It does not sink back. But it can be built over and will be built over. Few grasp my tower, since it stands on a high mountain. But many will see it and not grasp it. Therefore my tower will remain unused. No one scales its smooth walls. No one lands on its pointed roof. Only he who finds the entrance hidden in the mountain and rises up through the labyrinths of the innards can reach the tower, and the happiness of he who surveys things from there and he who lives for himself. This has been attained and created. It has not arisen from a patchwork of human thoughts, but has been forged from the glowing heat of the innards; the Cabiri themselves carried the matter to the mountain and consecrated the building with their own blood as the sole keepers of the mystery of its genesis. I built it out of the lower and upper beyond and not from the surface of the world. Therefore it is new and strange and towers over the plains inhabited by humans. This is the solid and the beginning.*[38]

The tower resembles the body in only being accessible 'from inside' and not outside. It is also the outcome of successive layers of conditioning experience, represented by the Cabiri (already discussed in chapter 6) who 'carry up what slumbers in the earthly'.[39]

---

38 LS 171–2, LFT 321–2, RE 429.
39 LS 166, LFT 321, RE 426.

One could liken the constructive process of the Cabiri to the process of the refinement of meaning from undifferentiated early experience, to image schemas, and then by metaphorical extension to more abstract language. The tower has thus been forged from 'the innards' of the body and right-hemisphere experience rather than the constructions of belief that we get from society, an indivisible experience combining the gradual refinement of meaning with the basic visceral experience of bodily energies.

The image of the tower has, of course, previously been used to symbolise pride built on certainty. The Tower of Babel from the Bible is a symbol of arrogance based on false certainty, whilst for Freudians the tower is a phallic symbol. Jung, however, subverts this tradition to turn it to positive ends, by making the tower a symbol of rooted and embodied confidence developed through integration. From 1923 Jung started to turn this symbolic tower into a stone one, by actually building a tower at Bollingen on the shores of Lake Zürich.

9.i. The dancing devil

There is one more final important symbol of embodied meaning in the *Red Book*. That's the way in which the Red One (already discussed in chapter 6) takes to dancing. In his conversation with Jung, laced as it is with petty polarisations, the Red One himself comes up with the importance of dancing: 'It's better to dance through life'[40] rather than be over-solemn. Dancing is obviously a highly embodied activity, whilst solemnity may be a product of dwelling too much within the limited context of left-hemisphere meaning. Dancing may thus be a highly integrative activity.

However, the *Red Book* also considers the dangers of dancing. The Red One claims to be 'joy', and Jung is troubled by this. The joy of the devil turns out to be a rather heedless joy.

> You dispute the fact that your joy is your devil. But it seems as if there is always something devilish about joy. If your joy is no devil for you, then possibly it is for your neighbours, since joy is the most supreme flowering and greening of life.[41]

---

40 LS 4, LFT 260, RE 216.
41 LS 5, LFT 261, RE 219.

It is not difficult to imagine how one's own joy can become a devil for one's neighbours. A loud party continued through the night may be the product of spontaneous joy, but in its heedlessness of others' feelings is also the product of narrow assumptions, according to which one's own short-term pleasure is of overwhelming importance, and the feelings of others not worthy of consideration. Jung thus raises the problem of hedonism as a moral value.

This issue re-emerges when Jung meets the Red One again, this time in unholy alliance with Ammonius (as discussed in chapter 1). There the Red One explains how he was influenced by Jung into an obsession with dancing – which becomes 'serious' and leads the Red One to joining the church and becoming a dancing abbot. However, even in the context of the church this obsession with dancing becomes 'hellish', apparently a sort of addiction. The Red One is only cured of his dancing addiction by meeting Ammonius.[42]

This development offers an elegant opposing parallel with the limitations of Ammonius. Both the Red One and Ammonius are engaged in a process of gradual integration that reflects aspects of Jung's own integration, but at the same time the incompleteness and asymmetry of that integration process allow them to get stuck in new kinds of absolute assumption along the way. Ammonius developed in such a one-sided way in his solitary life, that he was initially overwhelmed by his return to society and 'wallowed in pleasure'.[43] The Red One, on the other hand, became a solitary because he could no longer pursue his dance-obsession sufficiently in the context of the church. Each appears to have provided the other with an initial balancing sense of perspective, in which they could start to combine social and solitary, hedonistic and dutiful elements in a more integrated life, even though they were still combined in unholy alliance against Jung.

Both also illustrate that engagement with the body's meaning may be a vital part of a process of integration, but is not sufficient. By getting into better contact with the body through a practice like dancing, we may come to recognise assumptions and feelings that we had previously repressed, and thus be in a better position to integrate them. However, it is quite possible for bodily awareness to nevertheless remain associated with narrow and absolute

---

42 LS 33, LFT 276, RE 271.
43 LS 33, LFT 276, RE 270.

assumptions, which then hold us back from the next possible stage of integration. The stories of Ammonius and the Red One provide a particularly multi-layered and complex model of the integration process, because each is both part of Jung in one sense and separate from him in another. Their separate journeys reflect Jung's journeys as well as the obstructions to be encountered on those journeys. Yet at the same time, it is also clear that Jung's own journey rapidly moves beyond these limitations.

10. Complaints of the Dead

10.a. The effects of the dead

Engagement with death and the dead is an important recurring theme of the *Red Book*. Due to a mother with psychic tendencies and a spiritualist cousin who believed she could communicate with the dead, interest in the dead was an influential aspect of Jung's early life.[1] However, in the *Red Book* we can see a move to integrate both death itself, and the dead as Jung encountered them, within a framework of assumptions that, though still ambiguous in some respects, primarily values integration and the Middle Way. Jung has conflicts with regard to the dead that he needs to integrate.

However we choose to categorise the experiences of the dead recorded in the *Red Book*, we can learn from Jung's developing attitude to them without adopting any definite beliefs about the independent existence of souls or ghosts after death. Jung expresses himself on this point with a characteristic trenchancy:

> Do you think that the dead do not exist because you have devised the impossibility of immortality? You believe in your idols of words. The dead produce effects, that is sufficient. In the inner world there is no explaining away.[2]

The *effects* of the dead can take a variety of forms. They may remind us of our own mortality. They may continue to exert influence, whether individually or collectively, as images in our experience. Towards the end of the *Red Book*, though, the dead seem to increasingly come to represent closed loops of assumption and behaviour. The dead are those who have fallen off the developing tree of life and ceased to learn, and it is thus this quality of being stuck that makes the dead problematic. As Jung puts it:

> The dead who besiege us are souls who have not fulfilled the principium individuationis [the principle of individuation or individual integration], or else they would have become distant stars.[3]

1 Bair (2003) pp. 46–52.
2 LS 106, LFT 298, RE 347.
3 Black Book extract, Appendix C: LFT 370, RE 579.

This particularly suggests that the dead are primarily an image within ourselves, just as are the archetypal figures encountered by Jung in his visions. In effect they represent an aspect of the shadow archetype, because they might otherwise be repressed as negative and threatening. If our image of the dead is that of fulfilled and integrated beings, they become 'distant stars' because we may still be symbolically aware of them but they have no disruptive impact on us. However, the dead besiege us in the meantime in the form of a relentless anxiety about a lack of fulfilment before death, with our anxieties about ourselves indistinguishable from our awareness of the limited integration of others.

Nevertheless, though we might need to initially correct a Western cultural habit of externalising the dead by thinking of them instead as internal, in the end we need to remain agnostic about the continued 'existence' of the dead in themselves. Though it is impossible to coherently imagine how the dead could see without eyes, think without brains or position themselves without bodies, in the end we must allow that we do not know, because the ways in which they might potentially 'exist' or 'not exist' lie entirely beyond our experience. It is an important aspect of the practice of the Middle Way never to confuse rigorous agnosticism with denial.

10.b. Acceptance of death

The acceptance of death itself provides the starting condition for Jung's engagement with the dead, as without that acceptance he would effectively be a ghost himself, disturbed by anxiety about death into the same closed loops, and he would not be attractive to the dead.

Jung's acceptance of death becomes clear in the chapter of the *Red Book* headed 'Death', where Jung follows streams flowing out to the sea, and there stands on the margins beside the cold figure of Death, watching the dead as they are scattered and dissolved. The 'densely pressed multitudes of men, old men, women, and children…clasping themselves rigidly with their hands and arms…are all flowing past in an enormous stream'. The sea then whirls and scatters them 'and ever new droves dissolve into black air'.[4] The clear implication

---

4   LS 30, LFT 274, RE 264.

seems to be that Jung sees death as the dissolution of the individual into something larger, whether one understands this primarily in a physical or in a mystical sense.

The reflections that follow this vision of death also suggest strongly that there is an interdependent relationship between death and life, and thus that there would be an incongruity in wanting life without also wanting death.

> *We need the coldness of death to see clearly. Life wants to live and to die, to begin and to end. You are not forced to live eternally, but you can also die, since there is a will in you for both. Life and death must strike a balance in your existence.... For the completion of life a balance with death is fitting. If I accept death, then my tree greens, since dying increases life. If I plunge into the death encompassing the world, then my buds break open. How much our life needs death!*
>
> *... Without death, life would be meaningless, since the long-lasting rises again and denies its own meaning. To be, and to enjoy your being, you need death, and limitation enables you to fulfil your being.*[5]

One of the things standing in the way of our integration is thus the non-acceptance of death, whether that takes the form of anxiety about death or craving to maintain life. Many traditional myths point out the ways in which we would be deluding ourselves if we imagined ourselves as happier if we attained immortality, as it is only by having a temporal limitation on our lives that we are able to appreciate them. For example, in the Celtic myth of Oisin, the hero goes to live with his lover Niamh in Tir Nan Og, the land of eternal youth, but nevertheless longs to come back to the mortal lands. Eventually Niamh gives him a horse to revisit mortal lands, but warns him not to dismount from it. When he disobeys this instruction and dismounts to help someone, extreme old age immediately catches up with him, shortly followed by death.[6] Immortality remains an abstract fantasy, not one that the embodied conditions of our lives could actually endure.

This basic acceptance of death as an aspect of the practice of the Middle Way is also found in the accounts of the way that the Buddha faced up to his death. The *Mahaparanibbana Sutta*,[7] which

---

5 LS 31, LFT 274–5, RE 266–7.
6 Rolleston (1990).
7 *Digha Nikaya* 16, Walshe (1995) pp. 223 ff.

gives an account of the period leading up to the Buddha's death, shows him not only accepting death with equanimity, but also resisting the temptation to make a premature departure before his teachings were sufficiently established for others.[8] In an echo of Jung's vegetation images of the inter-relationship of death with life, the Buddha is said to have died under twin sal trees that burst into untimely blossom.[9]

10.c. The irruption of the dead

The dead first appear in the *Red Book* quite suddenly, whilst Jung is in the kitchen talking to the intuitive cook about the imitation of Christ.

> *I hear an odd swishing and whirring – and suddenly a roaring sound fills the room like a flock of large birds – with a frenzied flapping of wings – I see many shadowlike human forms rush past and I hear a manifold babble of voices utter the words: 'Let us pray in the temple!'*
>
> *'Where are you rushing off to?' I call out. A bearded man with tousled hair and dark shining eyes stops and turns towards me: 'We are wandering to Jerusalem to pray at the most holy sepulchre.'*
>
> *'Take me with you.'*
>
> *'You cannot join us, you have a body. But we are dead.'*[10]

The bearded man goes on to explain that he is Ezechiel, an Anabaptist, and that he and his fellows are internally driven to make pilgrimages to all the holy places.

> *'What drives you to this?'*
>
> *'I don't know. But it seems that we still have no peace, although we died in true belief.'*[11]

Ezechiel is unable to explain any further what important thing it is that they neglected in life to make them so driven in death, but he asks Jung if he knows. Jung then replies 'Let go, daimon, you did not live your animal.'[12]

---

8   See Ellis (2019) 2.f for a fuller discussion.
9   *Digha Nikaya* 16.5.1–2, Walshe (1995) p. 262.
10 LS 101, LFT 294, RE 334–5.
11 Ibid.
12 Ibid.

This scene is both dramatic and revealing as to the nature of the dead. Firstly, the fact that they are dead seems in some ways incidental, or at least primarily symbolic. The Anabaptists show all the signs of obsession centred on absolute beliefs that are heavily focused on the left hemisphere, with insufficient ameliorating openness to the right hemisphere to be able to challenge or soften those driving beliefs. Thus it is not *despite* their 'true belief' but because of it that they are in such a state, characterised by an alienation from the body that seems uniquely possible for humans and sets us apart from animals. The Anabaptists thus do not necessarily have to be dead in any literal sense: the more important issue is that they are dead 'from the neck down' – rejecting their bodies and trapped in endless confirmation bias. Given the association of this type of state with many types of mental illness,[13] it is then ironic as well as apt that it is Jung who immediately afterwards envisions himself in a mental hospital.[14]

Jung's subsequent discussion adds further support to this line of interpretation. Jung speaks of the dead as of a type 'who ensnared themselves'[15] and 'fell prey to power'.[16] He goes on 'He who never lives his animal must treat his brother like an animal.'[17] However high the concepts in the mind of these dead, their absolutisations mean that they cannot relate to others as persons with bodies like themselves, but rather have to abstract their values and relationships into a conceptual scheme governed by a rigid set of beliefs.

However, in line with his recognition of the inter-dependence of life and death, Jung also recognises that his life is tied in with such dead, and that he cannot simply disown or avoid them. Rather, he acknowledges a compassionate mission to aid them, within the limits of what he can practically manage.

> *Live the life of the day and do not speak of mysteries, but dedicate the night to bringing about the salvation of the dead.*[18]

Since the dead are the unintegrated, it seems that the mission to aid the dead is nothing other than the quest for integration in general.

13 McGilchrist (2009) pp. 393 ff.
14 LS 102, LFT 295, RE 337–8.
15 LS 103, LFT 296, RE 340.
16 LS 103, LFT 296, RE 341.
17 LS 104, LFT 296, RE 342.
18 Ibid.

10.d. The instrumentality of the dead

There is much continuing discussion of the nature of the dead later in the *Red Book*, in 'The Magician' and in 'Scrutinies'. The impression given of their narrow left-hemisphere dominance is particularly reinforced by the account given of their instrumentality with regard to the earth. In the light of the modern environmental crisis, it is difficult to believe that the following passage was written a hundred years ago.

> *These dead have given names to all beings, the beings in the air, on the earth and in the water. They have weighed and counted things. They have counted so and so many horses, cows, sheep, trees, segments of land, and springs; they said, this is good for this purpose, and that is good for that one. What did they do with the admirable tree? What happened to the sacred frog? Did they see his golden eye? Where is the atonement for the 7,777 cattle whose blood they spilled, whose flesh they consumed? Did they do penance for the sacred ore that they dug up from the belly of the earth? No, they weighed, numbered and apportioned all things. They did whatever pleased them. And what did they do! You saw the powerful – but this is precisely how they gave power to things unknowingly. Yet the time has come when things speak. The piece of flesh says: how many men? The piece of ore says, how many men? The ship says, how many men? The coal says, how many men? The house says, how many men? And things rise and number and weigh and apportion and devour millions of men.*[19]

This passage is remarkable for recognising the close relationship between representational language and manipulation, as well as recognising its effects on the environment and on other animals. As McGilchrist explains, left-hemisphere linguistic abilities probably developed for manipulative purposes, and the regions of the left pre-frontal cortex concerned with tool-using and linguistic representation are adjacent.[20] This recognition is also combined with the Jungian understanding of projection. If we put so much emphasis on the categorisation and use of things for our purposes, we simultaneously give them power over us, because of the strength of our identification with them. We begin to feel our most important values to lie, not in our own bodies, but in the things that we manipulate with those bodies. Consequently, if those things are no longer

---

19 LFT 352, RE 527.
20 McGilchrist (2009) pp. 113 ff.

available to us because of our environmental depradation, we will suffer. Even without such external effects, though, the takeover of our minds by externalised obsession with things could be seen as amounting to the devouring of millions of men that Jung writes about. In Jung's specific historical context, this may also be closely related to the First World War, which was almost literally devouring millions of men at the time.

Of course, this instrumentality of the dead also extends to their attitude to the living. Jung suggests that they wish to drink the blood of the living, which is a graphic way of depicting the unacknowledged reliance of left-hemisphere meaning on the right hemisphere. 'Give blood, so that I may drink and gain speech,'[21] Jung is implored by one of three shades who approach him. If they were to succeed, there would be a danger that the living, drained of blood, would join the dead, condemned to endless depressed constriction and searching obsessively for new sources of living sustenance. The dead offer nothing back to the living in exchange for their blood, making the relationship entirely parasitic.[22]

The shade who approaches Jung tries to persuade him with all the power of instrumentality, to give her blood and to be buried with her, because he is to her 'of unspeakable worth, all my hope'.[23] She craves the symbol HAP, which she describes as 'The word..., the symbol, the mediator...terribly simple, initially stupid, naturally godlike, the God's other pole.'[24] This God is both 'in the light' and simultaneously in the body:

> He is the flesh spirit, the blood spirit, he is the extract of all bodily juices, the spirit of the sperm and entrails, of the genitals, of the head, of the feet, of the hands, of the joints, of the bones, of the eyes and ears, of the nerves and brain; he is the spirit of the sputum and of excretion.[25]

No doubt many metaphysical speculations could be (and have been) read into HAP, but to me it seems obvious that this God is the Middle Way. The dead need the Middle Way, because the painful absolutisation of their fixed, rigid belief structures can only be relieved by access to broader meaning in which those rigid categorisations, with

21 LFT 340, RE 486.
22 LFT 340, RE 488.
23 LFT 340, RE 486.
24 LFT 339, RE 484.
25 Ibid.

all their dualistic oppositions, can be questioned and reformulated. That broader meaning lies in the body, in all the particularity and viscerality of the shade's description. Without bodies, the dead are stuck. So they crave bodies with a pornographic intensity.

10.e. The hanged man

A slightly different view of the dead comes from Jung's conversation with a hanged man in 'The Magician'. At Jung's request, his serpent brings up the hanged man from hell, as a sample of what death is like. The hanged man was judicially executed for the murder of his parents and wife – motivated, he says, by a desire to transport them more quickly to eternal blessedness.[26]

The hanged man's position in hell is vague:

> 'I suspect that I'm in Hell. Sometimes it seems as if my wife were here too, and sometimes I'm not sure, just as little as I'm sure of my own self.'[27]

The hanged man goes on to say 'there is no time with us, so there is none to spend. Nothing at all happens.'[28] He speaks to his relatives only about trivialities, and dwells in a state of boredom. 'Everything here is impersonal and purely matter of fact.'[29] The conversation with Jung ends abruptly as the hanged man gets bored with it.

Here we have an illustration of various other aspects of extremely left-hemisphere dominated states. Rather than the craving of the shade, we instead have indifference, boredom and alienation. The hanged man maintains the habits of life only insofar as he is prepared to offer a rationalisation of his actions as a murderer, and Jung also sees this rationalisation as involving a projection: 'A murderer is one who wants to force others to blessedness, since he kills his own growth.'[30] However, beyond this his experience seems drained of meaning, just as a representational world can become when cut off from the embodied energies on which it depends. The vagueness of his relations with the other dead suggests that he does not meet them with the embodied experience of the living, but only

---

26 LS 173, LFT 322, RE 430.
27 LS 174, LFT 322, RE 431.
28 Ibid.
29 LS 175, LFT 322, RE 431.
30 LS 179, LFT 323, RE 434.

as concepts. The impersonality, above all, is characteristic of over-reliance on the left hemisphere, because personality arises from the particularity of embodiment and the ability to recognise others as living persons.

The boredom of hell, like the boredom of heaven,[31] arises from its isolation from embodied experience, and its reliance on conceptual theology using unquestioned cognitive models based on dead metaphors. Human experience is that of having a living body, with its drives, changing focus of attention, and constant relationship to bodily functions. It is thus impossible for humans to dwell in either heaven or hell whilst remaining humans – a point that Jung clearly recognises. What remains important about these afterlife states is thus their relationship to death, because we, for our part, reduce the after-death state to decontextualised conceptual beliefs over-dependent on the left hemisphere. Our beliefs about death are just another projection away from our living experience, that we need to seek to integrate.

10.f. Integration of the dead

At some points in the *Red Book*, Jung seems confident of having integrated the dead sufficiently to no longer be seriously troubled by them.

> *I built a firm structure. Through this I myself gained stability and duration and could withstand the fluctuations of the personal.... Therefore the demands of the dead disappeared, as they were satisfied.*

> *I am no longer threatened by the dead, since I accepted their demands though [German: in] accepting the serpent. But through this I have also taken over something of the dead into my day.... So long as I wanted to satisfy only my own demands, I was personal and therefore living in the sense of the world. But when I recognised the demands of the dead in me and satisfied them, I gave up my earlier personal striving and the world had to take me for a dead man.*[32]

The dead are part of life, not something separate from it, just as the representational left hemisphere is an essential part of the functioning human brain. Jung clearly recognises that although he

---

31 See Ellis (2016) ch. 13.
32 LS 177–8, LFT 323, RE 433 ('though' appears to me to be a mis-translation).

might refuse the grossest attempts of the dead to take over life, he cannot reject the dead altogether. To do so would be to continue to operate on the basis of projection, and to absolutise the dead, rather than recognising them as aspects of his own experience. It is by being integrated enough in his own experience that he can cease to be negatively affected by the dead, whether by their indifference or their outrageous demands.

If Jung had left his relationship with the dead at that point of an apparent degree of integration, we could rest content with his treatment of the dead as consistently reflecting the Middle Way, and as in harmony with his responses to the archetypes. Though Jung's degree of integration would of course remain imperfect and his ability to help the dead limited, we could nevertheless admire his treatment of the dead as offering a model for an integrative response to them. However, as discussed above in chapter 3, the role of Philemon appears not to be as fully integrated as the other figures he encounters in the *Red Book*. Jung continues to at least partially project Philemon as something beyond himself, and as a result adopts Philemon's attitude to the dead, which goes beyond Jung's contentment in his own experience and offers something more like a mission.

> *Are you laughing, Oh ΦΙΛΗΜΩΝ? Alas, I understand you: humanity has completely faded for you, but its shadow has arisen for you. How much greater and happier the shadow of humanity than it is itself! The blue midday shadows of the dead! Alas, there is your humanity, Oh ΦΙΛΗΜΩΝ, you are a teacher and friend of the dead. They stand sighing in the shade of your house, they live under the branches of your trees. They drink the dew of your tears, they warm themselves at the goodness of your heart, they hunger after the words of your wisdom, which sounds full to them, full of the sounds of life. I saw you, Oh ΦΙΛΗΜΩΝ, at the noonday hour when the sun stood highest; you stood speaking with a blue shade, blood stuck to its forehead and solemn torment darkened it.*[33]

Philemon does not seem to be under any illusions about the nature of the dead, and recognises their craving for power,[34] but nevertheless seems to have a special role in speaking to them and helping them. It is Philemon who delivers the Seven Sermons to the

---

33 LS 152, LFT 316, RE 411–12.
34 LFT 342, RE 495.

Dead in 'Scrutinies', 'dressed in the white robe of a priest'.[35] A 'dark crowd' has arrived at Jung's door, of the dead who have returned from Jerusalem, but did not find what they sought. They are asking for light rather than blood. Jung's initial response is to dismiss them, but his soul insists that he lets Philemon speak.[36]

When Philemon began to speak, and to deliver his Seven Sermons to the Dead, Jung (according to the records of his later interviews with Aniela Jaffé) 'grasped' Philemon, so that he began to lose his autonomy.[37] Jung, it seems, took on the persona of Philemon, and with it his mission to the dead.

> Jung said to Aniela Jaffé that the discussions with the dead formed the prelude to what he would subsequently communicate to the world, and that their content anticipated his later books. 'From that time on, the dead have become ever more distinct for me as the voices of the unanswered unresolved and unredeemed'. The questions he was required to answer did not come from the world around him, but from the dead.[38]

Why did Jung identify himself so fully with Philemon's mission to the dead? Why, rather than merely integrating his experiences of the dead, did he feel required to *answer* their questions? To try to explain this will require another chapter in which wider questions are asked about major inconsistencies in Jung's work as a whole – inconsistencies that are not much evident before this point late in the *Red Book,* but which make the Seven Sermons out of harmony with the rest of the *Red Book,* and which then become a major source of confusion in the interpretation of Jung and his legacy. The underlying problem here will not only be Jung's attitude to the dead, but, closely associated with it, his attitude to metaphysics.

---

35 LFT 346, RE 507.
36 Ibid.
37 LFT/RE, 'Scrutinies' footnote 80; Notes made by Aniela Jaffé p. 25.
38 LFT/RE, 'Scrutinies' footnote 78; Jung (1989) p. 217.

11. Gnostic versus Agnostic

11.a. The two Jungs and the trouble with metaphysics

The *Red Book* confronts us with a major contradiction between Jung the gnostic and Jung the agnostic – a contradiction that then runs through the rest of Jung's work like a fault line. This chapter aims to explain why I think that contradiction is important, and why it is vital to give credibility to the agnostic Jung rather than the gnostic without appropriating one to the other. The enormous value of the *Red Book* is that up until the Seven Sermons it is the agnostic Jung who is dominant. However, the Seven Sermons seem to indicate something of the story of how the gnostic Jung began to cloud the picture.

I am not the first person to note major inconsistencies in the basic assumptions that underpin Jung's work. Renos Papadopoulos writes:

> *It is important to appreciate that there are two Jungs – the one with an open epistemology and Socratic ignorance, and the other Jung who, following Gnostic epistemology, was, in fact, essentialist and universalist.*[1]

I have already said something about the open epistemology of the agnostic Jung in chapter 1, because open epistemology is crucial to the Middle Way. The Middle Way consists in an avoidance of absolutisations, whether these absolutisations are positive or negative, and these absolutisations are associated with projections in which we fail to acknowledge our own contribution to shaping the 'facts' we think we perceive about the world, ourselves and others. Absolutisation is often unconscious, but can take the form of implicit or explicit assumption. Metaphysics is a form of absolutisation, and rigidifies claims founded on projection; so the adoption of any metaphysics, whether Gnostic or otherwise, is contrary to the Middle Way and has the effect of confusing and undermining it.

---

1 Papadopoulos (2006) p. 48.

Gnostic versus Agnostic 171

Papadopoulos, too, recognises at least some of the negative effects of Jung's indulgence in metaphysical thinking:

> The detrimental aspects and implications of Jung's Gnosticism have not yet been sufficiently appreciated: besides an elitist attitude, these include a closed system of circular tautology: people believe something to be true and whatever they see around them they interpret according to those beliefs, while all the while they also believe that they are open and that their beliefs are based on real evidence. This approach cannot be enriched by new elements and therefore it cannot develop further.[2]

Papadopoulos here identifies some of the key features of metaphysics in general which I have written about in more detail elsewhere:[3] circularity and ad hoc reasoning is just one indicator of a more basic confirmation bias, which is accompanied by the exclusion of alternative possibilities from consideration. Though we are all subject to confirmation bias, the belief in underlying or essential metaphysical truths accentuates it, by cutting off the possibility of alternative explanations that do not accord with these supposed essential truths.

However, even beyond these negative effects of metaphysics, the standpoint of embodied meaning (which, as I argued in chapter 9, has a close fit with Jung's attitudes in the *Red Book*) has a basic incompatibility with metaphysics. According to embodied meaning, our propositional beliefs are formulated within cognitive models that are dependent on assumed metaphors. The very way in which our language is significant for us thus does not depend on a relationship with any kind of essential truths, actual or hypothetical, but rather our very ability to think in such terms is due to an often unacknowledged process of left-hemisphere abstraction from an embodied meaning on which our abstract claims continue to depend. General claims (like this one) can be useful to us, but they are based in non-absolute cognitive models. Belief in the general truth of absolute claims can only be based on the deluded assumption that our claims gain their meaning from a representational relationship to reality.

Confusion in this area is often created by philosophers asserting that metaphysical assumptions are unavoidable, in the process defining metaphysics in terms of its framing priority rather than

---

2 Papadopoulos (1997).
3 Ellis (2015) 3.a–e.

its absoluteness. It is correct that we all tend to assume that, for example, objects can be separated in space and time. However, the test of absoluteness for such assumptions will lie in whether we are willing to consider alternatives when they are available and understand justification in incremental terms. If there is no possible alternative available to human beings, we can neither think about it nor repress it – however, with most metaphysical claims, there *are* possible alternatives, and the problem with metaphysics lies in the way it cuts off those alternatives. If we identify with a certain metaphysical position and then find it challenged, when we assume we have no alternatives available to us, we then tend to react as though the negating opposite of that metaphysical position has been proposed: for example, any challenge to our conception of what is good is taken to be evil, and any challenge to our conception of 'reality' to be idealism. Metaphysics tends to trap us in a series of dualisms or false dichotomies, according to which we can only frame our thinking in terms of certain battle lines.

To avoid such dualisms, the only helpful attitude to take towards metaphysics is rigorously agnostic. If one merely rejects one type of positive metaphysics, there is a danger that one will only fall into the opposite negative metaphysics: e.g. atheism instead of theism or determinism instead of freewill. Agnosticism on issues where there is social pressure towards the extremes requires a consistent effort at even-handedness.

In response to such points about metaphysics, however, it tends to be only philosophers who want to defend metaphysics in general. Jungians are perhaps more likely to cast doubt on whether the Gnostic assertions made in the Seven Sermons are indeed metaphysical. This is thus something that I will go on to discuss next. A third possible response is to argue that not all metaphysics has the negative effects I have outlined, or that Gnostic metaphysics is an exception. This again I will consider below.

11.b. Gnostic metaphysics

In the 'Seven Sermons to the Dead', Philemon plunges straight into the most abstract metaphysics. At the same time there is a complete change of tone from the discourses, imaginative experiences, and exploratory reflections that fill most of the *Red Book*. Philemon is telling us how things are, straight and from on high. It is indeed a sermon.

> 'Now hear: I begin with nothingness. Nothingness is the same as the fullness.... We call this nothingness or fullness the Pleroma.... In the Pleroma there is nothing and everything. It is fruitless to think about the Pleroma, for this would mean self-dissolution.'[4]

Philemon later goes back to try to explain the obvious self-contradiction in this.

> 'You say, "what use is there in thinking about it at all?" Did you yourself not say that it is not worth thinking about the Pleroma?
>
> 'I mentioned that to free you from the delusion that we are able to think about the Pleroma. When we distinguish the qualities of the Pleroma, we are speaking from the grounds of our own differentiated state and about our own differentiation, but have effectively said nothing about the Pleroma. Yet we need to speak about our own differentiation, so that we may sufficiently differentiate ourselves. Our very nature is differentiation. If we are not true to this differentiation we do not differentiate ourselves enough. We must therefore make distinctions between qualities.'[5]

Very similar language is used here to that of Mahayana Buddhist texts speaking of the doctrine of emptiness. The argument goes that, despite appearances to the contrary, it is helpful to make entirely abstract and absolute claims about things that lie entirely beyond our experience, because in doing so we are actually talking indirectly about things that do lie within our experience – in this case differentiation. Differentiation is indeed something we can experience, whenever we distinguish a male blackbird from a female one or a square from a triangle. The complete ultimate absence of differentiation, however, is not within our experience. If we want to talk about differentiation we can talk about differentiation – we don't have to talk about its ultimate absence instead!

To talk of the Pleroma is not meaningless: though the meaning is highly abstracted and stretched from its bodily base. It might have an archetypal meaning similar to that of God, but then it is difficult to see why it should be used instead of God. Philemon is evidently not talking at the level of meaning, but that of belief, challenging the orthodox Christian beliefs of the dead and offering Gnostic ones in

---

4 LFT 346-7, RE 509-10.
5 LFT 347, RE 511.

their place. The more he tries to relate the Pleroma in some way to experience, the stranger the beliefs get.

> 'We are, however, the Pleroma itself, for we are a part of the eternal and the endless. But we have no share therein, as we are infinitely removed from the Pleroma; not spatially or temporally, but essentially, since we are distinguished from the Pleroma in our essence as creation, which is confined within time and space.'[6]

This becomes even more garbled when Philemon tries to explain why we shouldn't, after all, just strive for differentiation, rapidly covering the patches over his incoherent attempts to reduce integration to absolutes with more patches, until the effect becomes thoroughly risible.

> 'You must not forget that the Pleroma has no qualities. We create these through thinking. If, therefore, you strive for distinctiveness or sameness, or any qualities whatsoever, you pursue thoughts that flow to you out of the Pleroma. Inasmuch as you run after these thoughts, you fall again into the Pleroma, and attain distinctiveness and sameness at the same time. Not your thinking, but your essence, is differentiation. Therefore you must not strive for what you conceive of as distinctiveness, but for your own essence.'[7]

There is lots more of this kind of material, and to go through it all attempting to attribute some helpful sense to it would be extremely tedious. Jung evidently thinks he is providing a framework for practical integration, but at every stage he undermines such a goal by giving us only thoroughly empty and abstract reasons for doing it – reasons that are much more likely to provide new bases of absolutisation than to help anyone find the Middle Way. He discusses pairs of opposites, which we are evidently supposed to be able to overcome because they 'do not exist'.[8] God, despite the important archetypal role he has played hitherto, is supplanted by Abraxas, a merely abstract figure who represents 'effect' and incorporates a whole list of things representing everything.[9] Monotheism is supplanted by monism with many gods who are one, as though this formality made any difference to our ability to integrate contradictory divine qualities.[10] The portentousness continues, lending a

6 LFT 347, RE 510.
7 LFT 348, RE 513–14.
8 LFT 347–8, RE 512–13.
9 LFT 350, RE 521–2.
10 LFT 351, RE 525.

false sense of profundity (for the unwary) to a set of crude generalisations about gender and sexuality.[11]

There are lots of rude names that it occurs to me to call all this, but the insults I would like to apply would be projections of how I feel about it. Strictly speaking I know nothing about how right or wrong this is, only that it is profoundly irrelevant to human life and human integration. But how it makes me feel, after the heights of the *Red Book* that have preceded it, is betrayed, upset, and mortified. How can a man who has done so much to work with his own projections, who can be such an inspiration on the path of human insight and integration, project onto the whole universe instead? How can he do it, not ironically or even in what he later recognised as a lapse, but in all seriousness? How can a man who has done so much to help us recognise our own multiplicity and non-essentiality, go on about essences? How can a man with such an alert sense of the limitations of our knowledge and the constructedness of our intellectualisations, go in for such transparent ad hoc excuses to try to justify his recourse to metaphysics?

The answer is, of course, that Jung is flawed. He is not as integrated as the reader up to this point in the *Red Book* might think. Too many of us have projected the Wise Old Man archetype onto him, and here is the reminder of our mistake. Jung was a fallible, mixed-up human being, and his integration was asymmetrical, proceeding much more in some areas than others. As a result, he was apparently just unable to resist the temptation to develop a metaphysical scheme in which to try to encapsulate his insights, even when all his efforts up to that point had gone into defying such schemes and their effects. From his accounts, it seemed that the scheme flowed out of his pen very readily and intuitively, and that it made the ghosts go away. But its intuitiveness for him does not prevent this from being a false solution. It is clearly the result of a long process of gestation in which he read about Gnosticism and reflected on it, not merely a moment's inspiration.

11.c. Philemon's inadequate answers

After each sermon is concluded and the dead have temporarily gone away, the more agnostic persona of Jung himself asks questions of

11 LFT 352–3, RE 528–31.

Philemon. Though these questions are critical, the inadequacy of the answers is well worth surveying, because it seems that too many Jungians may have been rhetorically taken in by these answers.

First Jung asks Philemon why he offers such strange teaching to the dead. Philemon replies:

> 'These dead ended their lives too early. These were seekers and therefore still hover over their graves. Their lives were incomplete, since they knew no way beyond the one to which belief had abandoned them. But since no one teaches them, I must do so. That is what love demands, since they wanted to hear, even if they grumble.'[12]

Philemon's assumption seems to be that, given the 'incomplete', narrow existence of the dead, the most loving thing to do would be to give them what they crave – namely, the certainty of metaphysical teachings. But this is a highly questionable assumption. One cannot completely rule out that in some possible circumstances a metaphysical teaching might be the most appropriate, but in practice this is extremely unlikely, given that metaphysical teachings are fixed and the conditions we encounter in experience are constantly changing.

Much, then, depends on whether the dead are subject to change. Within the world created by Jung's account of the sermons, they are indeed subject to change, because their attitudes change as a result of the sermons. The dead who are literally dead are no longer subject to any change, and cannot listen to sermons, but if we take the 'dead' to represent extremely left-hemisphere dominant people (whether these are seen as images in the minds of others or externally), then they are subject to change. In such a case, more metaphysics is the last thing they need. The dead need some contact with life, perhaps in limited quantities at first to gradually break them in whilst avoiding reaction. The dead may be aided by some critical perspective on their deluded beliefs, but only if that perspective can enable them to be agnostic about them rather than merely flipping into the opposite deluded beliefs. Psychiatrists dealing with the psychotic, or even therapists dealing with the merely neurotic, do not begin by preaching them metaphysical sermons, and not even Jung himself did such a thing, as far as we know. So how could it possibly be the 'loving' thing to do here?

---

12 LFT 348, RE 514.

Jung then asks Philemon if he believes what he teaches, and then whether he is certain of what he says. Philemon replies

> '*How could I teach what I believe? Who would give me the right to such belief? It is what I know how to say, not because I believe it, but because I know it. If I knew better, I would teach better.*
>
> '*I do not know whether it is the best that one can know. But I know nothing better and therefore I am certain these things are as I say.... There are no mistakes in these things... only different levels of knowledge. These things are as you know them.*'[13]

This explanation raises the issue of Jung's distinction between belief and knowledge, famously used in a BBC TV interview when Jung was asked if he believed in God. Jung replied, 'I don't need to believe. I know.'[14] In terms of knowledge as normally defined in philosophy – as justified true belief – this makes no sense, as clearly one can only know something if one also believes it. For a long time, for this reason, I have interpreted Jung's famous statement in terms of what philosophers call knowledge by acquaintance, indicating that Jung was *acquainted* with God by finding God meaningful through (archetypal) experience – experience that might be quite distinct from holding (at least) conscious, propositional beliefs about him. However, at length it occurred to me that if Jung meant knowledge by acquaintance in the *Red Book*, this would have been clear in the original German, which distinguishes between *kennen* (to be acquainted with) and *wissen* (to have propositional knowledge of). It turns out that Jung is using *wissen*.

So, the alternative is that by 'believe' Jung means 'merely believe', whereas by 'know' he means believe with certainty. This interpretation is reinforced by Philemon's claim here to be certain, and that there can be no mistakes in 'knowledge'. There seems to be no avoiding the unpalatable recognition that Jung believed that intuition, just because it is based on more profound and meaningful experience than ordinary conceptual understanding, must offer a kind of shortcut hotline to absolute knowledge.

Though this is a common assumption on the part of those who make heavy use of intuition, there is no justification for it, as already discussed in chapter 4 and evidenced by research into the reliability

---

13 LFT 348, RE 515.
14 McGuire and Hull (1987) p. 428.

of intuition.[15] This assumption seems to arise from a confusion between the *meaningfulness* of intuitions, particularly when they are connected with archetypes, and the reliability of those intuitions as the basis of beliefs. This assumption is presumably behind Jung's evident belief in a number of other phenomena that he investigates at first entirely in terms of meaning, such as astrology and alchemy. For example, both in the *Red Book* and elsewhere he shows apparent belief in the system of 'Platonic months', with the transition from the Age of Pisces (which began around the time of Christ) and the Age of Aquarius (beginning about now).[16] In the questions following the second sermon Philemon claims that the dead have no choice because 'the world, without these men knowing it, entered into that month of the great year where one should only believe what one knows'.[17] Nobody can deny that such astrological material may be of interest because of its symbolic meaningfulness, but in his detailed scholarly investigations into such symbols, as here, Jung often makes no clear distinction between their meaning and the adoption of beliefs justified by them. In Philemon's case he is clearly using such astrological claims as a basis of reasoning from which to reach other beliefs.

If the metaphysics of the Seven Sermons was intended to be justified by intuition, there is also a gulf between the kind of material they represent and the embodied basis of intuition. Intuition gains its prima facie justification (or 'validity') from its relationship to our most basic embodied experience. We may well have good grounds for confidence in an assumption that we never reflect upon, just because our bodies are familiar with it – such as the reliability of the chair we sit on for bearing our weight. However, the abstract claims of Gnostic metaphysics are the very opposite, being completely abstract in nature and a long way from anything we can have embodied confidence in. It is for that very reason that belief in metaphysics can be so damaging, regardless of the precise content of the metaphysical assertions being made.

It's also surprising that Philemon here claims 'to know nothing better'. This is hardly a credible claim, whether you see it as made by Philemon or by Jung. That Philemon knows better, we can judge

---

15 Kahneman (2010).
16 CW 9ii §147 ff.
17 LFT 349, RE 518.

from his earlier persona as a recalcitrant magician reluctant to talk about magic. That Jung knows better, almost more than anyone else, we can tell from the remainder of the *Red Book* up to this point. We can also see that he knows better from the quotation at the end of this chapter.

After the second sermon, Jung asks Philemon how people could unite under such a God as Abraxas, who 'blasts everything human'. This is a very important question given the role that God has had as an integrative archetype earlier in the *Red Book*. Philemon replies that the dead have already rejected a God of love, so he needs to offer them an alternative.[18] This, again, is a completely unconvincing response. The fact that the dead have rejected something does not necessarily imply that they will benefit from the opposite. Perhaps, on the contrary, the only possible way forward for them is to come round in a more experiential fashion to the integrative path they earlier rejected because they interpreted it metaphysically.

After the third sermon, Jung asks Philemon why he calls incomprehensible nature by the term 'God', and Philemon replies 'How should I name it otherwise?' He then argues that all possible terms for it imply some contradiction and then says unhelpfully that 'this God is and is not'. Yet this returns to the very conception of God as an object of belief that Jung rejected earlier in the *Red Book* (as discussed in chapter 3) in favour of the 'new' God as an integrative archetype. Such an archetype does not have to be identified with nature at all, and identifying it with nature is a projection, not an integrating recognition. It makes no difference whether God is seen as a loving metaphysical being or as a heartless metaphysical being, since both are delusions likely to be supportive of dogmatic beliefs. Agnosticism should lead us to avoid beliefs about Abraxas just as much as about the Christian God, and thus is in direct conflict with Jung's Gnosticism.

In response to Jung's questions after the fourth sermon, Philemon again seems to suggest that the dead should be judged by special standards and treated differently because of their conflictual adherence to Christianity. He also gives a long and vivid account of the instrumentality of the dead that I have already quoted in chapter 10.[19] But this time he seems to think that these conflicts make

18 LFT 349, RE 519.
19 LFT 352, RE 527.

the dead suited to polytheism, a claim that again is baffling, as it assumes without justification that the dead would be served better by a new religion than they were by the old one. He also appeals again to the Platonic calendar ('A new month stands at the door') to apparently justify a changed approach. This underlying appeal to determinism also recurs after the sixth sermon, when Philemon says 'Everything is running its usual course'.[20]

In the Seven Sermons, Jung is attempting to offer philosophy by shortcut. Although philosophers are often literalistic and caught up in their own limiting assumptions derived from projection, this is no justification for ignoring the need for rigorous scrutiny of abstract claims. The more general and abstract a claim is, the further it lies from embodied experience and thus the more rigorously critical the treatment of it needs to be. Jung's questions to Philemon go nowhere near far enough in their examination, and allow him to get away with far too much. When examined more closely, Philemon's justifications for his position amount to ad hoc reasoning, special pleading, non sequiturs, irrelevant appeals to intuition, and astrological determinism. Whilst the rest of the *Red Book* indicates a helpful underlying philosophy by showing it, but avoids explicit philosophy, the Seven Sermons naively wade straight into such territory, with disastrous results for the clarity and consistency of Jung's subsequent work.

11.d. Psychological interpretations of the Seven Sermons

I'm fully expecting that this rejection of Jung's metaphysical turn in the Seven Sermons will scandalise many Jungians, who may accuse me either of misinterpreting Jung or of failing to understand the insights that they see in the Seven Sermons. The idea of 'misinterpreting' Jung seems to me to make little sense in this context. Who is the 'real' Jung? What are the standards by which we can separate correct from incorrect interpretation in relation to such a text? I think we can only make *helpful* interpretations which fit a practical and inspirational purpose, and helpful interpretations will also need to be distinguished from unhelpful ones. To insist on the rightness of everything Jung wrote, regardless of its value to us, is

---

20 LFT 353, RE 533.

dogmatic, and thus we must be prepared to critically sort what we read. My chief concern is actually that readers of the *Red Book* do go through a critical process which both recognises its positive value and also does not assume that everything in it must be of positive value – for the Middle Way does not just consist in lapping up the words of the Wise Old Man. If you reach different conclusions from mine about what is helpful and unhelpful, then fine (I'm not the Wise Old Man either), but at all costs do differentiate. The method is far more important than the results.

It is, of course, possible to interpret the Seven Sermons, like any other ostensibly metaphysical material, in relatively helpful ways. Drob, for example, offers what he calls a psychological reading.

> *We can understand the 'Seven Sermons' as a discourse on the human psyche. As we have seen, in this view, the 'dead' are not so much those who have literally died, but rather the living, who have completely identified with reason and the material life, have become dead to their souls. When Jung/Philemon speaks to the dead about the Pleroma and Abraxas, it is not only to awaken them to the infinite and terrifying foundation of the cosmos, a foundation that can neither be 'rationalised' nor 'explained', but, more importantly, to awaken us to the ineffable ground of our own being in an unconscious that is infinitely wider than any of our individual selves and about which nothing definite can be said or understood. Talk about the infinite Pleroma and its transcendence yet immanence within the human psyche is designed to awaken us to the great mystery of our own being and shake us from our rational/ scientific and skeptical slumbers.*[21]

However, this supposed 'psychological' reading is still riddled with metaphysical language, as well as being embedded in Drob's perpetual dualism between religious metaphysics and 'reason'. So further interpretation yet will be required to make it genuinely phenomenal. The supposed 'foundation of the cosmos' to which the deluded are to be awakened presumably refers in experience to an embodied awareness, and 'the ineffable ground of our own being in an unconscious' to our sense of potential identifications in a wider psyche beyond our current egoistic identifications. Drob goes on

> *Jung compared the relationship of the unconscious (Self) to the conscious ego with the relationship between the Gnostics' 'blessed, non-existent God' and the 'demiurge', whom the Gnostics disparaged as being ignorant of its pleromatic origins. The demiurge, which…the Gnostics identified with the*

---

21 Drob (2012) pp. 245–6.

> *Creator God of the Bible, represents the conscious, rational ego, which in its arrogance believes that it is both the creator and master of the human personality.*[22]

Yes, it is possible to interpret the Seven Sermons in experientially relevant ways, and perhaps that is what Jung would have wanted us to do. But why should we, or indeed, the dead (in the sense of the most deluded people in modern society), *wish* to do such a thing? The advantage of reinterpreting symbols such as that of Christ in Christianity is culturally dependent, and allows the archetypal resonances of that symbol, for those rooted in Christian culture, to be linked to psychological experience. But nobody is rooted in Gnostic culture. Gnosticism is effectively a dead religion, and its revival can thus at best be a deracinated and somewhat forced exercise. Once again, the dead gain no advantage by swapping Christian metaphysics for Gnostic metaphysics, and if Gnostic metaphysics is to be psychologically interpreted as a matter of symbol, it loses the rooted value of Christian symbols for the Christian dead, without offering any alternative rooted or experiential value for the vast majority of people in modern society. A practical argument for Gnosticism depends on practical effectiveness, but it has practically none, and an abstract allegorical equivalence between Gnostic symbols and elements of the psyche can hardly substitute for the practical meaninglessness of those symbols.

Again, a parallel with Western Buddhism may be obvious. The importation of Buddhism into the West has borne some resemblances to Jung's project of reviving Gnosticism, except that it has had far more practical success. Just as in Jung's use of Gnosticism, the metaphysical elements in Buddhism (such as enlightenment, the Four Noble Truths, karma, and rebirth) can be interpreted psychologically. Unlike Gnosticism, however, Buddhism was not a dead religion, but merely a culturally remote one in the context of the West. Nevertheless its adoption has raised similar issues. You can interpret it psychologically, but why should one prefer the reinterpretation of a culturally strange metaphysical language to the reinterpretation of a culturally familiar metaphysical language? It is hard to resist the conclusion, in both cases, that a projection of positive qualities onto the exotic often plays an unhelpful part.

---

22 Ibid. p. 247.

11.e. Jungian agnosticism

However, let me finish this chapter on a more positive note. The Jungian Middle Way, as a positive insight, is a positive achievement beside which Jung's aberration right at the end of the *Red Book* is of scant significance. We have already traced the Jungian Middle Way in a host of different ways, but its strongest expression throughout is its practical realisation through Jung's own path of integration. As part of that path he continually adjusts his awareness of the archetypal figures with which he interacts – Elijah, Salome, the Soul, Ammonius, the Red One, and so on – from projected assumptions to gradually more adequate recognition of his own desires and assumptions. In avoiding those assumptions he is continually tacking from one extreme of interpretation to another and finding middle ground. Is Elijah the fount of all wisdom, or just a deflated old man? Is Salome an object of love or hatred? Is Ammonius a saint or a deluded obsessive?

It is only by *not knowing* these extremes that Jung can return to the ambiguous ground in between, in which he can acknowledge the constructed nature of these figures and the ways in which his portrayals of them are effects of his own desires and beliefs. An integrative process is one that can only occur by *not knowing* at each new stage, to avoid rigidification of one's responses. The Jungian Middle Way, like the Middle Way in any other context, is overwhelmingly *agnostic*. Jung's process and method very clearly do not involve penetrating to ultimate truths beyond delusion, but rather casting off delusions in order to adopt new provisional beliefs at each turn. There is no deduction from a final truth in his method, but rather an open journey.

So, if Jung really thought he was a Gnostic, he was deluded or confused in that respect, and in that respect he betrayed his own best insights. Let us be clear about that, for practical purposes: the Jungian Middle Way is not Gnostic, it is agnostic. Let's quote Jung himself once again:

> *The only true basis for philosophy is what we experience ourselves, and through ourselves, of our world around us. Every a priori structure that converts our experience into an abstraction must inevitably lead us to erroneous conclusions.*[23]

---

23 CW Supplementary volume A §175.

12. Towards a Jungian Integrative Ethic

12.a. Jung as a moral thinker

That Jung was strongly motivated by ethical concerns from early in his life is brought out by Papadopoulos in a discussion of Jung's early Zofingia lectures:

> Following Kant's primacy of morality, Jung criticised science and materialism for 'poisoning morality' (§137) and declared that 'no truth obtained by unethical means has the moral right to exist' (§138). Jung's strong feelings are reflected in the emphatic language he used in order to press his point; he went as far as advocating 'a "revolution from above" by forcing morality on science...for after all scientists have not hesitated to impose their scepticism and moral rootlessness on the world' (§138). The strong moral foundation of epistemology that Jung established in these lectures was to remain with him until the end of his life. Throughout, he was passionate that no production of knowledge should be placed above ethical considerations.[1]

While most scientists and analytic philosophers to this day rely on a crude fact-value distinction that is not adequate to the complex interaction of factual and value beliefs in experience, Jung from the beginning was clearly unwilling to accept this simplistic model. Even if his early expressions of this approach were crude, we can see that by the time of the *Red Book*, he was beginning to gather the resources he needed to develop a credible alternative model of the relationship between 'knowledge' and 'ethics' in the shape of the Jungian Middle Way.

Jung is an overwhelmingly moral thinker, and his thinking has enormous moral implications, but one could completely miss this point by reading most of the existing literature on Jung. On the one hand, Jung has been largely discussed and interpreted by therapists who see the paradigmatic practice in which Jung is applied as a therapeutic one – even though Jungian therapy is a highly specialised pursuit engaged in only by a very small minority of people.

---

1   Papadopoulos (2006) p. 17.

On the other hand, those academics who have engaged with Jung more philosophically are likely to either interpret him in line with a metaphysical system that they favour (e.g. Drob), or defend him as a scientist whom they see (at best) as having a distinctively balanced attitude to gaining an understanding of the facts (e.g. Kotsch[2]). Ethicists, for their part, also seem to have totally ignored Jung as a source of ethical thought – with very few exceptions.[3] Jung's own self-presentation in the works published during his lifetime have also probably not helped people to see his moral relevance, but in the *Red Book* these moral dimensions become increasingly clear. Jungian ethics, unlike Jungian therapy, is potentially relevant to everyone in all circumstances.

The 'way' as Jung describes it in the *Red Book* is implicitly ethical throughout, because it involves *normativity* – the belief that it is better to follow the way than to deviate from it. Those who assume that it is not ethical may do so on the basis of various narrow assumptions about what 'ethics' consists in. Some assume that 'ethics' involves only the application of moral rules, or the cultivation of particular virtues in limited social context or tradition where those virtues are valued. In modern parlance a complex web of substitutes for explicit ethics has developed, where normative judgements are instead masked by spirituality, political correctness or progressiveness, rationality, the valuing of evidence, empathy, professionalism, or aesthetic fulfilment – all of which tend to use the ethical vocabulary of 'good', 'right', 'ought', and 'should'. Jungian integration is yet another of these potential masks for ethics. It is important to face up to this and develop adequately open and experiential models for ethics in the face of Jung's work, rather than denying its ethical importance on the basis of an impoverished model of what ethics consists in, or seeking refuge behind any of these various masks.

In doing so we will be improving on the confusion Jung himself created in his vain pursuit of academic respectability by claiming that his work was solely empirical. Despite this, even in his psychological works Jung's language is often implicitly moral, and occasionally explicitly so. For example, he calls the 'union of conscious and unconscious in the individuation process' 'the real core of the

---

2 Kotsch (2000).
3 Two striking exceptions are Neumann (1990) and Colacicchi (2015).

ethical problem'.[4] In the *Red Book*, though, we have the privilege of seeing a Jung prepared to engage more consistently in moral language, even though he never goes as far as explicit moral theory.

That moral language is usually rooted in personal experience of an integration process, which is then universalised in a prophetic style. The moral element may appear as an imperative, for example

Quietly look into everything that excites your contempt or rage.[5]

Will yourself, that leads to the way.[6]

Or it may take the form of a universal wish, using models like 'may' or 'must':

May the frightfulness become so great that it can turn men's eyes inwards, so that their will no longer seeks the self in others but in themselves.[7]

But there is occasionally even the explicit use of terms like 'good' in a prescriptive sense:

If you succeed in making a terrible evil out of this war and throw innumerable victims into this abyss, this is good, since it makes each of you ready to sacrifice himself. For as I, you draw close to the accomplishment of Christ's mystery.[8]

To make a coherent moral perspective out of the moral language of the *Red Book*, however, requires me to build on the discussions in the rest of this book on the Middle Way and the process of integration, drawing out their moral implications and highlighting the specific points where Jung does make statements that cast light on that moral approach. The ethics of the *Red Book* is a Middle Way ethics.

12.b. Middle Way ethics

A Middle Way ethics recognises ethical valuation as an important part of our experience, indivisible from the rest, but at the same time avoids the acceptance of absolute statements of such ethical valuation. Much of the Western ethical tradition has laboured under the unnecessary assumption that ethics is intrinsically absolute, and in

---

4 CW 18 §1419, also quoted by Colacicchi (2015) p. 6.
5 LS 11, LFT 265, RE 232.
6 LP vii(r), LFT 254, RE 204.
7 Ibid.
8 LP vii(r), LFT 254, RE 203.

that respect thus intrinsically distinct from non-absolute empirical claims. However, ethical valuation, understood in terms of embodied meaning or the Jungian image, is *the valuation of an embodied person at a specific time*, just as a factual claim forms the belief of a specific person at a specific time. Whether we see them primarily as 'facts' or 'values' the conditions for the justification of our beliefs are similar: namely an avoidance of absolute assumptions as well as the support of evidence and/or consistency with our other beliefs. Far from being an unobtainable and therefore 'queer' absolute,[9] a moral belief thus gains greater justification from the *avoidance* of absolutes.

Those absolutes in the moral realm can be analysed in terms of the three dominant theoretical formulations of normative ethics: deontology (ethical values expressed by rules or principles), consequentialism (ethical values expressed by goals), and virtue ethics (ethical values expressed by states of character). Any of these can be interpreted absolutely, *or* in relation to other values. For example, a moral conviction that lying is always wrong constitutes an absolute deontological belief, making a prohibition on lying into an iron rule. However, if one also recognises that the value we attribute to the avoidance of lying can be compromised in relation to other values (such as important goals or virtues), one can still maintain a general appreciation for the wrongness of lying without this being absolute. Thus, one might compromise the prohibition of lying in order to avoid traumatising someone (a valuable goal), or to reinforce a sense of compassion for someone who would suffer from tactless honesty. A mature and relatively *integrated* ethics acknowledges all these different values and the complexity of the moral experience that surrounds them, avoiding a simple representational view about the overriding nature of a particular principle – one that after all depends for its interpretation on our bodies, metaphors, and context.

Such an account of ethics also reflects the interdependency of the different elements of the Noble Eightfold Path taught by the Buddha. Some elements of that path are obviously 'ethical' in a narrower sense, such as Right Action, Right Speech, and Right Livelihood. Buddhists have traditionally thought of these elements of the path in terms of the following of precepts, which are deontological in structure even though they are often thought of as more flexible than

---

9   The analytic philosophical perspective of Mackie (1977) pp. 38 ff.

moral rules. However, these moral practices need to be interpreted in terms of other elements of the path that are related to wisdom and meditation: Right View, Right Aspiration, Right Concentration, Right Mindfulness, and Right Effort. These imply that rule-following cannot be an end in itself, but that our judgements about how to act also depend on the cultivation of our habitual mental states and the avoidance of bias and delusion. The more that Buddhist Ethics is interpreted in the wider context of the path as a whole, rather than the narrow context of specific rules governing behaviour, the more we tend to move towards a Middle Way ethics.

So far, this account of Middle Way ethics is the one that I have developed myself, with some Buddhist inspirations, and articulated in more detail in previous books.[10] However, what I hope to do in the remainder of this chapter is to show how much Jung's implicit ethics in the *Red Book* reflects it. In his valuation of the messy middle ground, Jung constantly warns us off absolute interpretations not only of moral rules or principles, but also of goals and virtues. The result is not a set of final answers about how to act – that is not the nature of Middle Way ethics – but rather a set of warnings about moral prejudices we need to avoid if we want to lead our lives in a more adequate fashion. It is the avoidance process of the Middle Way that constitutes the universal element of Middle Way ethics, but within the extremes avoided, an area of discretion remains, so that positive moral choices can still vary between each individual in each situation without being any less justified in Middle Way terms.

12.c. Integration and responsibility

The extent of our responsibility is one of the most central moral issues tackled by Jung in this way in the *Red Book*. Where a philosopher might begin by looking for metaphysical grounds for responsibility (of a kind that he would never be able to find), Jung deals rather with the sense of responsibility that we already experience as embodied beings. That spontaneous sense of responsibility in a particular case can be unhelpfully absolutised either as a total responsibility or as its absence if we only focus on abstract metaphysical ideas about responsibility. Jung, on the other hand, is at pains to

---

10 Ellis (2012a) section 7.

encourage recognition of both the potential extent and the potential limitations of that responsibility in practical experience.

One extreme of responsibility is shown in the sacrificial murder scene already discussed in chapter 4. Here Jung acknowledges that he shares in the guilt for the sacrificial murder, ritually enacting this acknowledgement by eating the liver. As Jung explains this,

> *Man must recognise his complicity in the act of evil. He must bear witness to this recognition by eating from bloody sacrificial flesh. Through this act he testifies that he is a man, that he recognises good as well as evil.*[11]

In other words, there can be no absolute boundaries, and no denial of our moral experience, if we are to adopt attitudes that are adequate to recognising our embodiment. The greatest atrocities have their place in my psyche because they are meaningful to me, just as they are meaningful to others. Even if I never personally commit such atrocities, the shadow in my psyche encompasses them, so I take greater responsibility by integrating the shadow and acknowledging this, rather than repressing that meaning.

At the other extreme of responsibility, however, lies Jung's recognition of the personal limitation on what we can actively take responsibility for. We cannot take responsibility for the whole world, for that involves an implicit denial of the limitations of our bodies and a merely abstract extension of our agency to that of the whole of humanity. That way lies neurotic guilt, in which my sense of responsibility is in conflict with my sense of powerlessness.

> *You know how extravagantly nature strews human life and force on barren deserts. You should not lament this, otherwise you will become a prophet, and will seek to redeem what cannot be redeemed. Do you not know that nature also dungs its fields with men? Take in the seeker, but do not go out seeking those who err. What do you know about their error? Perhaps it is sacred. You should not disturb the sacred. Do not look back and regret nothing. You see many near you fall? You feel compassion? But you should live your life, since then at least one in a thousand will remain. You cannot halt dying.*[12]

Jung here portrays a crucial element of Middle Way ethics, that along with no *a priori* bounds to responsibility, there is also a full recognition of the embodied limitations of our action. This offers a strong challenge to, for example, those utilitarians who insist that

---

11 LS 77, LFT 291, RE 323.
12 LS 74/5, LFT 289–90, RE 318–19.

we should take responsibility for every starving child on the other side of the world, since every omission is a morally culpable act. Such claims are psychologically naïve, since if we want to develop a psychologically realistic understanding of how we can actually improve our moral practice, a recognition of our psychological as well as our physical limitations is important. If I give attention to helping starving children on the other side of the world, that will be good, but at the same time I will be omitting some other praiseworthy, and equally possible, use of my attention and energy.

Jung also here urges a recognition of the limitations of our knowledge of others. We never know for sure that others are wrong, so the energy put into correcting them is probably wasted, unless they are motivated to change and are on a sufficiently similar path to yours. The biases of responsibility, by which we tend to attribute total responsibility to others when they do badly but zero responsibility when they do well,[13] here need to be counteracted by wider awareness.

The balancing process between these two extremes of responsibility is also reflected in the striking scene in which Jung asks his soul 'to dive down into the floods' and pledges to accept everything she brings up. The soul finds all sorts of things from 'old armour' and 'rusty gear' to 'fratricide' and 'epidemics', and Jung says he will accept it all until she finds the positive things too – 'treasures of all past cultures'. Jung then realises that he must limit himself, and his soul instructs him to 'Be content and cultivate your garden with modesty'.[14]

The development of responsibility is a function of our integration, with different conditions being associated with potentially conflicting desires and beliefs that we can thus address better by reconciling them. We become integrated so as to deal with more conditions by accepting everything, but effective in responding to those conditions by limiting ourselves. Yet it is so easy to absolutise either our acceptance or our restriction. The extent of the garden that we can cultivate will vary hugely between different individuals, yet to keep stretching both its extent and its degree of cultivation is the practice of the way.

---

13 Discussed further in Ellis (2015) 3.f.
14 LS 124, LFT 305–6, RE 374–5.

12.d. Self and other

In the *Red Book* there are also a number of references to the extremes of assumption about the relationship between ourselves and others. The popular moral model that evil consists in 'selfishness', and that good is 'selfless' is effectively revealed as simplistic and confused. This popular model may lead to people objecting to internal reflection or assuming it to be self-indulgent, when 'internal' reflection may be precisely what is needed to develop the awareness required to overcome projection. If we are caught up in projection, then 'external' action that is apparently other-directed may have very narrow and deluded motives that treat others only in terms of one particular limited construction of who they are.

> *If you give up yourself, you live it in others; thereby you become selfish to others, and thus you deceive others.*[15]

Jung here tries to appropriate and adapt the vocabulary of 'selfishness', and interpret it in terms of a lack of self-awareness that leads us to project onto others.

However, the habit of thinking that our 'thoughts' (or internal experiences) are intrinsically ours, and things perceived through our senses are 'other' is deeply rooted. Jung begins to engage with it in his first discussions with Elijah.

> *E: Will you therefore confuse yourself with a tree or animal, because you look at them and because you exist with them in one and the same world? Must you be your thoughts, because you are in the world of your thoughts? But your thoughts are just as much outside your self as trees and animals are outside your body.*
>
> *I: I understand. My thought world was for me more word than world. I thought of my thought world: it is I.*[16]

Jung's 'more word than world' offers a reminder of the relationship between this assumption and representationalism. If the meaning of my language is taken to depend on a relationship to reality, symbols that appear internally can only get their meaning hypothetically, so that the meaning of Elijah's words is only meaningful in the sense that we could potentially relate it to reality. Elijah becomes a mere

---

15 LP vi(r), LFT 249, RE 188.
16 LP vi(r), LFT 249, RE 186.

hypothetical shadow of actual wise old men. However, if the meaning of Elijah emerges from the bodies of those who meet him or read about him, there is no intrinsic difference between the meaning of an 'internal' or an 'external' wise old man. On the one hand, then, internal figures can be outside the 'self' in the sense of challenging the ego, whilst on the other, external figures can be inside the 'self' in the sense of being mere constructions of the ego.

The moral implications of this become clearer in quotations like the following:

> *If you are aggravated against your brother, think that you are aggravated against the brother in you, that is, against what in you is similar to your brother.*
>
> *As a man you are part of mankind, and therefore you have a share in the whole of mankind, as if you were the whole of mankind. If you overpower and kill your fellow man who is contrary to you, then you also kill that person in yourself and have murdered a part of your life.*[17]

We should care about others *because* we care about ourselves, and we should care about ourselves because we care about others. This is not just an appeal to enlightened self-interest, that we will benefit in the end from a better attitude to others, nor is it an appeal to consistent rationality in our view of self and others, of the kind Kant put forward. Rather it is a recognition of the ways in which the very meaning of another, and thus the strength of our emotional responses to them, depend on our own inner representations of them. By conflicting unnecessarily with another, we conflict with a part of ourselves, and by integrating that conflict either internally or externally we follow a moral imperative.

Jung's view of self and other thus provides us with a helpful reinterpretation of the traditional association of moral goodness with love for others. That reinterpretation allows us to see integration, instead, as the moral goal, and that often integration of projected archetypes is what enables us to love others and avoid what is commonly seen as 'selfishness'. We have already encountered this point in chapter 7, where I linked its resolution to the Buddhist practice of the Brahmaviharas. Nevertheless, given the individuality of the path, there may also be occasions when conflict with others is an unavoidable part of the conditions (as often with a conscripted

---

17 LP vii(r), LFT 253, RE 200.

12.e. The Middle Way on moral rules

The implication of Jung's ethical stance in the *Red Book* on moral rules is plainly that they are not absolute, but nevertheless that we should not turn to a perverse antinomianism in reaction to them. The rules address certain conditions, but clearly those conditions also vary.

> *If you act from your humanity, you act from that particular situation without general principle, with only what corresponds to the situation. Thus you do justice to the situation, perhaps at the expense of a general rule. That should not be too painful for you, because you are not the rule. There is something else that is human, something all too human, and whoever has ended up there will do well to remember the blessing of the general rule. For the general rule also has meaning and has not been set up for fun. It comprises much venerable work of the human spirit.*[18]

It is clear from this that the only justifiable basis of a moral judgement is a response to the particular conditions of that situation. Any moral rule, after all, will be based on a representation of the situation that is dependent on a cognitive model and metaphorical structure, and we cannot rely on it being an accurate representation of reality. However, in arriving at the best response to that particular situation, an important part of the meaning resources we draw on will consist in moral rules. Given the importance of moral rules to social behaviour and the fact that they have been inculcated into us from childhood, this is hardly surprising. In many cases, we will obey a moral rule because it provides by far the best available response to a situation, drawing on a great weight of previous social experience. For example, the general taboo on sexual behaviour between adults and children is highly meaningful to us because of the weight of social experience on which it is based, and belief in its importance can be further buttressed in more recent times by the psychological evidence of the degree of harm to children that may well result if that taboo is broken. Such a rule, then, may remain overwhelmingly strong in practice even when it is not absolute in theory. Its strength

---

18 LS 10, LFT 264, RE 230.

in practice means that we would most probably produce a great many conflicts, both in ourselves and others, by disobeying it.

If the rule is followed, however, it is *because* of its human implications, rather than despite them. The abstract imposition of left-hemisphere based rules is clearly rejected. In *Scrutinies*, Jung identifies absolute left-hemisphere rules with the rule of the gods.

> There is no longer any unconditional obedience, since man has stopped being a slave to the Gods. He has dignity before the Gods. He is a limb that even the Gods cannot do without. Giving way before the Gods is no more. So let their wish be heard. Comparison shall accomplish the rest so that each will have his appropriate part.[19]

'Comparison' here is important. It is not that the gods are necessarily disobeyed, as that their rules are subject to comparison with alternatives, introducing an element of provisionality. This looks like rebellion, which shocks the character of Elijah and even the character of Jung's soul, but his soul then admits that 'the Gods need a human mediator and rescuer',[20] because otherwise the rules of the gods become absolutisation. 'The Gods are even happy to turn a blind eye from time to time, since basically they know very well that it would be bad for life if there were no exception to eternal law.'[21] Here we need to think about the more common examples of rigid rules that are more evidently in need of breaking: perhaps occasions when pointless honesty would be unkind, or killing would bring relief from great suffering, or stealing would sustain life.

One of the major problems created by reliance on moral rules, however, is their tendency to conflict. The problem of moral dilemmas is one that has long exercised philosophers. The conflict between principles is one that is symbolised in the *Red Book* by the battle between two serpents.

> The rock separates day and night. On the dark side lies a big black serpent, on the bright side a white serpent. They thrust their heads towards each other, eager for battle. Elijah stands on the heights above them. The serpents pounce on one another and a terrible wrestling ensues. The black serpent seems to be stronger; the white serpent draws back. Great billows of dust rise from the place of struggle. But then I see: the black serpent pulls itself back again. The

19 LFT 358, RE 549.
20 LFT 358, RE 548.
21 LFT 359, RE 551.

front part of its body has become white. Both serpents curl about themselves, one in light, the other in darkness.[22]

The result of this battle seems to be a dialectical one. It is not that the light simply conquers the dark, or just that the white serpent is adapted to the light and the black serpent to the dark. Rather the black serpent takes on some of the features of the white even in the dark. In the same way we should not treat principles of good as absolute nor principles of evil as wholly to be rejected. The 'good' may have something to impart to 'evil' that takes into account wider conditions, but that does not consist in a simple victory. There are principles of 'good' that we would be better following in general – for example, to look after our health, to care for our ageing parents, or to refrain from anger – but these gain their power from addressing conditions that include the dark and immoral, not from the verbal rule alone. Those who do not obey them would do well to take them on board and thus address wider conditions, but only in relation to the conditions of darkness in which they need to operate.

Jung's account of the solution to the battle between the serpents seems to rely very strongly on intuition:

> *If you will one of these principles, so you are in one, but far from your being other. If you will both principles, one and the other, then you excite the conflict between the principles, since you cannot want both at the same time. From this arises the need, the God appears in it, he takes your conflicting will in his hand, in the hand of a child whose will is simple and beyond conflict. You cannot learn this, it can only develop in you. You cannot will this, it takes the will from your hand and wills itself.*[23]

Jung expresses a similar point later in his psychological works:

> *If one is sufficiently conscientious the conflict is endured to the end, and a creative solution emerges which is produced by the constellated archetype and possesses that compelling authority not unjustly characterized as the voice of God. The nature of the solution is in accord with the deepest foundations of the personality as well as with its wholeness; it embraces conscious [sic] and unconscious and therefore transcends the ego.*[24]

If one thinks only in terms of immediate action, moral action to reconcile contradictory principles may well seem beyond willing, a

---

22 LP vi(v), LFT 251, RE 194.
23 LP vii(r), LFT 254, RE 204.
24 CW 10, §856.

matter of creatively stepping back and allowing new understanding to arise. The main reason for this, if one understands the situation in relation to embodied meaning, is that our immediate thinking is likely to be left-hemisphere driven and to remain contained within a particular cognitive model and/or assumptions about the situation. It is only by stepping back and relaxing the conflict in that currently conceptualised form that new ways forward may occur to us.

However, as Colacicchi argues,[25] this approach probably puts more emphasis on intuition than Jung needs to place, and gives insufficient attention to the role of conscious reasoning, because Jung is thinking of what we 'will' in the immediate context as limited by convention (or perhaps just by habit). What Jung often does not seem to take into account is that we can become consciously aware of the limitations of a particular cognitive framework and thus aware of the need for an alternative, even if we do not have access to it at that moment. We can overcome moral conflicts through a combination of deliberate strategy and tactical relaxation, but rarely just through one or the other, as recognised in the Buddhist concept of 'balanced effort', which places relaxation of the conscious will within a consistent wider framework of intention.[26]

If we want to follow an overall ethical principle that we recognise as overriding, then, but find it clashing with alternatives, we should not simply recruit one serpent to conquer the other. Rather we need to become sufficiently aware of both principles and the context in which they operate. It may become clear to us just in the context of reflection that a reframing of the principles is required to reconcile them with each other, or alternatively that one principle is overwhelmingly superior but perhaps just needs to be applied differently in a different context. If we do not easily find such a resolution, a deliberate relaxation of that reflection, with wider integrative practice, may be needed, after which a new creative resolution may emerge more intuitively.

12.f. Forethinking and the paradox of hedonism

Apart from going a fair way towards finding a Middle Way on rules (or deontological ethics), the *Red Book* also goes a good way towards

---

25 Colacicchi (2015) p. 69.
26 See Ellis (2012b) 4.a for further details.

finding a similar balance on goal-oriented approaches to ethics, otherwise known as consequentialism. Consequentialism takes certain types of goals, corresponding to a certain description, as being good goals: the most common form being utilitarianism, which in its classic form takes 'the greatest pleasure of the greatest number' to be definitive of good goals. Consequentialism very much raises the question of how we know those goals to be good, as well as how we identify them in practice, and the *Red Book* discusses some of the underlying psychological conditions of this in the context of Jung's reflections on his first encounter with Elijah and Salome.

It is here that Jung discusses 'forethinking', which seems to mean goal-driven representational planning, in relation to pleasure, which is the actual appreciative feeling for the thing one had as a goal. This distinction is very much a left hemisphere versus right hemisphere distinction, with the goal-driven left hemisphere maintaining an abstract view of the object of desire that it is focused on achieving, but not an appreciation of the desire itself.[27] It is the right hemisphere that is actually capable of engaging in sensual appreciation.

The 'paradox of hedonism' or 'hedonic treadmill' is the product of this disjunction, as supported by more recent psychological research. This is the phenomenon that we tend to undermine our experience of pleasure by the pursuit of it. Research by Fujita and Diener identified a tendency of stability in our levels of pleasure regardless of the fulfilment of our goals: thus, for example, a rise in income is unlikely to make us happier in the long-term, because we merely normalise the new levels of wealth and these produce the same levels of pleasure that we had before. The set point of happiness fluctuates in the long term for only about 9% of the population.[28] Anyone who believes that it is definitively good to achieve pleasure needs to face up to the basic difficulty this creates, namely that our action to produce pleasure is overwhelmingly fruitless, and we often deceive ourselves by mistaking the formally represented attainment of goals for actual appreciation of the fruits of those goals.

For Jung, forethinking is symbolised by Elijah and pleasure by Salome, particularly because he is perplexed by their mutually-dependent relationship. How can the seductive but murderous

---

27 McGilchrist (2009) p. 55.
28 Fujita and Diener (2005).

Salome, who demanded the head of John the Baptist as the reward for erotic dancing, be so linked to the wise and morally severe prophet? But Elijah affirms that 'I and my daughter have been one since eternity'.[29] Jung ends his first discussion with Elijah and Salome in a confused state: 'Doubt tears me apart'.[30] At one and the same time he recognises that he loves and fears Salome, and he associates this with his murder of the hero, but he also 'stuck to Elijah as being the most reasonable of the lot'.[31]

Of course, the hero represents the goal-driven ego, and, as discussed above in chapter 8, by 'murdering' the hero Jung has deprived forethinking of the absolute status it likes to assume, given the general dominance of the left hemisphere. In the goal-driven world, the object of desire itself – the experience of pleasure – must either be idealised or rejected. However, the maturation of the hero into the wise old man allows him to accept pleasure as not merely reducible to these extremes, and maintain a wider awareness of the experience of pleasure itself as opposed to merely the goal-driven relationship with the idea of it. The loving relationship between Elijah and Salome represents the reconciliation of ends and means, of goals and process. The hero rescuing the stereotyped passive maiden has matured into a symbolic subject who appreciates process as well as goals, together with an anima figure who reflects the complexity and ambiguity of pleasure as we actually experience it. Coming to respect and appreciate this relationship reflects Jung's own integration process.

This symbolic process of integration is also reflected in Jung's more theoretical reflections on forethinking and pleasure:

> *One cannot live with forethinking alone, or with pleasure alone. You need both. But you cannot be in forethinking and in pleasure at the same time, you must take turns being in forethinking and pleasure, obeying the prevailing law, unfaithful to the other so to speak. But men prefer one or the other. Some love thinking and establish the art of life on it. They practise their thinking and their circumspection, so they lose their pleasure. Therefore they are old and have a sharp face. The others love pleasure, and they practise their feeling and living. Thus they forget thinking. Therefore they are young and blind. Those who think base the world on thought, those who feel, on feeling. You find truth and error in both.*

29 LP v(v), LFT 246, RE 176.
30 LP v(v), LFT 246, RE 177.
31 LFT/RE footnote 161, quoting from Jung's 1925 seminar.

> *The way of life writhes like the serpent from right to left and from left to right, from thinking to pleasure and from pleasure to thinking. Thus the serpent is an adversary and a symbol of enmity, but also a wise bridge that connects right and left through longing, much needed by our life.*[32]

Jung's reflections here foreshadow his theory of character types, with the disjunction between thinking types and feeling types. The old people with sharp faces also prefigure the scholar discussed in chapter 9. More striking than anything about this passage, though, is Jung's degree of anticipation of the roles of the left and right hemispheres. As he says, we cannot 'think' and 'feel' at the same time – because, in the sense they are being used here, one implies a left-hemisphere dominant state and the other a right-hemisphere dominant state. The integration of the two perspectives, then, can only allow us to use the wider awareness offered by the right-hemisphere perspective to connect the isolated assumptions on the basis of which the left hemisphere thinks. The 'wise bridge' is one that has to be constructed by awareness over and over again.

The implication of this for consequentialist moral thinking, then, must be that our calculations for reaching future goals cannot be relied on, even when those future goals are formulated as a result of rigorous thinking about the widest possible benefits. Goals, however carefully justified, are always followed by fallible humans. The paradox of hedonism suggests that these goals are most unlikely to be experienced in quite the way we represent them even when they are 'achieved'. Just as a professional who works hard all her life in anticipation of a pleasant retirement may find herself unable to appreciate that pleasure when she gets there, so a government calculating the economic benefits of a particular policy may find that the actual effects of the policy prove quite different. To more effectively achieve desirable ends, we need to integrate our pursuit of ends with appreciation of the means.

If we consider the ways that such integration may actually impact our judgements, then it has to modify the naïve idealism with which we may become attached to big plans. There is a type of basic conservatism offered here, not necessarily implying political conservatism, but nevertheless incorporating an appreciation of the complex ways in which organic processes operate. Very often we

---

32 LP v(v), LFT 247, RE 181.

need to stop trying to fix things, and simply appreciate that they are as they are in adaptation to a set of complex conditions. The action of the Cabiri represents this slow, silent adaptation of both things around us and our own confidence: 'We complete what is impossible for you,'[33] they say. Jung also offers us a more explicitly counter-revolutionary message:

> *Do not throw yourself against what has become, enraged or bent on destruction. What will you put in its place? Do you not know that if you are successful in destroying what has become, you will then turn the will of destruction against yourself? But anyone who makes destruction their goal will perish through self-destruction. Much rather respect what has become, since reverence is a blessing.*[34]

If you destroy something that has a particular function without having an alternative means of fulfilling that function, then this is obviously self-destructive in the sense that that function will no longer be fulfilled, whether we are talking about order provided by governments, traditional moral theory, family structures, or personal relationships. This point can also be applied to emotional channels: for example, if you merely prohibit some form of sexual expression without providing any substitute, you are likely to merely repress, and thus cause the sexual feeling to seek expression in some other way. Morally, then, we need to think of shifts between alternative goals rather than simply in terms of the moral desirability of one goal or the need to avoid another.

Jung's discussion of magic also reinforces similar conclusions about our relationship with goals. On the face of it, magic is a means of the instant gratification of goals, of a kind that is impossible for psychological as well as physical reasons, because we have right hemispheres that involve process as well as left hemispheres focused on goals. But Jung is led to reconsider this naïve view of magic as he becomes more integrated, especially through his initial expectation-busting conversation with Philemon.[35] Magic is instead a form of creation involving elements of the unexpected: not a mere reproduction of ideas into fulfilment, but the setting in train of an organic process that extends beyond our initial representations. It

---

33 LS 166, LFT 321, RE 426.
34 LS 104, LFT 297, RE 344.
35 LS 139, LFT 139, RE 395 ff.

A Jungian Integrative Ethic 201

does not require us to give up our wishes, but it does require us to allow those wishes to be modified in relation to conditions, so that our destination may end up being quite different from our initial goal. Magic is thus another way of talking about integration.

> *Great is the power of the way. In it Heaven and Hell grow together, and in it the power of the Below and the power of the Above unite. The nature of the way is magical, as are supplication and invocation; malediction and deed are magical if they occur on the great way. Magic is the working of men on men, but your magic action does not affect your neighbour; it affects you first, and only if you withstand it does an invisible effect pass from you to your neighbour. There is more of it in the air than I ever thought. However, it cannot be grasped.*[36]

In another passage, Jung reflects on the image of the charioteer, presumably referring to the image from Plato in which the rational soul is likened to a charioteer driving two horses that represent the passions.[37]

> *But how do I create my charioteer? Or do I want to be my own charioteer? I can guide myself only with will and intention. But will and intention are simply part of myself. Consequently they are insufficient to express my wholeness. Intention is what I can foresee, and willing is to want a foreseen goal. But where do I find the goal? I take it from what is presently known to me. Thus I set the present in place of the future. In this manner, though I cannot reach the future, I artificially produce a constant present. Everything that would like to break into this present strikes me as a disturbance, and I seek to drive it away so that my intention survives. Thus I close off the progress of life. But how can I be my own charioteer without will or intention? Therefore a wise man does not want to be a charioteer, for he knows that will and intention certainly attain goals but disturb the becoming of the future.*[38]

The charioteer model is thus rightly rejected, along with the model of 'rational' ethics that it represents. Reason only ever being as good as the assumptions with which it begins, we have no justification for assuming that a belief reached through 'reason' is adequate to the conditions. Rather, it is our awareness of those prior assumptions and our ability to look beyond them, whether through critical or intuitive awareness, that offer us greater adequacy in our beliefs.

---

36 LS 130, LFT 308, RE 384–5.
37 Plato *Phaedrus* (1973) §246.
38 LS 138–9, LFT 311, RE 394–5.

The charioteer should not simply impose his will on the horses, for sometimes the horses know the way better than he does.

12.g. Cultivation of the integrated self

Much as the *Red Book* has to say about our responses to moral rules and goals, it is perhaps most centrally concerned with virtue. Virtue, after all, is the development of morally positive qualities or tendencies in the individual, and involves a much more holistic and long-term attitude to ethics. To become more virtuous is to become a *better* person than one was before, and the Jungian Middle Way offers a framework for becoming *better* – that is, more integrated or individuated.

One common traditional path for the cultivation of a more integrated self is that of solitude, and it is clear that this is central for Jung. Early in the *Red Book*, the retreat into solitude in pursuit of integration is represented by the desert. In the desert, projection is laid bare, because there is nothing else there to project onto, so one is forced to acknowledge one's conflicting assumptions and thus begin to integrate them. There is no distraction from confrontation with one's motivations. First, as Jung explains, there is boredom.

> *My soul, what am I to do here? But my soul spoke to me and said 'Wait'. I heard the cruel word. Torment belongs to the desert.*[39]

One has to wait and see what arises, rather than forcing the process and imposing goals. For goals will only come from your current awareness, and will not allow the arising of new awareness from beyond it. The torment of the sun in the desert is also a metaphor for the kind of mercilessness with which one must keep waiting and looking without distraction in order to develop further awareness. It is a metaphor for a meditative or contemplative state of a kind that Jung must have entered here. Jung writes that he spent twenty-five nights in this desert,[40] watching and waiting, until finally he encountered his soul, the deeper experience that he had repressed.

Much of Jung's description of his process at this stage will sound familiar to anyone who has ever tried meditation. He struggles

---

39 LP iii(r), LFT 236, RE 141.
40 LP iii(r), LFT 237, RE 145.

with insistent distracting thoughts, because of a conflict between his desire to meditate and to think about other things.

> *How can I order my thinking to be quiet, so that my thoughts, those unruly hounds, will crawl to my feet? How can I ever hope to hear your voice louder, to see your face closer, when all my thoughts howl?*[41]

There is also inspiring language reflecting the delights that can be glimpsed in meditation, addressed to his soul:

> *Let me persist in divine astonishment, so that I am ready to behold your wonders. Let me lay my head on a stone before your door, so that I am prepared to receive your light.*[42]

Later on, too, Jung describes the way in which this waiting on experience can result in a peak of frustration potentially leading into creativity.

> *The way is a highly peculiar standstill of everything that was previously movement, it is a blind waiting, a doubtful listening and groping. One is convinced that one will burst. But the resolution is born from precisely this tension, and it almost always appears where one did not expect it. But what is the resolution? It is always something ancient precisely because of this something new....*[43]

Jung's experience here is so universal that it does not in any way have to be necessarily bound to the specific practice of 'active imagination' that he was using. Rather there are a wide variety of integrative practices that could help to confront us with these unacknowledged parts of ourselves. For example, they could include mindfulness or meditation, immersion in wilderness, artistic practice of many kinds, shamanic journeying, visualisation, focusing, or psychotherapy of various types. All of these kinds of practices may enable new symbols to arise, providing us with new expressive and emotional resources that can be used to help broaden our understanding and thus make our beliefs more adequate.

A moral dilemma remains, however, as to how much emphasis to give to these sorts of practices. The popular prejudice that they are 'self-indulgent' is obviously wide of the mark, as is the idea that internally focused practices are 'solipsistic' (see chapter 2). Most

---

41 LP iii(v), LFT 238, RE 148.
42 LP iii(v), LFT 238, RE 149.
43 LS 138, LFT 311, RE 393.

people need to do *more* internally focused practice, and for them it is social activity that is the soft option. Nevertheless, internally focused practice is not an end in itself, and needs to be part of a balanced integrative practice that also recognises our role in society. Much of Jung's exploration of practice in the *Red Book* deals with the difficulties of finding such a balance. He often emphasises the danger of losing the effectiveness of one's individual practice by trying to fix all the conditions of the world, but nevertheless recognises that social conditions are part of that practice.

On the one hand, Philemon says 'You should not act on the other but on yourself, unless the other asks for your help and opinion',[44] suggesting a limitation of responsibility to cultivating your own garden with modesty (as discussed earlier in this chapter). It is ourselves we can most easily change, whereas the conditions influencing others are overwhelmingly beyond our power in most cases. On the other hand, though, Jung's alarming vision of 'the solitary' in 'the gift of magic' suggests a somewhat ironic view of the extreme lengths to which a sense of solitary mission can go.

> *The solitary speaks: 'Will no one stand by me in this need? Should I leave my work to help you so you can help me again? But how should I help you, if my brew has not grown ripe and strong? It was supposed to help you. What do you hope from me?'*
>
> *Come to us! Why are you standing there cooking up marvels? What can your healing and magical potion do for us? Do you believe in healing potions? Look at life, behold how much it needs you!*
>
> *The solitary speaks: 'Fools, can you not keep watch with me for an hour, until the difficult and long-lasting achieves completion and the juice has ripened?*
>
> *'Just a little longer and fermentation will be complete. Why can't you wait? Why should your impatience destroy the highest opus?'*
>
> *What highest opus? We are not alive; cold and numbness have seized us. Your opus, solitary one, will not be finished for aeons, even if it advances day by day.*
>
> *The work of salvation is endless. Why do you want to wait for the end of this work? ... We will not wait a single night longer; we have persevered long enough.... Abandon the work of salvation, and we will be saved.*[45]

---

44 LFT 343, RE 497.
45 LS 132-4, LFT 309, RE 386-7.

In the end, the solitary abandons his potion with ill grace, calling his critics 'a human swarm' but nevertheless yielding. 'My God, how difficult it is to leave a work unfinished for the sake of men. But for the sake of men, I abstain from being a saviour.'[46] Though tinged with irony, this suggests Jung's recognition that the claims of solitary development are far from absolute and often subject to delusion. Perhaps the most balanced statement on this point in the *Red Book* (ironically) occurs in the context of the Seven Sermons: 'Absence of community is suffering and sickness. Community in everything is dismemberment and dissolution.'[47]

On the one hand it would be easy to see the solitary as deeply deluded and quixotic, but on the other, the most creative responses to conditions often emerge from such solitary creative endeavours. The dilemma emerges from a more general human uncertainty that forms the condition for our moral judgements. The most we can say is that the Middle Way can be applied to this situation by thoroughly examining the arguments on each side in a particular case, rather than merely dismissing one side or the other. The first occasion when either side falls into ad hoc argument that is primarily defensive is a warning sign.

The dilemma of how far to follow an ideal of solitary development that is ultimately contributory to social good is one that also runs throughout the Buddhist tradition. At one extreme, Tibetan Buddhism offers examples of retreats lasting several years, or even the immurement of monks in caves when they are nearing death, so that they can remain entirely focused on the meditative pursuit of virtue in their remaining time.[48] At the other extreme, however, some forms of Buddhism (such as new forms of Ambedkarite Buddhism amongst Dalit communities in India) put a good deal of emphasis on social action to transform society, with individual development having a much more instrumental role. Only one thing seems clear here: that those who take only a purely social or purely individualist path and are dismissive of the alternatives are likely to have gone beyond a mere adaptation to their circumstances, and to have lost touch with the Middle Way as a wider framework.

---

46 LS 134, LFT 309, RE 387.
47 LFT 352, RE 530.
48 http://www.presscluboftibet.org/china-tibet-16/immured-anchorites.htm

12.h. Towards a Jungian integrative ethic

Throughout the *Red Book*, then, we have a fairly consistent attitude towards moral rules, goals, and virtues. This is that these are often important, and in a particular context may be good, but that we need to avoid absolutisation of these rules, goals, or virtues.

One way of understanding the need to avoid absolutisation in thoroughly Jungian terms is that each absolutisation involves a repression of the shadow. Though the maintenance of a particular moral motive may address conditions in a particular context, that will be at the expense of an unsustainable repression of alternative motives that may well address other conditions (in other times and contexts) better. Erich Neumann, who wrote in the late forties (and for whose book Jung wrote a prologue), recognised this problem, which must have been fresh in his mind after the Second World War, just as the similar recognition in the *Red Book* must have responded to the experiences of the First.

> *The absoluteness with which the opposing ideologies offer themselves as a solution to this problem [of confusion about values] is admittedly a 'help' to the conscious mind of an individual who can allow himself to be possessed by one of them. But the psychological law which requires that every fanaticism of the conscious mind shall be compensated by an equally powerful doubt in the unconscious explains why these ideologies have in fact contributed so much to the confusion of our time and so little to its reorientation.*[49]

Avoiding absolutes does not offer us a contrary absolute positive answer – as we would expect, otherwise the whole approach would be contradictory. Rather it yields a range of more justifiable options – options that might well be further prioritised on other, more debatable grounds. The basic human position of embodied uncertainty makes it impossible to recognise the sole 'right' option, because the basis on which it may be judged right depends on the prioritisation of virtues, goals, or rules and on many other contextual features. Nevertheless, we can be confident about the avoidance of *evils* in the form of self-defining absolutisations. We only recognise an evil in practice by moving beyond it, by finding alternatives, not either by emotional rejection or ideological anathema. Of course, our capacity to move beyond evil in this way is also positively boosted by our degree of integration.

---

49 Neumann (1990) p. 28.

It is precisely because of its lack of absolute answers that integrative ethics is also completely practical. Though it might seem superficially more practical to merely follow a moral rule that one believes to be derived from an infallible source, or absolutely prioritise a moral goal, the conflicts likely to follow from such an approach actually make them supremely *im*practical. For example, it is the absolute rules followed by the supposed Islamic State (at the time of writing, in 2017) that have brought almost the entire wrath of the world down on them in contestation, where more carefully interpreted rules of Islam might have avoided doing so. It is also the crude prioritisation of a moral goal, however apparently worthy (such as controlling population numbers, or building a hydroelectric dam), that produces conflict due to unforeseen side-effects, where consideration of the means together with the end might not. To be successful in the medium term, let alone the longer term, we need to address wider conditions as far as we are able, which means integrating the principles we are following. We can only do this *as far as practicable*, not to an indefinite degree, but usually practicability extends further than we initially think it can, because we simply haven't considered the alternatives.

Integrative ethics needs a good deal more development as an approach, but it should be readily apparent that it has strong social and political as well as individual moral applications. All social and political judgements are made by individuals, even if those judgements are then aggregated. When considering whether to vote for a new piece of legislation, for instance, or whether to vote for a party with a manifesto including a range of such legislation, we need to avoid absolutising just as much as we do in more obviously individual decisions. For example, a political candidate's programme is not wrong because of one recent mistake, or because of her association with regions or classes of society that you tend to dislike. Any of these types of reactions are projective absolutisations.

The fact that Jung never formally developed his approach into a formal moral theory, as well as the fact that there are some contrary elements that undermine Middle Way ethics even in the *Red Book* itself, let alone in Jung's other writings, should not undermine the development and practice of a Jungian integrative ethic, because the justification for it is pragmatic rather than being based on an appeal to Jung's intentions. The strength of that pragmatic approach, glimpsed by Jung in his theory of universal archetypes, is that it is reinforced by similar insights in many other contexts – whether Buddhist, Christian, from other religions, scientific, artistic, or from other schools of psychology or philosophy. The Middle Way provides an approach for embodied human judgement to best address conditions – whichever conditions they are and wherever they are found.

Conclusion

It is almost impossible to do anything approaching justice to the riches of the *Red Book* even in a commentary of this length. It is not only a multifaceted work, but also one that switches readily between modes and perspectives: prophecy and comedy; quest and reflection; despair, tension, and breakthrough. If you have not yet read it, I urge you to make your own engagement with it. It will be a different engagement from mine, just as your way is neither mine nor Jung's. That in turn could be merely a stimulus to a still greater challenge: of engaging in your own direct imaginative exploration of the integration process.

For some this book may have been a way into Jung, but for others a way into the Middle Way. The Middle Way for you will begin exactly where you are now and continue from there, with every new judgement an opportunity for integration rather than absolutisation. Jung can offer an inspiration to follow that way, but hardly a systematic guide to it. Though the individual nature of the path limits how much can be said, there is nevertheless a lot more that can be said, particularly about the different forms that absolutisation can take, whether in the form of ideologies, philosophies, religious dogmas, cognitive biases, fallacious assumptions, or social prejudices. There is also much that can be said positively about the different types of integrative practice, whether these work primarily in the sphere of desire, meaning, or belief, as well as the issues surrounding the integration model itself and the various ways it can be misunderstood. There is much more to say.

I have written other books to explore these issues, and founded a society, the Middle Way Society, to promote both the development and practice of the Middle Way. However, despite its antiquity in some respects, the development of clear thought and effective practice of the Middle Way, disentangled from authority claims in Buddhism or any other tradition, is still in its infancy. Academics rarely think in its terms, and it is not widely understood, though at the same time many other traditions of thought and practice connect with it. There is much more to do as well as much more to say. My hope is that Jung's *Red Book* will be a source of imaginative inspiration for many in setting out and continuing along that path for many years to come.

Bibliography

Bair, Deirdre (2003) *Jung: A Biography*. Back Bay Books, New York.
Bartholomeusz, Tessa and De Silva, Chandra, eds. (1998) *Buddhist Fundamentalism and Minority Identities in Sri Lanka*. SUNY Press, Albany.
Bodhi, Bhikkhu (2000) *The Connected Discourses of the Buddha: A New Translation of the Samyutta Nikaya* (2 vols). Wisdom Publications, Boston.
Bolte Taylor, Jill (2006) *My Stroke of Insight: A Brain Scientist's Personal Journey*. Penguin, London.
Cambray, Joseph (2014) '*The Red Book*: Entrances and Exits' from *The Red Book: Reflections on C.G. Jung's Liber Novus* (ed. Kirsch and Hogenson). Routledge, London.
Colacicchi, Giovanni (2015) *Jung and Ethics: A Conceptual Exploration*. PhD thesis, University of Essex. http://repository.essex.ac.uk/16857/1/Colacicchi_G_%202015_Jung%20and%20ethics_PhD%20.pdf
Drob, Sanford L. (2012) *Reading the Red Book: An Interpretive Guide to C.G. Jung's Liber Novus*. Spring Journal Books, New York.
Ellis, Robert M. (2001) *A Buddhist Theory of Moral Objectivity*: PhD thesis, Lancaster University. Also published by the British Library, London and Lulu, Raleigh as *A Theory of Moral Objectivity*.
Ellis, Robert M. (2012a) *Middle Way Philosophy 1: The Path of Objectivity*. Lulu, Raleigh.
Ellis, Robert M. (2012b) *Middle Way Philosophy 2: The Integration of Desire*. Lulu, Raleigh.
Ellis, Robert M. (2013) *Middle Way Philosophy 3: The Integration of Meaning*. Lulu, Raleigh.
Ellis, Robert M. (2015) *Middle Way Philosophy 4: The Integration of Belief*. Lulu, Raleigh.
Ellis, Robert M. (2016) *Parables of the Middle Way*. Lulu, Raleigh.
Ellis, Robert M. (2018) *The Christian Middle Way: The Case for Christian Faith but against Christian Belief*. Christian Alternative, Alresford.
Ellis, Robert M. (2019) *The Buddha's Middle Way: Experiential Judgement in His Life and Teachings*. Equinox, Sheffield.
Ellis, Robert M. (2020) *The Thought of Sangharakshita: A Critical Evaluation*. Equinox, Sheffield.
Ellis, Robert M. (2021) *Archetypes in Religion and Beyond: A Practical Theory of Human Integration and Inspiration*.
Fletcher, Joseph (1966) *Situation Ethics The New Morality*. Westminster John Knox Press, Louiseville.
Fujita, Frank and Diener, Ed (2005) 'Life satisfaction set point: Stability and change'. *Journal of Personality and Social Psychology* 88:1, 158–64. https://doi.org/10.1037/0022-3514.88.1.158

Hogenson, George (2014) 'The wealth of the soul exists in images' from *The Red Book: Reflections on C.G. Jung's Liber Novus* (ed. T. Kirsch and G. Hogenson). Routledge, London and New York.

Ireland, John D. (1990) *The Udana: Inspired Utterances of the Buddha*. Buddhist Publications Society, Kandy.

Johnson, Mark (2007) *The Meaning of the Body*. University of Chicago Press, Chicago.

Johnston, E.H. (trans.) (1972: 2nd edn) *Buddhacarita* of Ashvaghosha. Oriental Books Reprint Corp., New Delhi.

Jung, Carl, *Collected Works* (CW) in 20 volumes (1–20) plus supplements (A etc). Routledge, London.

Jung, Carl (ed. S. Shamdasani) (2009) *The Red Book: Liber Novus*. Norton, New York. (See note at the end of the introduction for bibliographic conventions used in referencing.)

Jung, Carl (1989: rev. edn) *Memories, Dreams, Reflections*. Random House, New York.

Kahneman, Daniel (2010) *Thinking Fast and Slow*. Penguin, London.

Kamalashila (1992) *Meditation: The Buddhist Way of Tranquillity and Insight*. Windhorse, Cambridge.

Knox, Jean (2003) *Archetype, Attachment, Analysis: Jungian Psychology and the Emergent Mind*. Brunner-Routledge, East Sussex.
https://doi.org/10.4324/9780203391525

Kotsch, W. (2000) 'Jung's mediatory science as a psychology beyond objectivism'. *Journal of Analytical Psychology*. 45:2.
https://doi.org/10.1111/1465-5922.00153

Kuhn, Thomas (1996: 3rd edn) *The Structure of Scientific Revolutions*. University of Chicago Press, Chicago.

Lakatos, Imre (1974) 'Falsification and the methodology of scientific research programmes' from *Criticism and the Growth of Knowledge* (ed. I. Lakatos and A. Musgrave). Cambridge University Press, Cambridge.

Lakoff, George (1987) *Women, Fire and Dangerous Things*. University of Chicago Press, Chicago. https://doi.org/10.7208/chicago/9780226471013.001.0001

Lakoff, George and Johnson, Mark (1980) *Metaphors We Live By*. University of Chicago Press, Chicago.

Mackie, J.L. (1977) *Ethics: Inventing Right and Wrong*. Penguin, London.

McGilchrist, Iain (2009) *The Master and His Emissary: The Divided Brain and the Making of the Western World*. Yale University Press, New Haven.

McGuire, W. and Hull, R.F.C. (1987) *Jung Speaking: Interviews and Encounters*. Princeton University Press, Princeton.

Milgram, Stanley (1974) *Obedience to Authority: An Experimental View*. Tavistock Publications, London.

Neumann, Erich, trans. Eugene Rolfe (1990) *Depth Psychology and a New Ethic*. Shambhala, Boston.

Nietzsche, Friedrich (1933) trans. Ernest Rhys, *Thus Spake Zarathustra*. Dent, London.

Nietzsche, Friedrich (1991) trans. Walter Kaufmann, *The Gay Science*. Random House, London.

Ñanamoli, Bhikkhu and Bodhi, Bhikkhu (1995) *The Middle Length Discourses of the Buddha: A New Translation of the Majjhima Nikaya*. Wisdom Publications, Boston.

Nyanaponika Thera and Bodhi, Bhikkhu (1999) *Numerical Discourses of the Buddha: An Anthology of Suttas from the Anguttara Nikaya*. Altamira Press, Walnut Creek, CA.

Olendzki, Andrew (2013) 'Skinny Gotami & the mustard seed'. *Access to Insight (BCBS Edition)*, http://www.accesstoinsight.org/noncanon/comy/thiga-10-01-ao0.html

Papadopoulos, Renos (1997) 'Is teaching Jung within university possible?' *Journal of Analytical Psychology* 42:2.

Papadopoulos, Renos (2006) 'Jung's epistemology and methodology' from *Handbook of Jungian Psychology* (ed. R. Papadopoulos). Routledge, London.

Payutto, P.A. (1992) *Buddhist Economics*. Buddhadhamma Foundation, Bangkok.

Plato, trans. Walter Hamilton (1973) *Phaedrus and Letters VII and VIII*. Penguin, London.

Price, A.F. and Mou-Lam, Wong, trans. (1969) *The Diamond Sutra and the Sutra of Hui Neng*. Shambhala, Boston.

Pullman, Philip (2011) *His Dark Materials* trilogy: *Northern Lights, The Subtle Knife* and *The Amber Spyglass*. Scholastic, New York.

Rolleston, T.W. (1990) *Celtic Myths and Legends*. Courier, Chelmsford, MA.

Saddhatissa, H. (1985) *The Sutta Nipata*. Curzon Press, London.

Salzberg, Sharon (1997) *Loving-kindness: The Revolutionary Art of Happiness*. Shambhala, Boston.

Sass, Louis A. (1994) *The Paradoxes of Delusion*. Cornell University Press, Ithaca.

Siegel, Daniel (2006) *The Mindful Brain: Reflection and Attunement in the Cultivation of Well-being*. Norton, New York.

Siegel, Daniel (2015: 2nd edn) *The Developing Mind: How Relationships and the Brain Shape Who We Are*. Guilford Press, New York.

Taleb, Nassim Nicholas (2012) *Antifragile: Things That Gain from Disorder*. Penguin, London.

Victoria, Brian (1997) *Zen at War*. Weatherhill, New York.

Walshe, Maurice (1995) *The Long Discourses of the Buddha: A Translation of the Digha Nikaya*. Wisdom Publications, Boston.

Zak, Paul J. (2012) *The Moral Molecule*. Bantam Press, New York.

Index

Abraxas, 174, 179, 181
absolutisation, 1, 4–5, 8–9, 17–20, 22, 24–5, **27–32**, 40, 52, 54, 66–8, 70, 72, 79, 83–4, 86, 94, 105, 112, 114, 124, 128, 132–3, 144, 147, 152, 154, 163, 168, 170, 174, 187–8, 190, 194, 206–7
abstraction, 28, 40, 70, 139, 146, 150, 171, 183
Achilles, 134
active imagination, 1, 203
ad hoc argument, 131, 171, 175, 180, 205
ad hominem argument, 108–10
Adam, 84
adaptability, 14, 130, 151
adaptation, 83–4, 200, 205
addiction, 157
adolescence, 118
aesthetic judgement, 97, 120, 185
agape (Christian love), 122
age, 57, 61, 131, 161
Age of Aquarius, 52, 178; see also Platonic months
agnosticism, 160, 170, 172, 175, 176, 183
Aion, 113
Alara Kalama, 18
alchemy, 178
alienation, 140, 163, 166
allegory, 57, 69
Ambedkarite Buddhism, 205
ambiguity, 1–2, 4, 12, 32, 38, 54–5, 64, 76–7, 86, 115, 140, 142, 147, **152–5**, 159, 183, 198
ambivalence, 52
Ammonius, 9, 34, 36, 86, **152–5**, 157–8, 183
amygdala, 32, 128; see also brain

Anabaptists, 3, 162–3
analytical psychology, 2
angel, 53, 151
anima, 7–8, 44–5, 96, 105, **112–26**, 134, 140, 198; see also daughter, maiden, Salome, serpent, soul
animal
  creature, 73, 101, 113, 130, 141, 163–4, 191
  daemon, 118
  'living your animal', 162–3
animus, 44–5, 113, 115, 124, 126; see also anima
Antichrist, 70
antinomianism, 193
anti-semitism, 110
anxiety, 30, 49–50, 72, **102–3**, 119, 153, 160
archetypal functions, 43
archetype, 5–8, 29–30, 36, **42–6**, 47–50, 52, 55–8, 60, 64, 65, 67–71, 73–4, 78, 82, 86, 88–9, 96–7, 100, 102, 105, 110, 113, 115, 125, 127–8, 131–5, 139, 142, 150, 160, 168, 173–5, 177–9, 182–3, 192, 195, 207; see also anima, God, hero, shadow, Wise Old Man
arrow (simile), 27–8
art, 1–2, 4, 44, 56, 84, 98, 119, 121, 203, 208
artwork, 113
asceticism, 9, 18, **22–4**, 34, 102, 116, 128, 143
assumptions, 4, 14, 21, **22–4**, 34, 36, 41, 43, 47, 59, 61, 72, 79, 83, 103, 105, 152, 157–9, 170–2, 180, 183, 187, 196, 199, 201–2, 209
astrology, 69, 178
asymmetrical integration, 157, 175

atheism, 50
atonement, 37, 75, 164
Auerbach, Erich, 76
authority, 4, 19, 20, 33, 59, **66–8**, 135, 195, 209
autonomy, 78, 121, 169
awakening, 19; see also enlightenment

balanced effort, 196
banality, 118–21, 147
baptism, 69
basic categories (of meaning), 142
Baucis, 61, 63
beauty, 38, 48, 101
Beijing, 94
bias, 5, 33, 36, **45**, 58, 67, 70, 111, 143, 163, 171, 188, 190, 209; see also confirmation bias, fallacy, hedonic treadmill
bidirectional tree, **85–7**, 92–3, 155
bird, 117, 122–3
black serpent, 194–5
bliss, 104
blood, 37, 69, 74–5, 79, 100, 155, 164–5, 168–9
Bodhi tree, 82, 103
bodily awareness, 103, 119; see also embodied meaning, embodiment
body, 4, 18, 40, 43–5, 48, 75, 77–9, 100, 105, 112, 119, 127, **140–50**, 151, 155–7, 162–3, 165–7, 191, 195; see also embodied meaning
Bollingen, 156
Bolte Taylor, Jill, 104, 211
boredom, 166–7, 202
Brahma
    abodes of ~ 124–5
    City of ~ 94
Brahma Sahampati, 47, 102
Brahmaviharas, 124–5, 192
brain, 5, **30–3**, 47, 72, 76–7, 79, 106–7, 119, 128, 132, 144, 146–8, 150, 165, 167; see also amygdala, brain lateralisation, left hemisphere, pre-frontal cortex, 'reptilian' brain, right hemisphere, synaptic connections, striatum
brain lateralisation, 5, 148; see also brain
bread, 75–6, 109

Buddha (Siddhartha Gautama), 1, 4, 7, 11, 13, 15, **17–19**, 20–1, 23, 25, 27–9, 31, 33, 35, 47–8, 52, 58, 62, 78, 82–3, 96–7, 102–4, 124–5, 131, 143–4, 161–2, 211–13
Buddha's Middle Way, The, 4
Buddhas, 42, 48, 56, 96, 98
Buddhism, 3–4, 7, **16–20**, 22–4, 27, 29, 40, 48–50, 58, 66, 89, 96, 102, 105, 107, 124–5, 131, 173, 182, 188, 192, 196, 205, 208–9, 211–13
Buddhist Ethics, 188

Cabiri, 106, 155–6, 200
Cambray, Joseph, 36, 88, 211
cannibalism, 74
castle, 118–21, 139, 147, 154
chaos, 72
character types, 199
charioteer, 18, 151, 201, 202
children, 113, 127, 160, 190, 193
Christ, 8, 42, 48, **69–80**, 109, 120, 123, 129, 137, 148, 152, 162, 178, 182, 186; see also Jesus
Christianity, 1, 2, 34–5, 54, 56, 69–70, **71**, 76, 78, 105, 109, 112, 121–2, 173, 179, 182, 208, 211
Christopher, St, 70
church, 34, 157
cinema, 107
circle, 36, 86, 89, 92
circularity of argument, 89, 171
city, 88, 94–6
class-consciousness, 120
cognition, 5, 9, 36, 102, 111, 119, 142, 145, 151, 153, 167, 171, 193, 196, 209; see also emotion, judgement, thinking
cognitive dissonance, 36
cognitive model, 153, 193, 196
cognitive psychology, 5, 111
Colacicchi, Giovanni, 185–6, 196, 211
Collected Works (of Jung), 10, 212
collective unconscious, 42
comedy, 209
Commentary on 'The Secret of the Golden Flower', 94
Communist revolution, 52
compassion, 125, 149, 187, 189; see also loving-kindness
conation, 122

Concerning Mandala Symbolism, 94
conditioning, 24, 155
conditions, 4, 13, 15, **18–19**, 21, 25, 28, 33, 40, 43, 47, 49, 58, 72, 78, 81–3, 88, 92, 101, 124–5, 128–32, 135–8, 141, 143–5, 153–4, 161, 176, 187, 190, 192–3, 195, 197, 200–1, 204–8
confidence, **21–2**, 41, 56, 72, 103, 106, 155–6, 178, 200
confirmation bias, 171
conflict, 5, 8, 15, 19, **20–1**, 30, 36, 41, 52, 54, 65–6, 96, 102–3, 115, 125, 127–8, 143, 148, 179, 189, 192, 194–6, 203, 207
connotation, 142; see also meaning
conscience, 47
consequentialism, 187, 197
conservatism, 199
container schema, 141–2
contemplation, 202
cook (figure in *Red Book*), 77–8, 120, 148, 162
correspondence (in meaning), 142; see also representationalism
cosmic justice, 102
craving (obsessive desire), 63, 72, **101–4**, 105–6, 119, 132, 139, 157, 161, 163, 165–6, 168; see also desire
creation, 90, 99, 174, 200
creativity, 38, 71, 84, 129, 203
credibility, 67, 170
critical thinking, 111; see also credibility, fallacy
crown, 81–2, 123, 136
crucifixion, 70, 72, 74

daemon, 118
Daily Mail, 67
Dalits, 205
dancing, 34, **156–8**, 198
daughter (in castle), 56, 115, **118–21**, 144, 146–7, 198
dead, 3, 9, 65, 71, 106, 127, 132, **159–69**, 173, 176, 178–82
dead metaphor, 31–2, 120, 145, 167
death, 2, 8, 12, 22–3, 25, 27, 31, 37–8, 54, 63, 73–4, 78, 82, 100, 109, 118–19, 127–9, 133, 137–8, 143, 159, **160–2**, 163, 166–7, 205

death of God, 37
death of the hero, 127–9
Deep Ecology, 83
demons, 101–2, 110
denial, 23, 30, 37, 53, 160, 189; see also scepticism
denotation, 142; see also meaning
deontology, 187
desert, 3, 152, 202
desire, 8, 15, 21–2, 25, 32, 34, 43–4, 63, 99, 101–4, **105**, 116–18, 122, 128–30, 133–4, 138, 166, 183, 190, 197–8, 203, 209; see also craving
destitution, **107–8**, 120, 149
destruction, 27, 49, 88, 90, 103, 106, 128, 154, 200
determinism, 24, 142, 172, 180
devil, 20, 34–5, 53, 100–1, 106, 108, 110–11, 156–7; see also demons, Red One, Satan
dialectics, 6, 70, 97, 124, 195
didacticism, 65
Diener, Ed, 197, 211
differentiation, 173–4
dogma, 5, 28, 65, 17, 77, 209; see also absolutisation, metaphysics
doubt, 27, **29**, 39, 47, 108, 198, 206
dragon, 133
Drob, Sanford, 6, 7, 10, 53, 130, 181, 185, 211
dualism, 15, 109, 166, 172, 181; see also false dichotomy

East, 11, 13–14, 18, 212
egg, 15, 46, 49–51, 88
eggs of the gods, 106
ego, 44, 48, 105, 112, 122, 127–8, 133, 138, 147, 181–2, 192, 195, 198
Einstein, Albert, 2
Elijah (figure in *Red Book*), 8, 56–7, **58–61**, 62–5, 67, 115–17, 135, 183, 191–2, 194, 197–8
embodied meaning, 5, 9, 26, 43–4, 69, 82–3, 106, 118–19, 123, 128, **141–3**, 144–6, 149–56, 161, 166–7, 171, 178, 180–1, 187–9, 196, 206, 208
embodiment, 81, 103, 124, **143–4**, 167, 189
embryos, 36

emotion, 40, 59, 102–4, 118–22, 125–6, 142, 144, 146–7; see also anxiety, boredom, craving, desire, fear, hatred, love, loving-kindness
emotive meaning, 9, 140; see also embodied meaning
empathy, 185; see also compassion
ends and means, 198
energy, 13, 21, 41, 43–4, 49–50, 52, 94, 103–4, 122, 124, 126, 143, 146, 190
enlightened self-interest, 192
enlightenment (nirvana), 17–19, **20–22**, 42, 47–8, 82, 96, 103, 128, 143, 182
entanglement, 106
environmental crisis, 164
epistemology, 28, 66, 170, 184, 213
equanimity, 125, 162
eros, 113
essentialism, 170
eternalism (Buddhist), 22–3
ethics, 8–9, 39, **184–208**; see also morality
eucharist, 72, 74–6
eudaimonia, 58
evangelism, 110
even-handedness, 172
evil, 8–9, 38–9, 45, 70, 74, 82, 84–5, **100–2**, 103–7, 111, 172, 186, 189, 191, 195, 206; see also shadow
evolution, 83
expertise, 67
eye, 100, **101**, 164, 194
Ezechiel (figure in *Red Book*), 162

facilitator, 61
fact-value distinction, 122, 184
fallacy, 67, 209; see also ad hominem, ad hoc argument, bias, false dichotomy, genetic fallacy, non sequitur, special pleading
fallibility, 65
false dichotomy, 147; see also dualism
family, 200
'fast' thinking, 22
fasting, 18
fear, 11, 18, 29, 32, 39, 49, 74, **102–4**, 116–17, 128, 131–2; see also anxiety

feedback loops, **32–3**, 72, 102, 119
feeling, 2, 9, 57, 73–4, 128, 148, 197–200; see also emotion
feminine, 2, 113–15, 118–19, 124, 146; see also anima
feminists, 101
final goal, **20–22**, 81, 105
fire, 12–13, 87–8, 90, 101
Fire Giants, 88
firefighters, 78
First World War, 135, 165
fish, 69, 149
fitness, 101
Five-Buddha mandala, 96
flattery, 109
Fletcher, Joseph, 122, 211
focusing (practice), 125, 144, 203
forest, 4, 18, 140
forethinking, 197–8
fortress, 94–6
Four Noble Truths, 182
four sights, 18
freedom, 30, 142
freewill, 24, 172
Freud, Sigmund, 28, 67, 142
Friar Tuck, 23
Fujita, Frank, 197, 211

Gandalf (Tolkien character), 68
garden, 22, 61, 71, 117, 141, 190, 204
Gay Science, The, 37, 212
gender identity, 114
genetic fallacy, 66–7
George, St, 133
gestalt, 26, 30, 120, 141–2
ghosts, 159–60, 175; see also dead
global warming, 84
Gnosticism, 9, 65, 71, 88, **170–83**
goal, 20, 42, 44, 82–3, 89, 101, 116, 119, 128–9, 174, 187, 192, 197–8, 200–1, 207; see also final goal, hero
God, 2, 7, 8, 15, 20, 25–6, 30, **37–55**, 56–62, 64, 67–71, 73–5, 77, 81, 86, 88, 96, 102, 104–5, 109, 115, 125, 129, 130, 132–3, 138, 165, 173–4, 177, 179, 181–2, 195, 205
golden seed, 106
good, 8–9, 36, 38–9, 45, 48, 70, 81, 84–5, 101–2, **104–6**, 107, 130, 172,

185–6, 189, 191–2, 195, 197, 205;
    see also ethics
gospel, 152
Greek, 63, 69
Groundhog Day (film), 137
growth, 39, 81, 83–4, 88–9, 137, 166;
    see also Tree of Life
guilt, 3, 75, 189
guru, 56, 66
Guru Nanak, 68

Haeckel, Ernst, 90
hanged man (figure in *Red Book*), 166
HAP, 165
hatred, 38, 124–6, 183
heaven, 81–3, 85–6, 92, 123, 167
hedonic treadmill, 197
hedonism, 157, 196–7, 199
hell, 8, 70, 81–2, 85–6, 92, 100, 107–8,
    111, 166–7, 201
hermit, 3, 34, 152; see also
    Ammonius
hero, 7–8, 31, 44–5, 69–71, 73, 96, 102,
    105, 115, **127–38**, 139, 161, 198
Herod, 56
His Dark Materials, 118, 213
Hogenson, George, 26, 141, 211–12
Holy Trinity, 21
holy war, 50
homeostasis, 84
homosexuality, 114
horse, 108, 161, 164, 201–2
hot-cold path, 13–14
hydro-electric dam, 207

idealisation, 37, 124, 126, 128, 138
ideals, 31, 38–9, 52, 123
ideology, 206, 209
image, 24–6, 36, 46, 56, 59, 70, 85–7,
    90, 94, 96, 112, 118, 123, 131,
    140–3, 145, 151, 155–6, 159–60,
    162, 176, 187, 201, 212
image schemas, 142, 145, 156
imagination, 40, 119, 146
imitation, **76**, 77–80, 82, 120, 131–3,
    138, 162
imitation of Christ, 76–80
immurement, 205
imperative, 153, 186, 192
incantations, 50

incrementality, 24, 172
individuality, 62, 64, 78–9, 108, 192
individuation, 5, **57**, 58, 130, 159, 185;
    see also integration
infallibility, 58–9, 64, 207
inspiration, 7, 30, 42, 50, 68, 77–8,
    108, 138, 146, 175, 209–10; see
    also archetype
instrumentality, 32, 135–6, 164–5, 179
integrated psyche, 105
integration, 1, 5, 8, 15, 22, 27, 29, 32,
    37, 39, 42, 45, 47, **57**, 58, 61–2, 65,
    74, 84, 88–90, 92, 94, 96–7, 99,
    102–5, 115, 119, 121, 124, 126,
    128–9, 132–7, 147, 151, 157–61,
    163, 168, 174–5, 185–6, 192–3,
    198–9, 201–2, 206, 209
integrative model, 105
internet discussion, 109
intoxication, 64–5
intuition, 2, 5, 16, 40, 50, 73, **77–8**,
    111, 177–8, 180, 195–6
irony, 205
Islam, 207
Islamic State, 207
Izdubar, **11–15**, 16, 18, 46, 49, 50, 62

Jaffé, Aniela, 169
Jerusalem, 9, 94, 162, 169
Jesus, 1, 69–70, 109, 131; see also
    Christ
Jews, 110
jhana (meditative state), 144
John the Baptist, 56, 116, 198
John's Gospel, 57, 152
Johnson, Mark, 5, 9, 141–2, 145, 151,
    212
joy, 125, 156–7
judgement, 4–7, 15, **16–17**, 19, 21–2,
    33, 40, 42, 57, 62, 67–8, 82–3,
    86–7, 105, 108, 110, 136, 208–9
Jung, Carl, *passim*
    approach to Christianity, 71
    approach to God, 37, 177
    concept of 'image', 141
    conflicting epistemology, 170–1, 183
    Gnosticism, 170–1
    'Liverpool' dream, 88–9
    moral motives, 184
    relationship to the dead, 159

Index

sexual stereotyping, 113–14
sources of scholarly information, 7
visions, 1–2
justice, 48

Kahneman, Daniel, 5, 22, 77–8, 178, 212
Kalamas, 62
Kant, Immanuel, 184, 192
karma, 182
karuna: see compassion
killing, 127–9, 194
king, 88, 129, 136–7
Kisagotami, 63
knowledge, 12–3, 29, 33, 84, 133–4, 140, 175, 177, 184
ko'an, 19, 131
Kuhn, Thomas, 153, 212

Lakatos, Imre, 153, 212
Lakoff, George, 5, 9, 120, 141–2, 145, 212
landscape, 113
language, 25–6, 31–2, 60, 64, 76, 78, 86, 104, 119, 132, 140–2, 144, 145–7, **152–5**, 156, 164, 171, 173, 181–2, 184–6, 191
Latin, 113
leaf-cutter ant, 141–2
left hemisphere of brain, **31–3**, 40, 76–7, 101, 104, 106, 116, 119, 128, 132–3, 144–9, 151, 153, 156, 163–7, 171, 176, 194, 196–9; see also brain, brain lateralisation
Liber Primus, 10, 25, 56 (excluding references *passim*)
Liber Secundus, 6, 10, 60, 64, 92, 94, 96 (excluding references *passim*)
liberty, 48
librarian (figure in *Red Book*), 3, 76–7, 148
library, 76–7, 119, 139, 148
life
  (as general value), 2, 20–1, 29, 36, 38, **39**, 54, 57–8, 74, 79, 88, 113, 119–20, 122, 124, 129, 132, 139, 146, 149, 153–4, 156–7, 159, 161–3, 166–8, 175–6, 181, 189, 192, 194, 198–9, 201, 204; see also Tree of Life

Buddha's ~, 4, 18, 82, 102, 124, 143
future ~, 23
Jung's ~, 7, 159, 184
meaning of ~, 18
period of living, 57, 139, 199
solitary ~, 157, 204–5
linguistics: see language
literalism, 152
literalness, 139
literary composition, 131
liturgy, 34
liver, 3, 75, 130, 189
Liverpool, 88, 94
locksmith, 107
logos, 57–8, 113, 152
love, 3, 13, 45, 50, 54–5, 61, 73–4, 102, 115–17, **121–6**, 132–3, 176, 179, 183, 192, 198
lover, 30, 53, 161
loving-kindness, 125; see also compassion
lying, 11, 59, 72, 100, 134, 149, 169, 187

madness, 106
magic, 3, 60–1, 70, 88, **133–6**, 138, 179, 200–1, 204
magician, 3, 61, 64, 134–5, 179
magnolia, 89
Mahaparanibbana Sutta, 161
Mahayana Buddhism, 19, 23, 173
maiden, 100–4, 110, 113, 118–21, 133, 140, 198; see also daughter, anima
male gaze, 101
Malunkyaputta, 27
mandala, 8, 48, 72, 73, 81, 83, 85–7, **88–99**
manipulation, 146, 164
Manjushri, 107
Mara, 102–3
marriage, 116, 121
Mary (mother of Jesus), 70
masculinity, 2, 114, 124; see also animus
maturity, 57
McGilchrist, Iain, 5, 31–2, 76, 120, 132, 145–6, 148, 150, 163–4, 197, 212
meaning, 3, 5, 9, 14, 25–7, 29, **30–3**, 42, 44, 46, 48–9, 76, 78, 86–7, 89,

92, 104, **118–21**, **139–58**, 161, 165–6, 171, 173, 178, 187, 189, 191–3, 196, 209
mediation, 2, 42, 70, 111
meditation, 18, 40, 79, 122, 125, 188, 202–3
mental illness, 163
Mephistopheles, 108
metaphor, **31–2**, 39, 94, 106, 140, 149, 202
metaphorical extension, 120, 142, 145, 156
metaphysics, 4, 6, 8, 16–17, 21, 28, 30, 46, 53, 65, 112, 153, 169, **170–2**, 175–6, 178–82, 185, 188; see also absolutisation
metta: see loving-kindness
Middle Way, *passim*; see esp. **3–5, 15–17**
 Buddha's ~, 17–19
 Jung's explicit references to ~, 15 (n.13)
 Jung's definition in *Psychological Types*, 16
Milgram, Stanley, 67, 212
mimesis, 76, 78, 132; see also imitation
mindfulness, 16, 40, 203
mockery, 72, 74, 109
modernity, 13, 15, 23, 32, 61, 66, 110, 112–13, **148–9**, 164, 182
modesty, 22, 190, 204
monism, 174
moral dilemmas, 194
moral theory, 186, **193–206**, 207
morality, 9, 23, 47, 53, 60, 75, 79, 86, 92, 104, 107, 121, 131, 136, 157, **184–207**; see also ethics
mortality, 159; see also death
mosaic, 36
Mount Meru, 94
mudita: see sympathetic joy
Muhammad, 1, 151
murder, 62, 127–32, 189, 198
murderer, 75, 153, 166
Muspelheim, 88
mythology, 42, 44, 64, 94, 107

Nanda (Buddha's monk), 62
Natural Law, 83
Naturalism, 83
Nature, 48, 52, 57, 83
needs, **43–4**, 67
negative metaphysics, 28, 172
Neumann, Erich, 185, 206, 212
neuroscience, 5, 31, 33, 145, 148; see also brain
neurosis, 176, 189
Niamh (mythical figure), 161
Nietzsche, Friedrich, 2–3, 28, 37–9, 212
night, 12, 56, 62, 69, 88, 107, 112, 123, 146, 157, 163, 194, 204
nihilism, 22–3
nirvana: see enlightenment
non sequitur, 180
non-linguistic symbols, 151
Non-Violent Communication, 111
normativity, 185
nothingness, 173
nous, 57–8
nymphs, 63

obsession: see craving
Odin, 123
Odysseus, 134
Oisin, 161
Old Testament, 56
omission, 190
optionality, 130
oracle, 56
originality, 119
Osho, 66
oxytocin, 150

paganism, 34, 49, 109
palace, 4, 18
Pali Canon, 4, 17, 125
Papadopoulos, Renos, 28, 170–1, 184, 213
paradox, 19
paradox of hedonism, 197, 199; see also hedonism, hedonic treadmill
parasitism, 165
particularity, 3, 166–7
perfection, 132–3
personal relationships, 200
personal unconscious, 42
phallic symbol, 156

Index

Philemon (figure in *Red Book*), 8–9, 37, 56–9, **61–6**, 67, 71, 134, 168–9, 172–81, 200, 204
philosophers, 9, 56–7, 171–2, 177, 180, 184, 194
philosophy, 3, 8–9, 23, 28, 177, 180, 183, 208–9
physics, 2, 67, 182
pilgrimages, 162
Pisces, 69, 178; see also fish, Platonic months
plants, 73
Plato, 105, 112, 201, 213
Platonic forms, 42
Platonic months, 178, 180
play, 36
pleasure, 7, 16, 18, 121, 144, 157, **197–9**; see also hedonism
Pleroma, 173–4, 181
poison, 12–13
political correctness, 185
politics, 4, 9, 34, 94, 107, 114, 134, **135–6**, 185, 199, 207
polytheism, 180
positivism, 28
poverty, 108
power
  energy or impact, 8, 15, 30, 39, 41, 45, 49–50, 52, 60, 65, 74, 77, 88, 117, 121, 124, 133–4, 149–50, 163–5, 168, 195, 201, 204
  socio-political ~, 4, 12, 47, 79, 96, 108, 120, **134–6**
practicability, 207
practicality, 1, 3–7, 9, 13–16, 19, 22, 25, 28, 32–3, 35, 42–3, 49, 70, 82, 84, 152–5, 174, 180, 182–3, 189, 207
pragmatism, 35, 140, 153, 207; see also practicality
prayer, 3, 40, 76
pre-frontal cortex, 32, 119, 142, 144, 164; see also brain
priest, 12–13, 169
priestess, 56
professionalism, 185
projection, 8, 30, **45**, 46, 52–5, 58–9, 64–8, 70, 96, 100, 103–4, 113–17, 121, 123–32, 139, 164, 166–8, 170, 175, 179, 180, 182–3, 191–2, 202

prophecy, 150, 209
prophet, 56–7, 59, 62, 115, 189, 198
provisionality, 2, 4, 17, 27, 183
psychological functions, 43–4
Psychological Types, 16, 73
psychosis, 176
psychosomasis, 80
psychotherapy, 203
Pullman, Philip, 118, 213

Qur'an, 151

raft, 4
rain, 89, 127, 129
Rajneesh, 66
rationality, 146–7, 185, 192; see also reason
raven, 123, 126
reality, 14–15, 19, 28–9, 45–6, 119, 140, 171–2, 191, 193
reason, 29, 57, 61, 81, 112, 122–3, 171, 174, 178, 180, 181, 196, **201**, see also rationality
reason-emotion distinction, 122
rebirth
  in Buddhism, 18, 182
  of God, 37–8
  of the hero 136–8
Red Book, passim
  overview of, 1–3
  interpretation issues, 5–6
  referencing, 10
Red One (figure in *Red Book*), 34–6, 108–10, 156–8, 183; see also devil
reductionism, 142
reframing, 18, 24, 29, 42, 111–12, 196
regeneration, 87–8
relativism, 82
relaxation, 196
religion, 2, 4, 9, 35, 44, 76–7, 100, 110, 180, 182; see also Buddhism, Christianity, God
representation, 86, 106, 116, 124, 132, **140**, 142–3, 145, 147–9, 153, 192–3, 200
representationalism, 9, 26, 104, 118–19, 128, **140**, 144, 147, 150, 152, 154–5, 164, 166–7, 171, 187, 191

repression, 4, 52, 88, 115, 118, 120, 136, 139–40, 146, 157, 160, 172, 189, 200, 202, 206
'reptilian' brain, 32, 119; see also brain, amygdala, striatum
reputation, 67
responsibility, 24, 52, 79, **188–90**, 204
resurrection, 70, 74, 109
retreats, 205
right hemisphere of brain, **31–3**, 40, 47, 76–7, 104, 119–20, 132, 144–51, 163, 197
ritual, 75
Romanticism, 117, 146
rootedness, 83, 144; see also embodiment
rose-apple tree, 144

sacrifice, 12, 100, 102, 106, 122, **129–31**, 186, 189
saints, 56
sal trees, 162
Salome (figure in *Red Book*), 8, 56–7, 61, 70, **115–17**, 121–4, 135, 183, 197–8
Sartre, Jean-Paul, 101
Satan, 7–8, 21, 34, 108, 123, 154; see also devil, shadow
saviour, 61, 151, 205
scarab, 86
scepticism, **27–30**, 148, 184
schema, 44, 141–2
schizophrenia, 53
scholar (figure in *Red Book*), 118–20, **139–40**, 143–4, 146, 154, 199
scholars, 2, 7, 9, 17, 76, 118–19, 139–40, 143, 148, 178
science, 1, 4–5, 9, 12, 14, 26, 33, 76, 84, 141, 153–4, 181, 184, 208, 212
scientific naturalism, 14
scientism, 28
Scrutinies, 10, 56, 61, 64, 71, 164, 169, 194
sea, 123, 160
Second World War, 20, 206
secularism, 43
Self (in Jung's sense), 7–8, **48–9**, 181; see also God, archetype
self-awareness, 191
self-censorship, 136

self-indulgence, 23; see also hedonism
selfishness, 191–2, 203–5
sensation, 57, 73
sense-organs, 101
serpent, 56, 60, 64, 83, 100, **117**, 122, 134–7, 166–7, 194–6, 199; see also black serpent, white serpent
servant, 113
Seven Sermons to the Dead, 2, 9, 37, 65–6, 168–9, **170–83**, 205
sexual temptation, 103
shades, 65, 165; see also dead
shadow, 7–8, 44–5, 62, 70, 73–4, 84, 86, 96, **100–11**, 115–16, 124, 130, 135, 160, 168, 189, 192, 206
Shakyas, 17
shamanic journeying, 203
Shamdasani, Sonu, 7, 212
Siddhartha Gautama: see Buddha
Siegfried (mythic hero), 127
signs and symbols, 150
silence, 4
simplicity, 54, 109, 120
sincerity, 109, 111
Sinhalese fundamentalists, 20
Situation Ethics, 122, 211
slippery slopes, 34
'slow' thinking, 22
Socratic ignorance, 170
soldier, 193
solipsism, 53, 203
solitude, 157, **202–5**
'son', 6, 88, 136–7
sophistication, 120, 135
soul, 3, 7–8, 21–2, 27, 57, 65, 75, 101, 107, **112–15**, 117–18, 122–3, 134, 139, 169, 190, 201, 202–3, 212; see also anima
special pleading, 180
spirit of the depths, 25–6, 38, 129, **148–50**
spiritualism, 159
spirituality, 185
stars, 159–60
stealing, 60, 194
stocks (financial), 78
Stoicism, 57–8
striatum, 32, 128; see also brain
stroke, 104

Index

sublimation, 63
substitution, 131
succession, 136, 152, 154
suffering, 7, 12, 18, 28, **71–4**, 79, 109, 125, 129, 194, 205
superego, 67
supernatural, 8, 38, 49, 52, 58, 102, 109; see also absolutisation, metaphysics
sword, 106-7
symbol , 14, 17, 20, 30-1, 38-40, 42, 47, 49, 52, 61, 64, 69, 81, 83, 85, 87, 88-9, 94, 96, 115, 118, 123, 148, **150-1**, 155-6, 165, 182, 199
symbolism, 48, 89, 92, 119
sympathetic joy, 125
synaptic connections, 145; see also brain, embodied meaning
synthesis, 71, 77
Syzygy, 113

taboo, 193
Taleb, Nassim Nicholas, 130, 213
Tantric guru, 61
theology, 167
therapists, 176, 184
therapy, 184-5
thinking, 2, 9, 22, 42-3, 53-4, 61, 73, 111, 116, 119, 121, 146, **148**, 149, 171, 173-4, 184, 196-9, 203
Thomas à Kempis, 76-8
Thus Spake Zarathustra, 37, 212
Tibetan Buddhism, 205
Tir Nan Og, 161
Tolkien, J.R.R., 60
tool using, 31-2, 164
totalitarianism, 136
tower, 108-9, **155-6**
Tower of Babel, 156
traditions, 1, 4, 58, 128, 209
trans-sexual, 114
Tree of Knowledge, 63, 84
Tree of Life, 8, 36, 48, 63, **81-8**, 89-93, 95, 97, 99, 122-4, 137, 159
trickster (archetypal motif), 36, 96, 134, 138
truth, 1, 4, 12-14, 16-17, 26, **27-30**, 31, 38, 48, 54, 61-2, 65, 71, 86, 120, 129, 147, 153, 171, 183-4, 198

Übermensch, 37
Udaka Ramaputta, 18
umwelt (von Uexküll's term), 141
uncertainty, 55, 84, 108, 205-6; see also scepticism
unholy alliance, **33-6**, 157
universalism, 4
universality, 2-5, 7, 15, 23, 25-6, 69, 81, 99, 119-20, 186, 188, 203, 207
upekkha: see equanimity
usurpation, 136
utilitarianism, 135, 189, **197**

vegetation, 36, 39, 81, 162
vested interest, 1, 67
virtue, 43, 129, 187, 202
virtue ethics, 187, 202-5
visions, 1-2, 11, 53, 56, 59-60, 63, 65, 76, 116, 138, 160
visualisation, 203
von Uexküll, Jacob, 141
vote, 207

war, 136, 186; see also First and Second World Wars
way of coming things, the, 25
weapon, 12, 49
West, 13-15, 18, 182
white serpent, 195
wine, 75-6, 99
wisdom, 2, 56, **57**, 58-61, 63-4, 68, 77, 107, 117, 120, 124, 135, 168, 183, 188
wisdoms, five, 96
Wise Old Man, 8, 37, 48, **56-68**, 69, 96, 116-17, 135, 139, 175, 181, 192, 198
Wise Old Woman, 56
witch, 136
wizard, 56
words, 3, 87, 144, 148, 151, **152-5**, 159, 191; see also language
Wordsworth, William, 137

Yggdrasil, 81, 87

Zarathustra, 37
Zen, 19-20, 131, 213
Zofingia Lectures, 28, 184